T0289245

DAYS OF CHALLENGE

DAYS OF CHALLENGE

THE MAKING OF A MODERN AMERICAN JEWISH LEADER

JACOB STEIN

Eshel Books
Washington • Baltimore

Copyright © 2007 by Jacob Stein
All rights reserved. No part of this book may be used or reproduced in any form whatsoever without written permission except in the case of brief quotations embodied in critical reviews and articles.

Printed in the United States of America

Special thanks to Walter Ruby

Published by:

ESHEL BOOKS
AN IMPRINT OF BARTLEBY PRESS
9045 Maier Road
Suite D
Laurel, Maryland 20723
(800) 953-9929
www.EshelBooks.com

Library of Congress Cataloging-in-Publication Data

Stein, Jacob, 1916-
Days of challenge : the making of a modern American Jewish leader / Jacob Stein.
p. cm.
Includes index.
ISBN-13: 978-0-910155-67-0
ISBN-10: 0-910155-67-4
1. Stein, Jacob, 1916- 2. Jews—United States—Biography. 3. Conservative Judaism—United States—History—20th century. 4. Jewish leadership—United States—History—20th century. 5. Jews—United States—Politics and government—21st century. 6. Jews—United States—Politics and government—20th century. 7. United States—Foreign relations—Israel. 8. Israel—Foreign relations—United States. I. Title.

E184.37.S74A3 2006
973'.04924092—dc22
[B]

IN MEMORY OF
MY BELOVED WIFE
JEAN

אֵשֶׁת חַיִל

A virtuous woman who can find?
For her price is far above rubies
The heart of her husband trusted in her
And he shall have no lack of gain

Contents

Preface

Shortly before the publication of this volume, I received a note from George H.W. Bush, our 41st President:

> Dear Jack,
>
> Many people will enjoy reading *Days of Challenge.* Your background is varied and productive, and all your work in the public sector has been highly successful. Your service in the White House, your membership on the United States delegation to the United Nations General Assembly, as well as your help on several special missions to the Middle East, were done with dedication and excellence.
>
> I value our thirty years of friendship and I wish you well in the future.
>
> Sincerely,
> George Bush

I first met George H.W. Bush in 1972 at a meeting with the Secretary General of the United Nations, Kurt Waldheim. As acting Chairman of the Conference of Presidents of Major American Jewish Organizations, I had asked Ambassador Bush to arrange a meeting for me with Secretary General Waldheim.

I was appealing for U.N. help in securing the release of four Israeli soldiers who had been captured by the Syrians.

Waldheim's answer to my plea was a standard "we will see what we can do." Yet, my friendship with George Bush was formed, and it grew from that day on.

I began to write this account of my more than four score years with the intention of focusing on the historic events I witnessed and in which I sometimes participated. I found that my memories of those events were dominated by the people I met and the friendships I developed. Even those who I did not consider allies or even friends left indelible marks on my recollections.

I have been privileged to work with some of the most influential men and women of my time. I have known presidents and prime ministers, generals, ambassadors, and kings. There have been many others without headlines to their credit, but who made valuable contributions. My personal relationships with all of them have been much more than byproducts of political alliances. They have been in large part the source of my pride and pleasure in serving the Jewish community and America.

My personal life has likewise been molded by the people around me. I often looked to my partners in the real estate business for fellowship, to the rabbi of my hometown synagogue for spiritual guidance, and of course to my family for love and support.

This is my first attempt at a book, but I have always enjoyed writing. Seventy-five years ago my parents sent me to Camp Mohaph in Glen Spey, New York, and today I still have copies of stories from the camp newspaper in my attic with my name in the byline. During my first year at Johns Hopkins I wrote a weekly column on University events for the *Baltimore Sun*, and for the past twelve years I have written a weekly column called "Musings" for the *Long Island Jewish World*, the

Manhattan Sentinel, and the *Jewish Tribune.* In "Musings" I write about topics of my choice, such as events in Israel, developments in Washington, and milestones in Jewish history.

I have tried to be as objective as possible, although I hope the reader will understand that like all human beings, I have certain biases. I have checked and re-checked my sources, but this is not a scholarly book, and if you find an error I ask you to please excuse it.

I write these words for my children, grandchildren and great grandchildren, for the many friends who have shared these events with me, and for you, dear reader. I hope this memoir will stand not only as a record of recent Jewish and American history and politics, but also as a testament to the achievements of Jews in America.

Growing Up American, Growing Up Jewish

I was born in Poughkeepsie, New York, on October 12, 1916. I grew up feeling very much a part of the Jewish community in Poughkeepsie, which was very well integrated into the larger Poughkeepsie community.

Both my parents were born in America. There are simply no superlatives that can adequately describe how much I loved my parents and admired their many positive qualities. They were deeply loving and caring people. Nor is there anything I can write here that would be sufficient to express my gratitude for the values they transmitted to me; values that have carried me through the rough-and-tumble of nearly nine full decades of life.

I also was blessed with two wonderful siblings; a younger brother Fred and a younger sister, Muriel, with whom I have shared many happy moments over the years.

My father's parents, Joseph and Fannie Horowitz, both from Hungary, were wonderful people. My grandfather was part owner of the Horowitz matzoh factory, now known as Horowitz-Margaretten. As I recall it, my grandfather together with his three brothers was left by their father, one-half interest in the Matzoh bakery, with the remaining half left to Regina Horowitz, his daughter. This uneven distribution was the cause of some family disagreements.

I had the exciting opportunity after we moved to Brooklyn for several years to respond to my grandfather's request shortly before the Passover Holidays to come to the bakery Sunday mornings. There I became part of the team on the truck that was delivering the matzohs across New York. What a pleasant memory.

Along with my parents, my paternal grandparents played a major role in helping me to build a strong and positive Jewish identity. They had come to the United States from Hungary in the late 1800s and moved up the Hudson River to Poughkeepsie shortly thereafter. Our family spent many a happy Shabbat morning together at shul followed by a delicious Shabbat lunch at Grandma and Grandpa's.

In those days, my father was into the ladies' dress manufacturing business, and my mother was a homemaker, as was usual for women at that time. My father's parents ran a clothing store.

Growing Up Jewish in Poughkeepsie

Although we lived and moved about in a secular milieu—Poughkeepsie had no Jewish section and we kids attended public school. Jewish beliefs and customs played a critical role in our lives. Starting at the age of about eight until we left Poughkeepsie six years later, I would leave school four times a week at the end of the school day and walk to my Hebrew School for several more hours of study. It was a very full day for an elementary-school kid, but I always relished my Jewish education and never resented spending my afternoons in Hebrew school.

Our family belonged to my grandparents' synagogue,

which represented a modern and comfortable Orthodoxy, where going to shul was a pleasure. Not that all of the practices at my Hebrew school would necessarily pass muster today. It was a rigorous and challenging place where a student was expected to learn. If he was not learning properly, the youngster would be forcefully reminded of his lack of progress by the instructor, who sometimes whacked students lightly on the fingernails with a ruler he carried around with him as he stalked the classroom. Despite all of that, the Hebrew school gave me a very good grounding in the Torah and Judaism, and I don't regret one minute I spent there.

Saturdays were filled with family. After shul and Shabbat lunch, we on occasion would spend all afternoon at my grandparents' home, which was above their clothing store. Other times my siblings and I would run off to the Saturday-afternoon matinee at the theater. (Of course we had bought our tickets Friday afternoon, before Shabbat.) Late in the afternoon, we sometimes would climb up onto the roof to wait for three stars to appear, signifying that Shabbat was over. Then we would go downstairs and help my grandfather to open his store.

What I recall of my bar mitzvah was that the bimah was in the center of the synagogue, so I didn't walk to a stage in the front of the synagogue, as is usually the case in synagogues today. I also recall that no women were on the bimah with me; they were all up in the balcony.

I don't remember much of what I felt the day of my bar mitzvah, probably because in that long-ago era, b'nai mitzvot were pretty much taken for granted. They were not celebrated with the big caterers and lavish displays that became common later on. In Poughkeepsie, after the *simcha* we went downstairs and had a simple, but festive, kiddush.

I would characterize my upbringing as well disciplined but not overly disciplined. I enjoyed my daily activities and felt comfortable amidst the constraints my schedule imposed upon me. That may sound strange in today's context, but it felt very natural to me at the time.

About fifteen years ago, my wife Jean and I drove up to Poughkeepsie to visit the house where I lived as a child. We knocked on the front door, and the present owners kindly invited us in. As we walked around the house, I felt a flood of pleasant memories washing over me. Following that, we visited the graves of my grandparents and then went to see the shul where my bar mitzvah had taken place 55 years ago. The synagogue building was still there, but in the intervening years had become an African-American Baptist church. My first reaction was sadness at the loss of my cherished synagogue, but I reflected that at least the building was still being used as a house of worship.

Brooklyn

About 1929, around the time of my bar mitzvah, my father joined his brother, Joseph Stein, in opening a chain of men's clothing stores, known, not surprisingly, as Stein Brothers. Stein Brothers' distinguishing feature was its prices; even during Depression days, $12.50 was a darn good price for a quality man's suit.

The rapid expansion of the Stein Brothers chain of stores to well beyond Hudson River towns such as Kingston and Newburgh led to a big change in our lives. My father and uncle moved the company's central office to mid-town Manhattan, New York City. When I was 14 my parents sold our house in Poughkeepsie, and we began a new life in an attractive apartment on Linden Boulevard in Flatbush, Brooklyn.

In Brooklyn, I attended P.S. 181 and then headed for Boys' High School, to which I traveled every day via the Nostrand Avenue Trolley Car. A vivid memory from this period is that of my father giving me lessons on his brand-new Dodge— one of the first cars in those days to have an automatic gear shift.

My family joined Sha'arei Torah synagogue, which was then headed by Rabbi Joseph Miller. A wonderful man, Rabbi Miller later presided at the marriage of my wife Jean and I. The late rabbi's son, Rabbi Amos Miller, later became a rabbi on Long Island and a dear friend of long standing.

At Boys' High, I joined the debating team and found myself to be well suited to the rhetorical training. I remember receiving a five-dollar gold coin as a reward for winning one particular event.

I felt motivated to do as well as possible academically in high school, which paid off in my being accepted to the highly regarded Johns Hopkins University in Baltimore.

Johns Hopkins University and Baltimore

About the time I headed to Johns Hopkins, my parents moved to an apartment on Central Park West in Manhattan. By this time, Stein Brothers had about 60 stores stretching from New York to California, and I spent summer vacations working at various stores. On one occasion, I worked at a clothing factory in Knoxville, Tennessee, from which our company bought a lot of our clothing. There, sitting at the sewing machine, I learned how to make men's suits; how to put cuffs on the bottom of pants, how to take in the waist. My father and uncle believed I should learn the trade from the bottom up, and I was, indeed, certainly starting from the bottom.

I did well academically during my two years at Johns Hopkins, from 1934 to 1936. My studies were generally difficult but by and large rewarding. My toughest subject was calculus, which gave me no end of trouble. My greatest joy at Johns Hopkins was becoming a weekly columnist for the *Baltimore Sun* concerning events taking place on campus. That was a great deal of fun and gave me my first taste of newspapering.

My Johns Hopkins years were especially happy for another reason: Just before leaving Brooklyn for Baltimore, my sister Muriel had introduced me to a lovely girl named Jean Cohen. From the moment Muriel brought Jean up to the house and asked me to make lunch for the three of us, I truly was smitten. After that first meeting, I remained in touch with her.

Finding the Love of My Life

Jean had grown up on Crown Street in Brooklyn, and her father was a can manufacturer. She lived about ten minutes from our home, so I used to hop a trolley to pick her up to go to see a movie together. Jean and I remained in close touch when I went away to college and of course when I came back to New York on many weekends.

What was it about Jean that made her so special to me? From the very beginning, the two us could deeply relate to one another; we were sensitive to each other's realities.

My bond with Jean was cemented during the difficult years of my father's illness leading to his death in 1942. When my father was diagnosed with cancer, it became obvious to me that I should be helping my mother. At the end of my sophomore year at Johns Hopkins, I transferred to Columbia University in New York City. Sad though I was to leave Johns Hopkins, I appreciated Columbia's top-notch academics and thrived there. I was especially interested in the study of geography. I also took quite a few business and statistics courses in preparation for the day, not too far up the road, when I would become directly involved in managing Stein Brothers. It simply never occurred to me that I should follow a different career path from that of entering the family firm. I don't recall ever having made an active decision to go into the firm; rather, my father *told* me I would do so, and I believed this was my destiny.

Being in New York, I now could spend more time with

Jean, who was by then a student at City College. I realized that finding Jean was the best thing that had ever happened to me. We discovered that we were deeply in love.

After I graduated from Columbia, my father sent me to Utica, New York, to train in management at the Stein Brothers store there. I learned a lot there, but my main focus at that time was on Jean. Almost every weekend I would return to New York City by train, and Jean would meet me at the elevated train station at 125th Street in Harlem.

In June 1939, one year after I graduated from Columbia, Jean and I married. Pledging ourselves to one another, as the Bible says, "We became as one." We would remain cherished partners and a strong team for 65 extraordinary years.

Kansas City

Shortly after our marriage, my uncle and father sent me to Kansas City, Missouri, to manage a recently opened Stein Brothers store. Jean and I packed our bags and drove out to Kansas City, settling in shortly before the High Holidays.

In Kansas City I experienced for the first time overt anti-Semitism. People would walk into our store and ask me, "Is this a Jew store?' Keenly aware that I was responsible for the success of the business, I would answer as calmly as possible, "Yes, this is a store with Jewish ownership that serves everybody." At such moments I would focus first and foremost on protecting the company interests. I would attend to the potential customer's intentions on buying a suit, sports coat, or pair of pants. But inside I would be boiling and thinking, "What the hell difference does it make whether this is a Jew store? You came in here to buy a suit!"

That Rosh Hashanah, Jean and I walked nearly an hour from our rented apartment in Kansas City to the nearest synagogue. There we were in for a rude awakening. We realized that it was a Reform synagogue—*terra incognito* for us. Everyone except us had driven to shul. I asked someone for a kippah, and he replied, "Oh, we don't wear them here." Jean and I looked at each other with our mouths open in astonishment. A synagogue where men didn't wear kippahs—we really were in Kansas! So our six months in Kansas City was a real culture shock.

1942: A Year of Sorrow and Joy

In 1940 my father sent me down South—Little Rock; Jacksonville, Florida; and Atlanta—to meet managers and get a feel for operations of Stein Brothers stores there. In particular the company had a big store on Peachtree Street in Atlanta, GA.

After several months, Jean and I returned to New York, where I began working full time in the company's main offices in midtown Manhattan. We rented a one-bedroom apartment on Riverside Drive.

Looking back, I feel blessed to have spent time nearby my parents in the last years of my father's life. It was a time of great emotional contrasts for our family. World War II raged on in Europe while our lives flowed along harmoniously, with the painful exception of my father's illness. And then, in 1942, we welcomed with great joy our first son, Richard, even as we mourned the passing of my beloved father.

The loss of my father had a deep impact upon me. I had loved and honored him for his teachings, and now he was gone, at much too early an age.

Settling In: At Home in Great Neck

Shortly after my father's passing, Jean and I moved to a house in Great Neck, New York—to the very house we would call home for some 60 years. The move was motivated primarily by a desire for more space and quality public schools. After a little coaxing, we persuaded my grieving mother to move into a house near us.

The house we selected was just being completed by the builder, Bob Rose, and by the middle of October 1942 we were settled in our new home.

I was given a medical deferment from joining our troops in Europe due to a bladder condition. For a time I worked at Purdy's Shipyard in Port Washington, NY building picket vessels that patrolled Long Island Sound to ward off German submarines. While it wasn't as exciting or as dangerous as being sent overseas to fight, I was pleased to have this opportunity to do my patriotic duty.

In the aftermath of my father's death, my uncle bought up Dad's share of the company, with the exception of stores in Kingston, Utica, and Glens Falls NY, and Burlington, VT which I inherited. Looking to make my own mark, I left Stein Brothers and started Stein Clothes from an office at 915 Broadway, at Broadway and 21st Street. Soon I was immersed in business, buying clothing in bulk for the stores and hiring and firing personnel.

Jean and I searched assiduously for a shul in our new home town. In particular I wanted to be able to say Kaddish for my father every day of the year after his passing. We joined a start-up Conservative synagogue in Great Neck named Temple Israel; we were the 35th members. At Temple Israel, we soon felt we had found a Jewish community where we could really put down roots.

One aspect of this synagogue that appealed to us especially, after coming from an Orthodox background, was that my wife and I were able to sit together during service. We could share the synagogue experience in every respect. Very quickly, I found myself on the board of directors, then editor of the synagogue paper, *Temple Light*, then chairman of the education committee, and finally temple president. When a synagogue is new and has few members, that's how it goes.

In the early and mid-1940s, Great Neck was not a very Jewish place, so Jews tended to seek out and form friendships within their synagogues. Jean and I greatly enriched our personal and professional connections through our synagogue involvement. We witnessed many changes in the Jewish community at large in the wake of World War II, as Jews joined in the mass movement to the suburbs. By 1950, Great Neck was experiencing "strong Jewish growth."

In any event, from the very beginning I enjoyed being actively involved in the life of Temple Israel. As the years went by, I also grew more and more impressed by the spiritual vitality and tremendous growth potential of Conservative Judaism.

Meanwhile, things were going well with my business. Within a few years, I expanded Stein Clothes from four stores to eleven, including one that we opened in our Manhattan office. That operation was particularly successful. Apparently people figured that if they were buying clothes at an industrial building like that one, located on the edge of the Manhattan Garment District, they must be getting it wholesale. They almost were, as I kept our overhead very low.

I traveled a lot during those days in order to keep my stores—which were scattered across upstate New York and one each in Vermont and Connecticut—running up to speed. For efficiency's sake, I secured a pilot's license and bought a single-engine plane. Flying my own plane also brought me much joy, and I took Jean along for the ride on occasion. I kept the plane in Roosevelt Field, which was then still a working airfield.

One day during the summer of 1950, I went tuna fishing off Montauk with a friend from Great Neck who was in the real-estate business. My friend spoke with me about the real-estate field, in particular about opportunities available to create a profitable business within short time. Not long thereafter, he showed me a piece of vacant property in Great Neck that was available. I bought the property and soon sold it for a substantial profit, without even having to take title. At that point, I asked myself what I was doing in a business based on the principle of selling one suit at a time.

I decided to look into real estate in a serious way and soon concluded that the real-estate field offered me much better prospects than the clothing business. I therefore began selling off my clothing stores and launched a new business venture—Jacob Stein Realty. In my new undertaking, I would drive around Long Island looking for properties with a future and then buy corner properties on intersections on different parts of the Island. Much of the land that I bought was undeveloped agricultural land on eastern part of the Island. I would divide it into lots, secure permits from local jurisdictions to develop the properties, and then finally sell the land at a considerable profit to builders.

Those were the days, of course, when the Island was experiencing tremendous population growth. Years into my business, Jacob Stein Realty came to own and operate commercial properties all over the Island. In fact, forty years later, I still own the first two buildings that I built, retail centers within a couple of miles from my home on Great Neck Road in Great Neck.

In the course of the 1950s, Jean and I welcomed two more children, Stuart and Linda. I had reached a level of financial security that allowed me to spend more time with my family and with Jewish community affairs. I devoted myself not only to my wife and children but also to the building up of Temple Israel, and, increasingly, of the United Synagogue of Conservative Judaism. Only in my-mid 30s, I had the opportunity to help chart the course of Conservative Judaism in America at the time of its fastest growth.

Temple Israel And the United Synagogue: A New American Judaism

Temple Israel swelled its ranks at the end of World War II when the GIs began returning home and Jews began moving from New York City to Long Island. The Temple moved it's original property atop a hill at 10 Preston Road in 1947 to a larger building at 108 Old Mill Road, Great Neck, NY.

Initially, in the late 1940s and early 1950s I concentrated on making Temple Israel an exemplar of what a suburban Conservative synagogue could be. I never imagined those efforts would lead me within two decades to becoming the de-facto leader of the American Jewish community; making the case on behalf of Israel, oppressed Soviet Jewry, and other aspects of our aspirations for the Jewish people on the world stage. Yet by 1969, I would become president of the United Synagogue, which led to my representing that body on the Conference of Presidents of Major American Jewish Organizations and within two years to my speaking on behalf of all of American Jewry as chairman of the Presidents' Conference. I would participate in discussions and negotiations with President Richard Nixon and Prime Minister Golda Meir and a host of world leaders ranging from the Soviet Union's Leonid Brezhnev to France's Georges Pompidou.

Our family had a natural growth. Our children, Richard, Stuart, and Linda, were busy with their public school and with the Temple Israel three-day-a-week school and a variety of athletic activities. Today they are bright and well educated, independent children who have given us six grandchildren who in turn have given us six great-grandchildren with number seven currently in the womb.

While Temple Israel has played an integral role in my life, we have had some nervous moments as a congregation. The late 1940s and 1950s were schizophrenic years, as we coped with the news out of Europe, rejoiced in the return to our historic holy land, welcomed a huge influx of Jews into our community, and generally reinvented ourselves as a new American Jewish community. In 1958, amid our Zionist fever, we sent our youth group to Israel for a tour. The travel arrangements called for them to sail from New York to Marseilles and then to fly on to Israel. While the Temple Israel youngsters were at sea, a sudden crisis developed in Middle East. The U.S. government dispatcbed Marines into Lebanon to help President Camille Chamoun to stamp out a rebellion. The State Department warned Americans of the dangers of travel to the Middle East. We dispatched urgent messages to our children to come home and not move on to Israel. Most did return, but some, who either did not receive the message in time or chose not to hear it, went on to Israel and had a great time there.

An American Zionist Debate

While Temple Israel wrestled with our postwar growing pains, the tattered remains of European Jewry festered in displaced person's camps and desperately tried to reach Eretz Israel. Support for the idea of a Jewish state soared throughout American Jewry, including among members of our own temple.

Nonetheless, the situation gave rise to a bitter ideological debate. On one side was our spiritual leader, Rabbi Asher Block, and on the other, much of the lay leadership, including myself.

Many of our members expressed a desire to sing the Zionist anthem, *Hatikvah,* at Shabbat services. Rabbi Block asserted the position that if we were to sing any national anthems in shul, it ought to be the *Star Spangled Banner.* The rabbi disdained nationalism in general (he adhered to Wendell Willkie's One World principles) and was lukewarm on the topic of Jewish statehood in particular. The rabbi was adamant.

As the 1948 declaration of the Jewish State drew closer, tensions came to a head between the Zionist congregants and those who supported the line of Rabbi Block. Two members, Joe Teich and Al Lazarus, got so heated up over the issue that they engaged in a physical confrontation, There was no knockout or even a knockdown, but fists were definitely used. The loser was neither man but rather Rabbi Block, as the Board of Directors formed a consensus that under the circumstances it would be best not to renew his contract.

The role of the recently formed United Nations regarding Palestine held a special resonance for the Great Neck Jewish community because the international body was then located in Lake Success, just a few miles away. We were busy Jews in 1947 as we watched the British position on the end of their mandate. In August of that year the United Nations report on the British Mandate recommended the prompt ending of the Mandate and by a 7-3 margin, with one abstention, the partition of Palestine into a Jewish state and an Arab state and an international zone containing the holy places. Zionists reluctantly accepted the plan which was rejected outright by the Arabs.

Many of our Temple Israel members gave money quietly to buy arms for the Haganah, the underground army of the Yishuv, the Jewish community in Eretz Israel. We listened breathlessly on our shortwave radios the latest reports on the deteriorating military situation in Palestine.

Our dispute with Rabbi Block mirrored passionate debates raging elsewhere in the American Jewish world. Personally, I considered Rabbi Block to be an agreeable person and a first-rate spiritual leader, but, like many others, I became caught up in the hope and expectations for the imminent emergence of a Jewish State. I felt that such a state would depend on American Jewry to provide the financial support and diplomatic clout to ensure its survival. Under the circumstances, it seemed to me to be in Temple Israel's best interests to have a rabbi who unequivocally supported Jewish statehood.

Rabbi Mordecai Waxman: Leader, Mentor, Friend

We temple leaders initiated a search committee, headed by George Schwartz (also known as Little George to distinguish him from another Board member named George Schwartz, a.k.a., Big George), to find a replacement for Rabbi Block. Little George went out to Chicago to interview a young rabbi named Mordecai Waxman. He came back highly impressed.

Rabbi Waxman, himself the son of a highly respected Conservative rabbi in Chicago, had served as a chaplain in the Army during the War. The Jewish Theological Seminary and and others far and wide recognized the rabbi for his scholarship. Rabbi Waxman and his charming wife Ruth were invited to come to Great Neck and meet the congregation. We were instantly taken with this handsome young rabbi with a dapper-looking moustache, charm, and evident erudition on matters Jewish and general. We installed Rabbi Waxman in late 1947. He guided the destiny of Temple Israel for the next 55 years, until his death in 2002.

Certainly, our lay leadership can take credit for wisdom in selecting Rabbi Waxman. Yet it was Rabbi Waxman's own skill, understanding, compassion, teaching ability, and inspirational skills that made him into one of the most revered rabbis—and outstanding religious leaders in general—of the last half of the 20th century. He proved to be both a giant of scholarship and a human being of great personal warmth and decency. Members of the congregation who soughts his counsel constantly remarked on his ability to connect deeply on a personal level.

Yet as indispensable a spiritual leader as Rabbi Waxman was to all of us at Temple Israel, his interests and involvement extended far beyond the synagogue. He went on to become, successively, the president of the Rabbinical Assembly; the Synagogue Council of America; and the International Jewish Committee for Inter-religious Consultation (IJCIC), the international Jewish body that consulted with the Vatican on the body of issues involved in Catholic-Jewish relations.

In the wake of the Holocaust, Rabbi Waxman focused heavily on strengthening relations between Jews and non-Jews. He left an inspiring legacy in the area of interreligious relations. He made a major contribution to the development of *Nostrae Aetate*, which, in 1965, after 2000 years of Catholic charges of deicide against the Jews, finally absolved our people of responsibility for the crucifixion of Christ. Pope John XXII announced *Nostrae Aetate* during the 2nd Vatican Council in 1965.

As president of IJCIC in 1988, Waxman hosted Pope John Paul II at a Jewish-Catholic "summit" meeting in Miami. I was among the Jewish leaders who had the honor to be presented to the Pope by Rabbi Waxman. That meeting was hardly free of controversy; some headline-driven Jewish leaders accused Rabbi Waxman of being too deferential to the Pope. These leaders felt that the rabbi should have publicly upbraided the Pope for having received Austrian President Kurt Waldheim, who had been revealed as having been at the scene of Nazi war crimes in Yugoslavia during World War II. They also thought he should have pushed the Vatican hard to recognize the State of Israel. Yet Rabbi Waxman was a consummate gentleman, and public denunciations of other religious leaders were not his style. Instead, Rabbi Waxman spoke forcefully to the Pope in their private meeting about Jewish disquiet over his positions on Waldheim and Israel. It later became clear that his intervention had yielded results, especially on the Israel issue.

Within a few years of that Jewish-Catholic summit in Miami, John Paul reversed decades of Vatican policy and finally recognized the Jewish State in 1993, clearing the way for his later historical visit in 2001 to Jerusalem, Bethlehem, and other Christian holy sites.

Rabbi Waxman was "knighted" by the Church in the mid-1990s as a Commander of the Order of St. Gregory at a ceremony in Baltimore presided over by Cardinal Keeler of that city, who was then chairman of the American Conference of Bishops. Jean and I were proud to attend that ceremony, which also honored Cardinal Willebrands, the Vatican's point man on relations with the Jews for many years.

Even as he engaged in countless activities on a global scale on behalf of the Jewish people, Rabbi Waxman remained deeply engaged with his congregation at Temple Israel. He certainly played an enormous role in the lives of my own family, presiding at the b'nai mitzvot of my two sons, Richard and Stuart, and the bat mitzvah of my daughter, Linda, as well as at two of the three weddings of my children.

Virtually every Saturday afternoon for nearly half a century, Rabbi Waxman opened his home to groups of 15-20 Temple Israel congregants for wonderful group discussions that were always free-spirited, yet civil, in tone. During those sessions, we focused on matters ranging from the Temple Israel and what else could be done to uplift and inspire the congregation to the State of Israel and why its prime ministers often felt the need to take stands in defiance of world opinion.

I remember several occasions during the early 1990s when Prime Minister Yitzhak Shamir was involved in an intense conflict with my friend, President George H.W. Bush. Prime Minister Shamir objected to the President's delay, out of opposition to Shamir's settlement building, to give loan guarantees to Israel. President Bush asked for 120 days approval of loan guarantee.

Some people criticized me strongly for supporting President Bush in the face of some unfortunate comments on the President's part about being "one lonely little guy" standing against the Jewish lobby. Yet at such moments, Rabbi Waxman took firm charge of the discussion so that there would be no expressions of personal animus despite sharp philosophical differences. He was a deeply civilized man who made sure that civility was always upheld and an amiable spirit manifested in all public discussions in which he was involved.

At the end of those invigorating discussions at the Waxmans' home, guests would be treated to some of Ruth Waxman's most delicious baked concoctions. Overall, those Saturday afternoons shmooze sessions were both intellectually enriching and deeply enjoyable. Even today, several years after the passing of both Ruth and Mortie, I miss those occasions intensely.

For me, Rabbi Waxman was a mentor and soul mate in matters of religious doctrine and philosophy who, like myself, supported an open and inclusive form of Conservative Judaism fully at home with both the rhythms of the modern world and the dictates of *halachah.* He was also a dear friend.

As we shall see, when I ran as a maverick for President of the United Synagogue, Rabbi Waxman put his full support and considerable political weight behind me. Without a doubt, his support made a major contribution to my surprise victory.

Sadly, it seems to me that today the Conservative movement has a dearth of leaders of the caliber of Rabbi Waxman.

We need more forward-looking people of great scholarship who are willing to grapple with the crises confronting the movement and the Jewish people as a whole. Rabbi Waxman was truly an irreplaceable leader, and his protean contribution to Conservative Judaism is profoundly missed.

Lessons of the Holocaust

During the late 1940s and 1950s, my religious outlook was profoundy influenced by not only the birth of the State of Israel but also by an unfolding awareness of the impact of the Holocaust on the Jewish people. This outlook colored my deepening involvement with the affairs of Temple Israel and the Conservative Movement.

Earlier, as a college student youth who was mostly occupied with his studies and a young man striving to build a business from the ground up, I had paid only intermittent attention to world affairs. At the time, it was my own dear father who alerted me to the ever-worsening plight of European Jewry.

During a trip to Europe in the mid 1930s, my father had befriended a Jewish clothing manufacturer in Vienna by the name of Klimt. Several years later, after the Nazis took over Austria, my father signed affidavits of financial responsibility that allowed several families named Klimt to receive life-saving documents that allowed them to emigrate to the United States. As World War II began and the Nazis occupied most of Europe, we had heard ominous reports suggesting that terrible atrocities were being committed against Jews. I remember clearly having read in the newspapers of the 1942 report by Gerhardt Reigner, the Geneva representative of the World Jewish Congress, that the Germans had begun the systematic genocide of European Jewry.

Still, like most American Jews, I had been stunned, sickened and appalled beyond words when the U.S. Army poured into Dachau, Bergen-Belsen, and other death camps, liberating the starving and desperately sick survivors and confirming our worst fears about the fate of Europe's Jews.

The lesson that I took from the overwhelming tragedy of the Holocaust, like many other young American Jews of my generation, was that, henceforth, I had to assume a personal responsibility for the welfare of our people in America, Israel, and throughout the world. I also felt a commitment to serve my synagogue and the larger community as a lay leader.

In those days, as today, I was not an emotional person given to grandiloquent declarations and promises. In any case, in the face of the revelation of the magnitude of the Holocaust, words seemed cheap and meaningless. For committed young American Jews like myself, there was little to be said, but a great deal to be done, if we were to achieve our goal of ensuring the Jewish people a sustainable future in America and also in the new State of Israel.

Then, as now, there were different paths to Jewish communal leadership. Some of my colleagues rose as star fund-raisers for United Jewish Appeal or as leaders of defense organizations such as the Anti-Defamation League or American Jewish Congress. My own focus as a budding Jewish leader was almost entirely on creating a vibrant Conservative congregation at Temple Israel and later on building a stronger Conservative movement through our lay arm, the United Synagogue.

The Battle for Egalitarianism

In the early 1950s, I was Chair of the Temple Israel Education Committee, and there I served as an advocate for co-education of boys and girls in our religious school. By that time, a schism had developed in the congregation between those who wanted us to continue to maintain a separate, but clearly not equal, Sunday School for girls and those who supported my efforts to close both of our ineffectual Sunday schools and to provide instead a higher quality co-educational four-days-a-week religious school.

The battle for a new co-educational Sunday school raged for about five years within the congregation before my position, strongly backed by Rabbi Waxman, finally carried the day. In an address to the Temple members on January 23, 1953, I sought to lay out as thoughtfully as possible the high stakes involved in the issue, not only for Temple Israel, but for the larger cause of sustaining the Jewish people in the wake of our shattering losses during the Holocaust. My message was in large part a response to a Board vote that I thought had been undertaken with too little consideration.

> "Nearly two years ago, your education committee made a study of the Sunday School as it then existed. Your committee discovered that the Sunday School as an instrument of teaching Conservative Judaism was totally ineffective, and so recommended to the Board of Trustees that it be abolished by the expedient of not starting new classes....A few people complained, and by a vote of 6-5 out of Board membership of 23, the Board approved the starting of a Sunday school program beginning in September 1953. It is my feeling this does not represent the wishes of the majority of our membership, and so before its final resolution, we are anxious to determine the wishes of the congregation in this matter.
>
> "Those who favor the Sunday School say that a girl does not need the same religious training as a boy; that a girl does not have to be bas mitzvah'd, a girl does not have to know how to read the siddur. We beg you to stop and think. The emotional pulse of Jewish life is very low.

> The rapid deterioration and almost total elimination of traditional observances in the American Jewish home, the appalling widespread ignorance in the field of Jewish learning coupled with the extermination of Jewish community life in Europe have made our situation critical. We are engaged in a war for survival; not survival in the physical sense as in bare group survival, but the survival of values, concepts, and significant ways of group behavior."

We won that battle, and by the mid-1950s, Temple Israel's youth education program was running firmly on the basis of co-education and increasing egalitarianism. Still, the rituals in the synagogue itself were lagging behind. In a speech to the congregation, probably in 1956 or 1957, I expressed concern about our congregation dragging its heels in terms of allowing women equality in our ritual life. I commented especially on girls' and women's right to have an *aliyah* during the reading of the Torah in the synagogue service. I reminded the congregation that the Rabbinical Assembly, the rabbinical arm of the Conservative movement had endorsed that change in 1955. My speech was as follows:

> "Many of us have parents who attended Orthodox synagogues, yet we choose not to follow in the Orthodox affiliations of our parents because we found it unbending, unyielding, and unrealistic. Many left Orthodoxy altogether, became unaffiliated or joined the Reform movement. [On the other hand] we [in the Conservative movement] wanted to keep the spirit and heritage of Judaism today and to reinterpret it to meet the challenges of life today. So we are training our children, giving boys and girls the same study opportunity, setting the same stan-

dards for bar and bas mitzvah. Our high school has more girls enrolled than boys. Every Saturday morning in our youth service, boys and girls are called to read from the Torah. But how can we justify the Temple Israel Youth Service observing one ritual form and the Adult Service observing another one?

"The consequences of our failure to recognize in our adult ritual the needs of our young couples and young adults can well nigh be disastrous. The time is not too distant when the youth of Temple Israel and the many Temple Israels around the country...will, if not granted the same worship opportunities in our synagogues, form their own synagogues...and we will have the very dubious distinction of having fathered a two-generation form of Judaism."

I stated emphatically,

"It is the women who are the backbone of the UJA campaigns, the Federation campaigns. It is the women who are the backbone of the financial support of the sisterhood of the temples in many cases through the activities of the sisterhoods. Is it not fair, then, that these women be given the role of participation in the Jewish life of the community by affording them at least equal worship opportunities with men?

"Now I suggest that we adopt aliyahs for women, not in a revolutionary way, but in an evolutionary way. I suggest that on the occasion of a wedding, perhaps the woman might be called to an aliyah. After the birth of a child. To commemorate a special event. On departing the community for college, a young adult woman

> should be called to the Torah. On Simchas Torah, how nice it would be to have not only a chasan Torah, but also a calla Torah, giving honor and recognition to a woman who has done outstanding work for the Temple community during the year."

Within a few years, the resistance to women's aliyot at Temple Israel had broken down, and by the time I assumed the synagogue presidency in 1959, aliyot were fully egalitarian. While I personally played a role in pushing that process to fruition, the main role in effecting such changes belongs to Rabbi Waxman, who quietly but effectively broke down resistance among an ever-dwindling minority of the Congregation to making the Temple more open, democratic, and egalitarian.

My own efforts to win equal rights for women in services at Temple Israel reflected my overall effort to help build a temple that served as a house of worship for all members on an equal basis and transmitted to members a sense of community. It was to help build that sense that we instituted a lavish kiddush—really a luncheon—after services every Shabbat.

I always encouraged, mainly through example, congregation members to speak out when they had a concern they felt was not being adequately addressed. I thought members ought not leave issues to the Seminary, the United Synagogue, or Temple Israel leadership to resolve. I transmitted a sense that each of us is an important player who could make an impact if he or she spoke out forthrightly and made a cogent case for change.

Yiddishkeit and Jewish Education

From the shul's early years, we developed a full social program. We held an annual bazaar on the lawn of Joe Teich's house. The sisterhood mounted splashy stage productions with names like "Carmen Shapiro" and "Spouse Pacific," which were takeoffs on Broadway musicals. A wonderful synagogue member named Sy Kleinman penned these off-off-off-Broadway extravanzas. Sy kept us laughing for many years.

We had a fiercely committed Board at Temple Israel. These individuals cared passionately about the Temple's welfare and devoted untold hours to making it one of North America's finest Conservative congregations. Our meetings often went on until well past midnight.

At nearly every Board meeting throughout the 1950s and 1960s, we would debate the school curriculum. The phrase we would use was *Yiddishkeit,* as in, "We have to teach *Yiddishkeit.*" We came to realize, during our sometimes heated discussions, that each of us translated the word *Yiddishkeit* to mean something different. Yet we we remained united our determination that our school should do the best possible job of transmitting Jewish knowledge and a feeling of Jewish identity to our young people.

During this period, Great Neck North High School, which many of our youth attended, decided to offer an advanced biology class on Saturdays. We objected strongly, and together with Rabbi Waxman and Rabbi Rudin of nearby Temple Beth El, we raised the issue forcefully with the Great Neck Board of Education. They quickly saw the light, and henceforth there were no more Saturday classes.

My zeal for improving Jewish education led me beyond my own shul to the cause of improving Jewish education throughout Long Island. I was among the founders and the first president of the Long Island Association of Jewish Congregational Schools. In a speech to the founding meeting of that body on April 30, 1953, I said,

> "Our problem is the whole of Jewish education—a problem made acute by the mushrooming growth of Nassau and Suffolk counties during

> the past eight years. In that short space, a migratory wave of young parents left the stability of urban living with its mature cultural and social institutions for suburban life with its immature institutional patterns, creating an ineffective, unstable and unsatisfactory educational system....To this end we are committed to a three-point policy: standardization, intensification, and expansion of [Jewish education]."

A Jewish Take on Intermarriage

Institutional change is not always an easy thing to bring about; certainly there were times when I was less than successful in my Temple endeavors. One area where I failed back in the 1960s and 1970s, both at Temple Israel and at the United Synagogue, and where I am still having little success today, is that of intermarriage. I believe strongly that Jewish institutions must accept the reality of intermarriage and learn to foster sparks of Judaism wherever they exist.

Today about half of American Jews marry outside of their faith. The Reform movement has found a way to welcome the non-Jewish partner as a *ger,* a stranger who is honored among us, and thereby allow the intermarried couple and their children to participate in synagogue life. The Conservative movement and associated synagogues, on the other hand, spend considerable energy passing edicts stipulating that the gentile partner in mixed marriages should be prohibited from serving on the Board of Directors and on committees of Conservative synagogues.

There was simply too much resistance at Temple Israel, the Seminary, and the United Synagogue for me to make much progress on my entreaty to the Conservative movement that we should discuss this subject sensibly and dispassionately. It remained one of those subjects we don't talk about.

Nevertheless, I often raised the subject of intermarried rights in off-the-record discussions among the movement leadership. I am more outspoken on the subject today, as a respected leader emeritus with no further personal ambitions for communal leadership posts.

I welcome our movement advocating the adoption of Patrilineage, whereby if one member of the couple is Jewish and the children are brought up Jewish, then the couple should be considered Jewish and welcomed in our synagogue. But I am also advocating that we open our eyes to the steady hemorrhaging of our number due to the soaring intermarriage rate. At a minimum, if we were to be more welcoming to intermarried couples in our temples, we would stop driving away those couples who desire to raise their children as Jews or at least to expose them to Judaism and raise their children as Jews.

Temple Presidency, 1959-1964

On September 7, 1958, we broke ground for our building on Old Mill Road, the same building we use today. Speaking on this occasion, I foreshadowed the platform for my Presidency ust a year later, as follows:

> "The synagogue has a threefold aim; as a House of Worship, House of Study, and House of Gathering. The Synagogue building, standing in the midst of the community, constantly proclaims that to be a Jew means to believe in something that is beyond Man. That we can grasp through our five senses and understand through the power of our own reason is not the totality of existence or of being. The rapid growth of Great Neck, the

> expanding program of our synagogue, the sincere desire of all of us to dignify our worship, our study, and our gathering with an environment worthy of our community; all these factors impel us to proceed with our new construction."

During that same year, I wrote an article in the *Temple Israel Light,* in which I staunchly upheld the right of individual synagogues to shape their own destinies. I warned the other institutions within the Conservative movement—including the Jewish Theological Seminary, the Rabbinic Assembly, and the United Synagogue—not to overstep and infringe on the prerogatives of the synagogue. My article included the following:

> "I believe that a congregation has the sovereign right to determine how it shall raise funds and what its relationship shall be with other synagogues in the community. Any attempts to dictate to the member institutions...may divide and splinter our Conservative movement. We may suddenly find ourselves with congregations, Conservative in spirit, that refuse to affiliate with the United Synagogue because they refuse to be told how to conduct themselves in those affairs that are clearly internal matters....Our growing Conservative movement needs leadership to strengthen it—not a Big Brother to oversee it."

During my five-year presidency, Temple Israel continued to grow at a steady pace. We experienced far fewer ideological problems than had existed during the tumultuous 1950s. With the synagogue running smoothly, I began dealing with issues farther afield. Somewhat ironically, given my insistence on maintaining the autonomy of individual congregations from the dictates of the United Synagogue, I was becoming ever more involved in shaping policy for that national body.

Serving the Metropolitan Region of the United Synagogue

My first major stepping stone toward the leadership of the United Synagogue was my assumption of the presidency of the organization's Metropolitan region, a position in which I served from 1958 to 1960. The Metropolitan region included all of Greater New York, where something like forty percent of the nation's Jews lived. So by dint of demography, it was the most powerful United Synagogue region.

It was natural that in my new capacity I formed a close relationship with Rabbi Louis Finkelstein, the veteran, much revered Chancellor of the Jewish Theological Seminary. I maintained this friendship even after leaving the Metropolitan region leadership to become a United Synagogue lay leader.

National Enrollment Plan Chairman

Rabbi Finkelstein initiated the idea of the Seminary's National Enrollment Plan (NEP), a newfangled concept for raising money for the Seminary that involved Conservative lay people more directly in Seminary affairs. Yours truly signed on as NEP chairman and initiated a whirlwind of travel together with Jean to Conservative congregations around the United States and Canada, where I would advocate forcefully on NEP's behalf. I felt passionately about the Seminary's importance as the indispensable intellectual resource that sustained the entire Conservative movement. I also understood that the NEP represented an opportunity to put right the Seminary's hitherto shaky finances, which hitherto had inhibited its ability to compete with other academic institutions for the best young minds in the Jewish community.

At venues across the country I regaled audiences about the importance of the National Enrollment Plan to the Seminary and to the entire Conservative movement. One such time was during a special convention of the National Enrollment Plan in Miami Beach in January 1961, which drew Conservative movement luminaries from around the country. Addressing the delegates, I asked,

> "What does the Seminary need the money for? For its rabbinical school? Yes, and here the Seminary must be in a position to compete for youth possessed of great intellect. The Seminary trains and teaches cantors; the seminary through its teacher's institute prepares our children's instruction—through the medium of radio and the Eternal Light program, the message of Judaism is brought to millions of non-Jews. And through this medium and the medium of the Frontiers of Faith on television, many non-Jews have their only contact and only information about our people, our way of life, and the high ethical standards we set for ourselves. The Seminary sponsors the Jewish Museum [and] five Ramah camps....The Seminary [projects] our voice onto the American scene and at various political functions, stating our position on *schechita,* on capital punishment, and on other issues.
>
> The *tachlis* of all of this is that it costs money. Gentlemen, we are the leaders of the communities, the presidents of our congregations, the opinion molders of our associates. We have a responsibility to commit ourselves to the support of our institutions. An annual deficit on $1 million is taken from funds that have been earmarked for endowments and other major purposes.
>
> Can anyone here conceive of a school of learning starting its academic year without knowing where its funds are coming from or how

> much money is coming in? Yet until NEP, this has been the way the Seminary School had to operate....We propose that every individual member of every U.S. congregation be a member of NEP supporting the Seminary. We propose that a $10 annual membership fee be added to the dues bill submitted by the congregation. Surely no one can say that for what the Seminary does, $10 is too much. $3.2 million can be raised in this way without one penny of it going towards paying the expenses of high-priced professional fund-raisers and expenses of an elaborate fund-raising structure. I hope that each of you through your temple Board of Trustees will pass a resolution adopting NEP by which the sum of $10 will be added to your membership fee bill and will be collected by you and forwarded directly to the Seminary to support its work."

My appeal was accepted by acclamation. Within a relatively short period, thanks in large part to my constant traveling and making the case for the indispensability of NEP for the Seminary, we were able to raise much of the money we had been seeking. After steadily increasing NEP proceeds, we succeeded in raising more than one million dollars in one year in 1969, my last year as NEP chairman.

I was extremely gratified to know that my efforts had helped put the finances of the Seminary on a more solid basis. What a thrill it was to see that superb institution of learning with the means to focus more fully on its main role, namely, that of giving the best possible education and training to our next generation of Conservative rabbis and cantors. In a show of gratitude for that achievement, I was invited to the Seminary by Rabbi Finkelstein, who presented me with seven leather-bound volumes of the Talmud. It was a high honor, and one I certainly appreciated.

Rabbi Finkelstein was a brilliant person, of whose scholarship I stood in awe and whose friendship I deeply valued, but he was also an individual whose anger could easily be aroused if someone disagreed with him. As we will see, he and I had a number of confrontations once I became president of the United Synagogue. Yet once he had his explosion and had calmed down, Rabbi Finkelstein would return to manifesting a feeling of close and loving friendship. He was a giant among Jewish leaders, who during his time as Chancellor did everything he could to broaden the base of the Seminary and make it relevant to the larger society. One on occasion, he invited Chief Justice Earl Warren to lecture at the Seminary. Much of what the Seminary is about today reflects the directions begun by Rabbi Finkelstein during his tenure.

Those almost continual journeys on behalf of NEP during the early and mid-1960s allowed me to build a wide web of personal connections. That network would prove indispensable when, a few years later, I would throw my yarmulke into the ring as a candidate for the presidency of the United Synagogue.

I was scarcely an unquestioning supporter of the United Synagogue. I perceived that the organization was failing to meet the challenges it was facing in the late 1960s, an era of rapid growth and societal transformation. Watching more and more of our youth being pulled away from Judaism by the lure of the era's youth culture, I wanted to help make the Conservative Movement more responsive. In my position as a lay leader, I advocated that the United Synagogue step up its efforts to communicate with Conservative Jewish youth on campuses across the country.

While the top lay and professional leadership of the organization listened respectfully and paid lip service to my appeals, they did next to nothing to turn my ideas into concrete programs. Therefore, it seemed to me, only by becoming president could I change the culture of the organization.

The Arduous Road to the United Synagogue Presidency

In 1968, I let it be known within the movement that I was interested in being elected president of the United Synagogue at the annual convention of the United Synagogue set for October 1969. I was the first-ever independent presidential candidate who did not have the endorsement of the United Synagogue's professional leadership and of the Jewish Theological Seminary leadership.

At that time, the United Synagogue clearly occupied the lowest rung in the triangular relationship with the two other premiere organizations of the Conservative movement, namely, the Jewish Theological Seminary and the Rabbinical Assembly. The United Synagogue was obviously under the Seminary's thumb, operating out of a small office in the headquarters of that institution. I believed it was time to shake up the United Synagogue's starchy and unimaginative leadership; I wanted the organization to advocate more forcefully on behalf of the Conservative lay population.

As the fateful annual convention approached, I was chagrined to learn that I had not been selected for the position by the nominating committee, which included the United Synagogue insiders as well as some of the top people at the Rabbinical Assembly and the Seminary. The committee chose instead Emmanuel Scoblionco, of Allentown, Pennsylvania. Scoblionco was a decent man who had contributed much time and effort to the United Synagogue over the years but who was hardly an innovator with ambitions to raise the profile of the organization in a serious way.

Clearly, the powers that be in the Seminary and the RA preferred a docile United Synagogue that would do the bidding of the other two branches of the movement without making much of a fuss. They saw to it that my candidacy was spurned precisely because I threatened to shake up that cozy relationship. Among those who did their best to try to deep-six my candidacy was Rabbi Bernard Mandelbaum, the Seminary's Provost, who served directly under Rabbi Finkelstein and directed the Seminary's relationship with the United Synagogue. Rabbi Mandelbaum campaigned actively for my opponent, giving the distinct impression that the Seminary was opposed to my candidacy.

At that point, about three months before the convention, I was faced with an immediate choice: either renounce my ambitions to be elected the United Synagogue president or mount a challenge to the nominating committee and take my case directly to the rank-and-file at the convention. The odds against success in the latter appeared long; there had never before been a challenge to the official nominee selected by the nominating committee (nor has there been since). Yet while it seemed likely that I would lose my appeal, I concluded that my staying in the race as an independent candidate would give a platform to the many people who believed the United Synagogue had to stop doing business as usual and instead address the serious issues impacting the Conservative movement.

I therefore moved vigorously into action, filing the necessary petitions with the signatures of people from congregations across the country, with the hundreds of lay leaders with whom I had formed connections and friendships during my peregrinations on behalf of the National Enrollment Plan. I put in a call to Rabbi Finkelstein and expressed my consternation that Rabbi Mandelbaum, his second-in-command at the Seminary, was exerting so much influence over the process. I said, with more emotion in my voice than I usually want to express, "I spent several years raising money for the National Enrollment Plan; if you recall, you held a luncheon in my honor after I raised one million dollars for the NEP—doesn't all of that qualify me to be President of the United Synagogue?!" Rabbi Finkelstein responded, "Don't worry. There will be no more interference." Indeed, from that point forward, Rabbi Mandelbaum kept quiet.

I also turned to my own beloved spiritual leader, Rabbi Mordecai Waxman, who, by this time, had attained considerable prestige as one of the most respected congregational rabbis in the movement. I was delighted that Rabbi Waxman gave me his very active support. He sent letters to every rabbi in the country speaking warmly about his years of getting to know me in the synagogue, about my work on the Jewish education committe, and about how we had worked together on the interfaith committee.

Considering that I was directly taking on the movement's establishment, this was a somewhat risky move on Rabbi Waxman's part. I was deeply grateful to him for supporting me so ardently. I also had a strong team who had served with me in the Metropolitan region—people like George Maislin and Henry Rapaport who campaigned actively on my behalf, sending letters to the leaders of the other regions endorsing my candidacy.

After I had gathered what I understood to be the requisite number of signatures, I submitted my petition to the nominating committee. The committee promptly informed me that they rejected my petition as "unacceptable" for having too few signatures and having failed to fulfill other arcane and never-before-invoked requirements. Keeping my cool, I went out and gathered the required number of signatures and met the other requirements, and then sent the nominating committee a thinly- veiled warning that they would be well advised to accept my petition if they did not want me to go to the podium at the convention and speak openly and candidly to the larger membership about what had been going on behind the scenes.

The United Synagogue convention opened at the Concord Hotel at Lake Kiamesha, New York, on Sunday, October 26, 1969, and for the first time in the history of the Conservative lay movement, there was an air of excitement and suspense as the proceedings opened. All of my friends and supporters from around the country were pumped up and predicting my victory; I myself, while hopeful, was less convinced that the delegates would overturn decades of precedent and elect as president of the United Synagogue a person who had not been endorsed by the nominating committee.

On the following day, my opponent and I both made nominating speeches. Unlike the speech of my opponent, which was characteristically cautious, my own speech was a clarion call for change. I urged an upgrading of the role of the United Synagogue in relation to the other wings of the movement and beckoned the United Synagogue to reach out much more assertively to our young people, especially to those on college campuses.

The vote was held by secret ballot—again for the first time in the organization's history—and several suspenseful hours ensued before the results were announced. I was elected president of the United Synagogue by a 2-1 margin. The delegates responded to the announcement with a sustained round of applause. I was then inundated by backslaps, handshakes and effusive congratulations, including a surprising number from insiders who had opposed me.

Befitting the significance of the moment in the history ofthe Conservative movement, Dr. Finkelstein called almost immediately from New York. He congratulated me and informed me that he would be coming up on Wednesday night at the culmination of the convention to install me officially as president of the United Synagogue.

Moving the United Synagogue Forward

On Tuesday, I met with three of my supporters among the lay leadership—Phil Greene, Harold Stubenhaus, and Ben Markowe—and asked them to peruse the United Synagogue budget for $40,000 that could be used for new programs I wanted to institute. By the following day, they had determined that there was a $20,000 surplus in the budget that could be used for new programs, which was at least a start. On Wednesday night, I was duly installed by Dr. Finkelstein and everything went very smoothly. All of my family was there, including my mother, who came up from Florida for the occasion.

On November 10, I had a pleasant luncheon with Rabbi Finkelstein at the Seminary where we discussed in general our aims and hopes for the Conservative movement. There was complete harmony, and we agreed it would be advantageous to continue this type of luncheon meeting throughout the course of my term.

Certainly, Rabbi Finkelstein readily accepted two of the principle changes I made; replacing Rabbi Bernard Siegel, who I believed had served as executive director for too long, and elevated him into another, more ceremonial position. I appointed Dr. Morton Siegel, who served ably as acting executive director until I was able to find a regular executive director, Benjamin Kreitman, who then served ably for many years. The other big change was moving the United Synagogue's main office out of the Seminary to a new space at 115 Fifth Avenue.

The move was a symbolic Declaration of Independence from the Seminary by the United Synagogue, which would now be better able to carve out its own identity without the Seminary leadership breathing down our necks. To his credit,

Rabbi Finkelstein readily accepted the move. I had the impression he was even relieved to have a strong United Synagogue President like myself who was forceful in insisting on cutting the apron strings after so many years.

To be sure, our declaration of independence was only a relative one, since United Synagogue's budget, for example, still came from the Seminary. It was at my meetings with Rabbi Finkelstein every year to plan the following year's budget that his well-known temper would sometimes boil over. Naturally, I would submit a somewhat larger budget request every year in order to pay for new programs, and at times, he would exclaim forcefully that it was a *hillul hashem* (a desecration of the name of God) to press the Seminary for money.

I learned not to take those explosions too seriously because after a little while, he would calm down and negotiate an agreement with me that invariably would meet the needs of the United Synagogue. Then we would shake hands amicably and depart from each other as the best of friends.

The initiative that I carried out as President of the United Synagogue of which I am most proud was the outfitting of a truck into a full-service bookmobile that traveled to campuses across the United States. The bookmobile's purpose was to reach out to our college youth and show them our caring and support at a moment of maximum tension between the generations across the United States. The bookmobile was a pioneer effort that was later copied by other Jewish groups. We implemented the program during a time when college campuses were consumed with extreme left-wing politics; with young people burning American flags and marching with banners of the Viet Cong.

In the wake of the 1967 war in the Middle East, the student left also had become militantly anti-Israel; they had begun accusing Israel of being an imperialist occupying power ruthlessly persecuting the Palestinians. Never mind that at the Khartoum Conference several weeks after the end of the 1967 War, the Arab countries had unanimously agreed on a hard-line statement categorically refusing to recognize Israel's right to exist.

On America's campuses, the Israelis were the bad guys, and pro-Israel Jewish students were feeling ever more lonely and isolated. Our bookmobile and other campus-directed programs I initiated helped to ease that sense among our students of being left alone, without support, in a bitterly hostile environment.

My principle joy at being president of the United Synagogue was traveling the length and breadth of the United States and Canada, with occasional visits to south-of-the-border locales such as Puerto Rico, Mexico, and Argentina, to discuss the future of the movement with our lay leaders. Almost invariably, I brought Jean along with me on those trips, and the connections we formed were family-to-family, rather just person-to-person between myself and a particular leader. Indeed, there was generally a warm sense during those meetings of being part of a larger family—the family of the United Synagogue—with most of us committed to a common agenda to reform and invigorate the lay arm of the Conservative movement.

I was able to carry out the bulk of my reforms during my first year as President of the United Synagogue. This proved fortunate because within a few months of my ascension, I found my time and energy more and more consumed by happenings at the Conference of Presidents of Major American Jewish Organizations, where, as first we shall shortly see, I rather quickly ascended to the position of acting president.

In the 1970s I found myself facing a situation in which it was critical to establish strategies to help as many Soviet Jews as possible to move to Israel, and to help coordinate the Jewish community's position vis a vis U.S. Secretary of State

William Rogers' plan for Middle East Peace. The work of the United Synagogue, as important as it was, began to take second place in my time and priorities.

Fortunately, I had built a capable team at the United Synagogue. Executive director Dr. Morton Siegel kept things running in the right direction while I negotiated with President Nixon and Secretary of State Henry Kissinger over the Soviets and the Jackson-Vanik Amendment or over moving American armaments more expeditiously during the Yom Kippur War.

In 1973, in turning over the office of president to my successor, I was able to say with pride that we had fulfilled the bulk of what we had set out to accomplish four years earlier. Thanks to the steps we had taken, the United Synagogue had become a serious player for the first time, not only within the Conservative movement, but in the larger Jewish community as well.

I remained active in both Temple Israel and the United Synagogue long after I retired as president of both places. I never forgot that it was those two wonderful institutions that launched me on a path that led me to the very highest positions of American Jewish lay leadership.

A Leap into Jewish Political Affairs: Acting Chairman, 1970-1971

At the time I was elected to be President of United Synagogue in October, 1969, I had no aspirations to rising higher in the councils of American Jewish leadership. Until then, my Jewish horizons had been limited to the world of Conservative Judaism—which seemed to me during the 1950's and 1960's to be more than enough of a challenge.

Certainly, I relished the opportunity to represent the organization on the Conference of Presidents of Major American Jewish Organizations. I quickly recognized the sacred trust of this umbrella body that espouses the positions of the American Jewish community to the White House and Congress, as well as foreign governments.

I never imagined that within two months I would assume the role of acting chairman of that august body—or that I would then twice be elected to be its chairman. I was privileged to serve in what is widely considered the most important leadership position in American Jewry during one of the most tumultuous period for Israel and world Jewry in the second half of the twentieth century.

The Conference of Presidents had its origins in the early

1950's, and, ironically enough, was not created at the initiative of the organized Jewish community but rather the U.S. State Department.

One day in late 1953, Henry Byroade, Assistant Secretary of State for Near Eastern and African Affairs, approached Nachum Goldmann, president of the World Zionist Organization to ask whether it would be possible for American Jewish organizations to create a single mouthpiece in its dealing with the Eisenhower Administration. This was to spare officials like himself and his boss, Secretary of State John Foster Dulles, from having to receive delegations from a multiplicity of organizations.

Working closely with the then-Israeli Ambassador to Washington, Abba Eban and Nachum Goldmann succeeded in convincing the heads of 15 key Jewish organizations to join together in a new body to be known as the Presidents Club (the name was changed in the 1960's to the Conference of Presidents of Major American Jewish Organizations).

As J.J. Goldberg narrates in his book, *Jewish Power,* the Presidents Club, which was headed at the outset by Goldmann, began as an informal body with virtually no staff or budget. Its very limited purpose was to express American Jewry's consensus of support for Israel to the U.S. government and other governments around the world.

Goldmann was a charming and savvy political operator of German birth who had represented the WZO in Geneva during the 1930's and the Second World War, and by the 1950's was the New York-based head of numerous organizations, including the WZO, World Jewish Congress and the Conference on Jewish Material Claims Against Nazi Germany. Goldmann realized he could not run the Presidents Conference on his own and persuaded Chicago real-estate developer Phillip Klutznick, International President of B'nai B'rith, to take over as chairman. Yehuda Hellman, an Israeli who had worked closely with Goldmann in the past, was hired as executive director. The high level of interest in the newly-created State of Israel brought Zionist leaders, and those working to secure U.S. aid in the release of Soviet Jews, to address their issue and seek government support.

Previous meetings between various Jewish organizations and government officials had been kept mostly discreet and secret. In contrast, the meetings of the Presidents Club with officials like Dulles, were widely publicized, so as to place maximum pressure on the Eisenhower and subsequent administrations to lend a sympathetic ear to the positions of Israel and American Jewry.

Throughout the 1960's, under the leadership of chairmen B'nai B'rith President, Label Katz (1960-61),, Rabbi Irving Miller 1961-63), Lewis Weinstein 1963-65), Dr. Joachim Prinz 1965-67), and Rabbi Herschel Schacter, the Presidents Conference transformed itself from a loose club of presidents to a representative bodies of organizations representing the overwhelming majority of American Jews.

The importance of the Presidents Conference as the voice of the American Jewish community in its dealings with both Congress and the Lyndon Johnson Administration was heightened during the tense weeks leading up to the 1967 Six Day War, and upgraded again after President Nixon came to power and became the first U.S. president in history to receive a delegation from the Presidents Conference in the Oval Office.

The ever-growing prominence of the Presidents Conference caused consternation among some within the Jewish organizational world, including, ironically, the Conference's aging founder, Nachum Goldmann, who had come to feel by the end of the 1960's that the Presidents Conference was putting his own World Jewish Congress in the shade. As we shall see, I was compelled to spend considerable time and energy during my first months as Presidents Conference chairman to counter a series of moves by Goldmann to strengthen the WJC's position in America so as to establish that body as the voice of an 'independent' American Jewish community rather than the voice of the Israeli Foreign Office, as he falsely characterized the Presidents Conference.

Originally, I had planned spending my first year on the Presidents Conference as a quiet listener and learner, but almost immediately events put me in a different direction. The chairman of the Presidents Conference at the time I myself assumed membership in the Jewish community's premiere umbrella body was William Wexler, the soft-spoken president of B'nai B'rith. Wexler was a resident of Savannah, Georgia, and with his wife's illness was often not in place in New York or Washington when crises erupted and emergency meetings of the Presidents Conference had to be called.

Wexler discerned the importance of appointing an acting chairman with the power to call emergency meetings in his absence when necessary, and within several months of his taking office as chairman in January 1970, he asked me if I would be willing to assist him as acting Chairman. I was surprised and gratified by the request and immediately accepted.

Bill Wexler never shared his thinking with me about why he passed over a number of Presidents Conference veterans and chose a newcomer like myself as acting chairman, but I do believe there were several important elements in his decision.

Outgoing chairman Rabbi Herschel Schacter told me shortly after I joined the Presidents Conference that certain longtime members were unhappy at the selection of Wexler as chairman earlier that autumn, such as President of the Union of American Hebrew Congregations Rabbi Maurice Eisendrath and President of the Rabbinical Assembly Rabbi Wolfe Kelman. They felt strongly that the chairman should have been a president of one of the denominational movements, which they considered the heart and soul of American Jewry.

Therefore, it seems likely that Wexler, keenly aware of this simmering resentment among Conference *vatikim* (veterans), preferred to choose a newcomer as acting chairman—someone who, like himself, was not a rabbi.

There was another factor; namely that one year after the Republican Party had reclaimed the White House after an eight year hiatus, I believe that I was the only member of the Presidents Conference who was an active member of the GOP.

My friendship with Max Fisher and the role he played in all my personal relations with the White House and with all the Conference of Presidents relations was most important. Max was a Michigan businessman and chairman of the Council of Jewish Federations who, over the preceding several years, had become the Jewish community's "Mr. Republican."

In 1969, Max moved into the White House as President Nixon's liaison to the organized Jewish community. Thus, it made political sense for Wexler to give a role in the Presidents Conference to an active Republican like myself, who had Fisher's ear and trust.

Yet neither Wexler nor I had an idea at the time he asked me to serve as acting chairman that he would soon be absent so frequently that I would become, in effect, de facto chairman of the body for much of the remainder of his presidency.

Shortly after his election to the chairmanship, Wexler's wife became gravely ill and passed away. It threw him into an extended period of mourning that clearly limited his ability to handle the heavy political lifting that came with being chairman.

After Wexler's election to a second one year term in late 1970 (since the origins of the Presidents Conference, all chairmen have customarily received a second one year term unless they request otherwise), he met and married an Israeli woman.

This much happier circumstance again diverted his attention from the world of politics and diplomacy.

In any case, by that time, Wexler had become accustomed to leaving in my hands considerable amounts of Presidents Conference business that would customarily have been on the chairman's plate. He was evidently satisfied with the balanced and self-confident way I ran the organization's business. Therefore, as the end of Wexler's second one year term approached, I had the inside track to be elected as Chairman of the Conference.

The Rogers Plan

I will never forget the first time I took part in a Presidents Conference mission to Washington—December 22, 1969.

My maiden mission came at a moment of high tension in U.S.-Israel relations. The crisis had been precipitated by Secretary of State William Rogers, who within a few months of coming to office found himself exasperated by what he felt was Israel's stalling of international mediation efforts during repeated missions to the Middle East by United Nations Special Representative Gunnar Jarring during 1968 and early 1969. Golda Meir had become Israel's Prime Minister in February 1969 after her predecessor Levi Eshkol died suddenly of a heart attack. Even more emphatically than Eshkol, Golda Meir made clear Israel's unwillingness to go beyond rhetorical affirmations of Security Council Resolution 242 to actually manifesting a readiness to withdraw from large parts of the territories it had occupied in 1967.

Concerned about deteriorating U.S. relations with the Arab world and Moscow's ever-growing influence there, Rogers became increasingly determined to turn up the pressure on Jerusalem. Secretary Rogers' strenuous efforts to create a more "even handed" policy between Israel and the Arabs, were, however, only intermittently backed by President Nixon, who during the course of his first year in office frequently undercut Rogers on a variety of issues, including the Middle East; seeming instead to favor the counsel of his National Security Advisor, Dr. Henry Kissinger.

On December 9,1969, Rogers, who undoubtedly felt driven in part by a desire to demonstrate through a bold initiative that he was the real arbiter of U.S. foreign policy, delivered a major Middle East policy address. Roger's speech contained a laundry list of policy initiatives that stunned Israel and the American Jewish community, neither of which had been consulted in advance.

The speech called for an Israeli withdrawal from the Sinai and the West Bank back to the 1967 borders; contemplated granting Jordan an ill-defined role in Jerusalem, which Israel had annexed and declared as its eternal and undivided capital in the immediate aftermath of the 1967 War. Rogers also advocated giving Palestinian refugees from 1948 the right either to return or to be compensated.

Within days, the main precepts of the speech were being referred to in the media as the "Rogers Plan" and the State Department was steadily putting pressure on the Israeli government to accept it.

Such an acceptance was, however, clearly not in the cards; as Israeli Ambassador to the U.S. Yitzhak Rabin made clear several days after Rogers' speech when he came to the Presidents Conference to tell us in unambiguous terms that the Rogers Plan endangered Israel's very survival and should be staunchly opposed by the American Jewish community. We needed little convincing on that score, and the cautious political signals coming from the White House during those December days indicated that, Rogers' advocacy aside, the Nixon White House Administration did not relish the prospect of trying to force the terms of the Rogers Plan down Israel's throat.

Clearly, there was reason to hope that if the Presidents Conference and other Jewish organizations engaged in some well-timed pro-Israel political advocacy on Capitol Hill and in the media, we might be able to alleviate the pressure on Israel to assent to Rogers' terms. First, however, we needed to meet with Rogers himself, to signal our complete rejection of his proposal.

Upon my arrival in Washington on the morning of December 22 for the meeting with Secretary of State Rogers, I took a cab to the B'nai B'rith Building on Rhode Island Avenue, where I and the 13 other members of the Presidents Conference who assembled in Washington that day received a briefing from Shlomo Argov, a top assistant to Rabin at the Israeli Embassy. Argov presented a very black picture—I thought overly black—of impending confrontation between Washington and Jerusalem as a result of the Rogers Plan. After that meeting, our 14 member delegation got into limousines to be transported to the Department of State, where we were ushered into the offices of the Secretary. Outgoing chairman Rabbi Schacter was our spokesman, while Rogers was flanked during the meeting by such State Department heavyweights as Roy Atherton and Joe Sisco.

What followed was a cordial but tough exchange, in which Rogers insisted that the fulfillment of the positions he had articulated in his December speech were necessary not only to prevent the radicalization of the then-600 million strong Muslim world, but also secure the long term survival of Israel itself. Roger's argument in this respect amounted to a classic exposition of a State Department mindset which George Ball later memorably described as "saving Israel in spite of itself." That outlook was radically at variance with the American Jewish community's core belief that the U.S. should give Israel the means to defend herself against a coalition of implacable Arab enemies with combined armies many times the size of her own, and should also grant the Jewish state the political independence to determine when her security "red lines" had been crossed.

Therefore, we took polite but firm exception to Rogers' position on each of the issues in contention; the U.S. calls for Israel to withdraw from Sinai and the West Bank; the contemplation of any sort of "return" to Israel by the 1948 Palestinian Arab refugees; and Rogers' assertion that Jordan should be given some kind of role in Jerusalem. Despite the deep and undisguised disagreement between the two sides, however, civility was maintained throughout the discussion and voices were never raised even during the sharpest moments of contention.

After our delegation left Rogers' office, we headed back to B'nai B'rith, where we hammered out a press release reflecting our deep concerns over Rogers' presentation.

Our public statement amounted to a signal to Jewish grass roots organizations across the country to commence a telephone and letter-writing campaign to President Nixon, Secretary Rogers and other key Administration officials making clear our community's disquiet over the specter of the United States pressuring Israel to retreat to what Israel's Foreign Minister Abba Eban called the "Auschwitz borders" of pre-1967. We made clear that we found such a demand upon Israel to be especially unfair and dangerous for her survival given that the entire Arab world had emphatically refused to accept Israel's existence within any boundaries whatsoever in their infamous "Four No's" declaration of July 1967.

As I flew back to New York, I vowed to myself to ensure that the 800-plus congregations affiliated with United Synagogue should be mobilized immediately so that we could play our part in the Jewish community's battle against the Rogers Plan. I reflected that I was now one of a handful of American Jews who had been empowered to present the position of the

Jewish community—as well as those of Israel—to the highest policy makers in the United States government. It was both an exhilarating opportunity and an awesome responsibility. True, I was only one individual, but it was also the case that the well-being of millions of Jews in Israel and other countries depended in no small part on how persuasively I and other members of the Presidents Conference would be able to articulate Israel's case, and how effective we would be in marshaling political resources on behalf of the Jewish state.

Fast forward one month to January 24, 1970. On that day, the other presidents and I were back at the B'nai B'rith building, preparing for the annual conference of the Presidents Conference the following day. As we deliberated, we were informed that President Nixon had prepared a message for delivery to the participants at the meeting. Hammered out by Nixon himself in collaboration with Max Fisher, it specifically named Israel as a "friendly state," a characterization with diplomatic significance that raised Israel's status vis a vis the U.S. as close to, although not yet at, the level of a NATO ally. The statement also made reference to arms and material assistance requested by Israel and, most importantly, denied categorically that there was any attempt ongoing to the U.S. government to impose a peace on Israel and its neighbors or to substitute negotiations between the superpowers for direct negotiations between the direct parties to the conflict.

While Nixon's statement left a great deal to be desired from a pro-Israel point of view, it nevertheless appeared to be much closer to our position, at least rhetorically, than to the Rogers Plan. The friendly tone of the statement appeared to be dramatic evidence that the Administration had responded positively to the tremendous wave of concern about undue U.S. pressure on Israel that had flooded into Washington from Jewish communities and organizations all around the country during the preceding month. The Administration's palpable shift in position as a direct consequence of that lobbying campaign seemed to me a powerful demonstration of our community's political weight and of how we could effectively respond as concerned American citizens to developments in U.S. Mideast policy we found potentially dangerous for Israel. I was particularly gratified with the prominent role played in that campaign by our United Synagogue congregations.

Tension between Secretary of State William Rogers and President Nixon's national security affairs advisor were sharp, and word came to me from Max Fisher that Leonard Garment, counselor to the President and advisor on Jewish affairs, had said that the President did not intend to advance the very initiatives he was advising in the Rogers Plan: initiatives for Israeli withdrawals. The plan presented ten points for Israel, Egypt, and the Soviet Union, which were to create a "final and reciprocal accord."

On December 22, 1970, Israel stated, "Israel will not be sacrified by any power or interpower policy and will reject any attempts at an imposed solution. The proposal submitted by the the USA cannot but be interpreted by the Arab leaders as an attempt to appease them at the expense of Israel." Israel, Egypt, and the Soviet Union all rejected the Rogers Plan.

Internal Politics

Not that the work of the Presidents Conference was all high geopolitics. As I was quick to find out, we had to deal with our own internal political issues as well. I met with Bill Wexler on February 5 to argue that the organizations within the Presidents Conference with the most substantial memberships—especially the denominational organizations—should be given some kind of weighted vote in determining the policies of the Presidents Conference. I also advocated that the Presidents Conference should more clearly distinguish its own mission from those of bodies like the World Jewish Congress and United Jewish Appeal, with which we sometimes overlapped and competed. The way to accomplish this, I asserted, was to restrict our activities to the dealings of the American Jewish community with Israel and with Jews abroad, primarily the Soviet Union. I said specifically that we should focus our attention and efforts on America's relations with Israel and our support for Israel and a strong American-Israel partnership, as we keep our members informed on our domestic problems.

Wexler was sympathetic to the views I was propounding, but also gave me the impression that given the delicate nature of organizational relationships within the Presidents Conference, any changes would have to be introduced slowly and piecemeal.

Looking back, he was correct, for today nearly 35 years later, the same kind of turf battles still resonate between the large and small organizations that make up the now much larger and more powerful Presidents Conference. The political reality is that it has proven devilishly hard to reform an unwieldy club of high-powered presidents, each of whom fights tenaciously to protect the interests of his or her own organization and most of whom come to the table with a healthy sense of self-importance.

As Abba Eban once quipped, "So, all of these people are Presidents of Major American Jewish Organizations? Aren't there any minor ones?"

I also learned during that my first months at the Presidents Conference that while international diplomacy often takes place behind closed doors inside the cozy corridors of power, it can also take place on occasion in chaotic fashion amidst swarms of shoving reporters and fired-up street demonstrators.

On the morning of March 2, a group of us convened in Dr. Wexler's suite in the Waldorf Astoria Hotel in New York for a meeting with President Georges Pompidou of France, who was completing a tour of the United States that had taken him to Washington, San Francisco and Chicago. Pompidou had long angered the American Jewish community by maintaining an arms embargo of Israel initiated in the wake of the 1967 War by his predecessor Charles De Gaulle and in uttering a string of pro-Arab and anti-Israel policies and statements that went even further than the unbalanced positions laid out by De Gaulle during his last two years in office.

Pompidou had asserted during his American trip that Israel "should cease taking advantage of its special racial ties," which appeared to be another way of saying that Diaspora Jews should not advocate on behalf of, or even feel any special relationship with, their fellow Jews in Israel. The Conference was deeply concerned with the tenor of Pompidou's positions and comments and we were primed to give him a major piece of our mind at the New York meeting. Instead, we were left stewing in our own juices all morning, until finally at 1:00PM we received official confirmation from the French consulate that Pompidou would not be coming to meet with us after all.

It developed that the reason Pompidou cancelled his meeting with us was that he and his wife had been frightened when participants in a pro-Israel and anti-Pompidou demonstration closed around the couple as they arrived for a dinner reception in Chicago the previous evening. The Chicago police reported that the 10,000 strong demonstration had been non-violent, but Mrs. Pompidou felt personally insulted by the incident, while the French president himself was angrily calling the Chicago protest "a stain on the forehead of America" and claimed the police had acted in complicity with the demonstrators.

Moments after learning of Pompidou's cancellation, we received a call from Max Fisher at the White House. Max informed us that President Nixon was concerned about the damage to Franco-America relations caused by the Chicago incident and had decided to fly to New York that evening to attend a dinner for Pompidou at the Waldorf Astoria. Given all of that, Fisher asked us to cancel, at the request of Nixon, anti-Pompidou protest rallies that were scheduled to take place that evening outside the Waldorf. We let Max know that we did not control the planned demonstrations and were hardly in a position to call them off.

Amidst all of this turmoil, several of us walked out of our suite at the hotel in a state of considerable irritation and were immediately confronted by a swarm of news reporters demanding to know what had happened. Our general line was that we felt Pompidou had been rude to cancel the meeting without any notice, and that if we had been actually been given the opportunity to meet him, we would have conveyed our distress over the sale of 110 Mirage jets to Libya and at the same time continuing an embargo of jets which had already been bought and paid for by Israel.

Later that afternoon, I spent about an hour and a half with a reporter from *Time* Magazine to whom I stressed that we objected to French foreign policy under Pompidou first and foremost as American citizens because a series of French actions including pulling its armed forces out of the military component of NATO, withdrawing its gold from Fort Knox, and stirring up nationalist leanings among French-Canadians in Quebec, had directly undermined U.S. interests. The French decision to sell such a large number of state-of-the-art jet fighters to a virulent enemy of the U.S. like Libya, certainly fit into that pattern, I concluded.

Alarmed that President Nixon was continuing to delay an Israeli arms request first submitted by Prime Minister Golda Meir the previous autumn, apparently as a means to pressure Israel to be less militarily assertive in the so-called War of Attrition with Egypt then raging along the Suez Canal, I decided, in the absence of Dr. Wexler, to convene an urgent meeting of the Presidents Conference in New York on March

20, 1970. The meeting, the first I chaired as acting chairman, proved to be less than memorable—we heard a report from an official of the Israeli Embassy who told us that while Israel had been heartened to learn that U.S. economic aid would continue unimpeded, no decision had been taken by Washington on Israel's request for military aircraft. Yet it set the tone for the many Conference meetings I would convene in the months ahead.

On March 31, I met for lunch with Maurice Eisendrath (Reform,) Wolfe Kelman (Conservative)and Earl Morse of the Union of American Hebrew Congregations. It was a kind of "burying the hatchet" session in which they tacitly assented to accept me in my enhanced position as acting chairman of the and I expressed personal agreement with their position that the Presidents Conference should be restructured to more adequately reflect the role of the religious institutions in the leadership and deliberations of the organization. I realized that any such restructuring was unlikely to happen anytime soon since it could not be done without the assent of Wexler and other key members who would be almost certain to oppose it.

The four of us agreed to work together on other projects like planning together the following year's observance of Israel Independence Day. It was agreed that Kelman and Eisendrath would each appoint a committee of rabbis to work on details of the event. In the meantime, Morse and I would issue a joint statement on the meaning of Passover in 1970. I left the meeting much heartened that I had reached a modus vivendi with Eisendrath and Kelman; writing in my diary that the meeting represented "a most fruitful beginning to what I hope will be a strengthening of the unity of the American Jewish community."

In my role as president of United Synagogue, but also keenly conscious that my words carried extra weight in my expanded role, I decided to speak out forcefully in early May after President Nixon's decision to send U.S. forces from South Vietnam into Cambodia led to widespread violent protests on campuses across the countries, culminating in the tragic killings of four student protesters at Kent State University by National Guard troops.

I sent a letter on the seventh to all of the presidents of United Synagogue congregations across the country expressing deep concern that "As a nation we stand in grave danger of losing the confidence and loyalty of our young people."

Noting that many students were now returning home from campuses that had been shut down to protect lives and property, I stated, "These students are returning disillusioned, confused, angered and vulnerable to demagogic appeals. They need leadership—the leadership of your synagogue in creating programs of involvement and action, affording them the opportunity to manifest their concerns, express their feelings and share in the decision making process—at least on the synagogue and community level."

Two days later I dispatched a telegram to President Nixon:

> "The million and a half members of the United Synagogue of America share your deep concern over the alienation of our youth. We offer the cooperation of the leadership of our 826 congregations across the country in developing and carrying forward programs to encourage our youth in the fullest expression of their concerns within the context of the democratic American tradition."

Fortunately, the protest and dissent over Cambodia in May, 1970 proved to be the high water mark of youth alienation toward America. In the ensuing years, millions of young people who had seemed to despair of "the system" during the late

60's, entered the job market, started families and left behind the revolutionary rhetoric of their youth. Nevertheless, that was a very scary time when the whole country seemed on the edge of unraveling, and it left scars that impacted American political and cultural life for decades to come.

Throughout the summer of 1970, the Nixon Administration was engaged in intensive efforts to end the so-called "War of Attrition" between Israel and Egypt. The Egyptian army, which had been largely rebuilt and rearmed via massive Soviet arms shipments, was by early 1970, also augmented by a rapidly growing force of so-called Soviet military "advisers" manning SAM-3 missile sites along the Suez Canal and around Egypt's main cities. The conflict was proving terribly costly in Israeli lives and threatened to portend a dangerous military clash between the IDF and the Russians

When I had dinner with the usually upbeat Abba Eban on May 21, he was in a grim mood, expressing to me the intense frustration Israel felt about the ongoing unofficial U.S. arms embargo of Israel, which was preventing the Jewish state from receiving badly needed U.S. fighter planes to replace those destroyed by the SAM-3's. Eban contended that America's recent incursion into Cambodia and the negative international and domestic response it evoked seemed to make the Administration less favorably disposed toward Israel's arms request. He said that Israel's attitude was "If the answer is no, tell us now," rather than leaving the situation in a state of ambiguity.

The Foreign Minister indicated that while he realized a few extra planes themselves would hardly tip the military balance in Israel's favor, not giving the planes would encourage the Arabs toward aggressive action and give Israelis a sense of isolation. Within a few weeks, our own efforts and those of other Jewish groups on this issue would lead 74 senators to sign an open letter urging the Administration to sell Israel the planes and other arms it had requested.

Two weeks later, Ambassador Yitzhak Rabin gave the Presidents Conference an in-depth briefing of the military situation that made clear how fearful Israel was that the ever growing Soviet involvement in Egypt was inexorably pushing Israel toward a situation of 'to be or not to be'. Rabin was a very different type than Eban; a shy, taciturn and sometimes gruff military hero turned reluctant diplomat, but his strategic understanding was outstanding, even if he invariably put the most pessimistic possible spin on Israel's situation—obviously in a bid to elicit greater U.S. military and diplomatic support. Yet on that occasion, Rabin appeared genuinely deeply apprehensive that Russia's ever-growing upgrading of Egyptian air defenses along the Canal might tempt the Egyptians to embark on ever more provocative military adventures and would inexorably lead to the long-dreaded Israeli-Russian military clash.

Rabin emphasized that Israel was not urging a specific course of action on the U.S., only that there was no real option available to the Administration of doing nothing. The sort of benign neglect often favored by U.S. foreign policy when few good options appeared available would be highly dangerous and destabilizing in this case, in that such a course would allow the ongoing negative trends to continue to the point that Israel might have no choice but to engage the Russians militarily along the Suez Canal.

The Nixon Administration had clearly come to the same conclusion because on June 19, 1970, it launched a major Middle East peace initiative which aimed at achieving a cease-fire on the Suez Canal, and threw in, mainly as a sop to the Arab side, a resumption of the Jarring Mission after a nearly two year hiatus. The Administration also promised the Israelis unofficially to end the arms embargo if a cease-fire agreement was reached. The Soviet Union, Egypt, and the other Arab states quickly announced their acceptance of the U.S. plan, forcing Israel to also publicly assent, agreeing, in the process, to some important concessions, including accepting for the first time the premise of indirect negotiations with its Arab neighbors, instead of direct ones, and agreeing to a 90 day limited cease-fire in place as a first step to closing down the conflict, instead of the unlimited cease-fire Israel had previously insisted upon.

Meanwhile, however, as the sides debated over the actual terms of the cease-fire agreement and United Nations Special Representative Gunnar Jarring prepared to commence another round of shuttle diplomacy, conditions on the ground continued to deteriorate, as the Soviet military advisers took an ever more aggressive role along the Canal. On July 25, the Russians provided cover for Egyptian air attacks east of the Canal and on July 30, the long feared military clash between Israeli and Soviet fighter pilots took place, with Israel shooting down four Soviet pilots in MIG-21's.

That humbling experience seemed to sober up the Soviet leadership in Moscow, and within two weeks the Soviets and Egyptians agreed to terms they had refused only a few weeks earlier and which made possible the signing of a cease-fire agreement on August 7. As noted, the cease-fire was originally set to last only 90 days, but was renewed every three months until the outbreak of the Yom Kippur War three years later. The agreement stipulated that both Egyptian and Israeli missiles and fighter planes be moved back 50 kilometers from the respective sides of the Canal.

The sudden death on September 28 of President Gamal Abdel Nasser and his replacement by the less bellicose and more western oriented Anwar Sadat served to turn down the temperature along the Canal. While Rabin complained bitterly to the Presidents Conference on August 18 that the Egyptians and Soviets were violating the cease fire by continuing to move missile sites close to the Canal and charged that the U.S. was ignoring Israel's evidence of these violations, by early 1971 both Rabin and Eban were acknowledging to us that, despite undoubted cheating by the Egyptians, the ongoing cease-fire left Israel in a better strategic situation than it had been in since shortly after the 1967 War.

Meanwhile, as Rabin predicted, the second Jarring mission, which Israel initially boycotted because of Soviet stalling on pulling back its missiles, but eventually agreed to participate in, accomplished nothing very much except allowing the U.N. negotiator to shuttle from Mideast capital to capital. The gap between the two sides was simply too wide to make possible the achievement of a breakthrough to a permanent peace settlement.

The Jews of Romania

Amidst all of these developments, Jean and I paid a visit to Israel in early July, and then flew to Bucharest, Romania for a visit to the Jewish community there. It was our first trip behind the Iron Curtain. It turned out that the flight to Bucharest was delayed for several hours, so all of the passengers were treated by El-Al to a dinner at a hotel in Tel Aviv. As we chatted with our fellow passengers, we learned that nearly all of them were Romanian Jews who had made aliyah over the past 20 years and were returning home to visit for the first time. Many also had concentration camp numbers on their arms, something that palpably brought home to us the meaning of Israel to thousands of people who without the Jewish state would likely no longer be around.

During our four day visit in Bucharest, Jean and I were escorted everywhere by the kind, resourceful and politically astute Chief Rabbi of Romania Moses Rosen, who almost single-handedly held Jewish life together in that totalitarian state for over a generation. Rabbi Rosen had asked me to address the Choral Synagogue community and I was ready. I handed my notes to Rabbi Rosen as he indicated that the notes need be cleared before I used them. All went well.

Rabbi Rosen also played a key role in maintaining contacts between the governments of Romania and Israel. Under Nicolai Ceausescu, an unreconstructed Stalinist in domestic affairs, Romania was the only Soviet bloc state that did not break off diplomatic relations with Israel after the 1967 war, but rather maintained those relations throughout the 1970's and 1980's and served as a go-between on issues of war and peace and concerning the situation of Soviet Jews.

We were received by the Romanian Minister of Religion, Professor Dogaru. I had a *maftir* during Shabbat services at the Choral Synagogue, and there was a *kiddush* in our honor after services were complete. Overall, I was impressed with the vitality of the-then 100,000 strong Romanian Jewish community, 50,000 of whom were in Bucharest, and the large number of community institutions it maintained, including a community newspaper, a kosher restaurant in Bucharest, a system for providing food and clothing aide to elderly community members in need and three summer camps for Romanian Jewish youth—two in the Carpathian Mountains and one on the Black Sea.

On September 20, 1970, the Presidents Conference played host to Prime Minister Golda Meir. Meir had hardly been a new quantity to American Jewry when she became Israel's top leader the year before; she had, after all, moved to Milwaukee from Kiev at the age of six and after making aliyah as a young woman, became, thanks in part to her perfect American English, the leading emissary of the pre-independence Yishuv to American Jewry. In early 1948, her stirring appearance at the Council of Jewish Federations during which she informed the gathering that the Yishuv stood poised to fight for its life with the Arab world and needed money immediately to purchase armaments, elicited a deeply emotional response from the delegates and the flow of millions of dollars that helped make it possible for the new State of Israel to emerge victorious from that life and death struggle.

As she appeared before us that day at the Waldorf in 1970, Golda seemed truly larger than life, and her weather-beaten face seemed powerfully evocative of Israel's determination to survive, whatever the cost. She was full of Yiddish-accented wit and wisdom, but her rather calculated "Jewish grandmother" shtick did nothing to disguise that this was one very tough lady.

Reporting on her meeting with Nixon in Washington two days earlier, Golda reported that she had forthrightly informed the President that the Rogers Plan call for Israel's withdrawal from occupied territories could not serve as the basis for negotiations; Israel would not take part in the Jarring talks until all the Soviet missiles were pulled back 50 kilometers from the Canal, and requested substantial economic and military aid without any tie-ins to the political situation. The last request might have been considered chutzpah considering Golda's flouting of U.S. policy on the other points, but she told us that Nixon had placed no pressure on her and evinced a warm and sympathetic manner. Nixon, who placed a premium on toughness, evidently felt a personal kinship with that "tough as nails" Jewish grandmother.

In her meeting with President Nixon, Golda stressed Israel's need for the new F-4 Phantoms. News soon came that Nixon had agreed to open the direct channel with Golda, and that her requests for Phantoms and A4 Skyhawk aircraft, along with two hundred million dollars a year to pay for them, would be considered. The decision, he indicated, would depend on Israel's actions: "Agree to our peace plans and arms supplies, and financial help will follow."

On December 3, 1970, I had lunch with Nachum Goldmann, and several of his lieutenants at the World Jewish

Congress, including Dr. Gerhardt Reigner, who in 1942, had sent to the U.S. from his listening post in Geneva the first hard evidence of the systematic mass murder of European Jewry by the Nazis.

During the meeting, Goldmann surprised me by making a detailed proposal whereby United Synagogue would become an affiliate of the World Jewish Congress.

He thought United Synagogue would benefit by virtue of the fact that it would have contact with Jewish communities around the world, but I felt we could achieve such contacts without putting our organization into the orbit of Goldmann, who seemed to be more erratic as he got older.

Goldmann did not take kindly to that rebuff, and would soon be pushing hard to undercut the influence of his own creation, the Presidents Conference, just at the time I was coming to power.

It was nonetheless quite an event to have lunch with Goldmann, a man who was influential in bringing the world's attention to the Zionist claim for a Jewish state and its recognition and equal treatment. Because of United Synagogue's efforts to build an international conservative Jewish base in Jerusalem, I knew, as President, that we were not of the mind to be a minor player in the World Jewish Congress. Goldmann and I debated the issue but reached no agreement. Still, we closed as friends.

On January 18, 1971, Rabin addressed us on the occasion of William Wexler's election as President for a second one year term. For the first time I could remember, Rabin expressed satisfaction with the military situation, noting that the Arab terrorists were at their lowest ebb in years. While it was understood that the U.S. was prepared to give Israel a guarantee of its borders if it withdrew from the occupied territories, Rabin said Israel was insistent that its borders should be such that they could be defended successfully by the IDF with or without any outside guarantees. He also noted that Israel was strongly opposed to the introduction of U.S. and Soviet forces along Israel's borders as part of a final peace settlement, because these countries' actions would be governed to some extent by issues in which the two countries were involved beyond the Middle East.

It was on these two points that the U.S. and Israel would come to loggerheads in the ensuing months, as the Presidents Conference would learn in March during a background meeting we held at the State Department with Undersecretary of State for Mideast Affairs Joseph Sisco. An affable man with considerable charm, Sisco evinced a "Lets cut through the bull and deal with the real issues" air that quite eluded his stiffer and more formal boss, Secretary Rogers. During that meeting Sisco pointed out forcefully that Israel's strategic position was infinitely improved as a result of the cease-fire, and reminded us that, beyond rhetorical statements, the U.S. was placing little real pressure on Israel to withdraw.

Given all of that, Sisco remarked, the U.S. frankly felt "embarrassed" by Israel's failure to respond seriously to peace proposals by Jarring. Israel, he said, should "put its conditions on the table" rather than employing a policy of dithering and delay. Urging Israel to seize the positive moment and launch a serious effort to reach a peace agreement with Egypt and Syria, Sisco responded to comments by Eban several days earlier that the situation was developing favorably but still amounted to "half ripe fruit" that should not be prematurely harvested, Sisco insisted that on the contrary, the fruit was indeed ripe, but would "soon become overripe and fall from the tree." For our part, the Presidents Conference delegation urged the Administration to show understanding of Israel's position; especially considering the Jewish state's bitter experience in 1957 and 1967 with international guarantees, which turned out short-lived and, when Nasser decided to dispense with them, be nothing more than worthless pieces of paper.

One week later, at a formal Presidents Conference session with Secretary of State Rogers that I chaired, it became clear that whatever its exasperation with Israel's stalwart stance, the U.S. was not prepared to push the Jewish state too far. In direct response to questions I posed, Rogers promised that the Administration would be less openly critical of Israel in the coming weeks and months, and that whether or not Israel took negotiating positions in variance with those of Washington, the U.S. would continue to support the Jewish state military and economically. In other words, Israel had a green light from Washington—or at least a flashing yellow one—to go on resisting efforts by Jarring and the world community to force it to withdraw back to the 1967 borders in exchange for a peace agreement with the Arabs.

That seemed to me good news at the time, and I was pleased that we at the Presidents Conference were fulfilling our role of helping to give the elected government of Israel the means to defend itself as it saw fit. A kind of complacency seemed to grow in Israel during those years that manifested itself in contempt for the Arabs' military capabilities and belief in its own invincibility. Those comfortable illusions came to a shattering denouement in October 1973 with the destruction of the Bar-Lev Line by the much derided Egyptians and a similar deep penetration by the Syrians of Israel's defenses on the Golan Heights.

But that stunning event was still far off, and 1971 was a quiet time when Israel seemed to be enjoying a well-earned break from conflict. On February 6, 1972, the Presidents Conference membership voted unanimously that I would become the body's new chairman.

Behind the scenes, however, there had been some opposition to my ascension. Several weeks before the vote I had been visited by supporters of Rabbi Eisendrath who urged me to step aside and allow him to be the candidate for the position of Chairman. In response I made clear I believed I could continue to do a good job as chairman and therefore had no intention of not seeking the position.

Rabbi Maurice N. Eisendrath was the leader of the Reform Movement - a great scholar and a popular leader. He worked against religious emptiness. His religious policy is best addressed by the sentence in his book, "Can Faith Survive?" where he writes, "Our generation needs God, but it must be a concept of God attuned to the best of our scientific knowledge as well as to the sharp demands of our reason and conscience." This was written in 1964 and the Reform movement (tbe Union of American Hebrew Congregations- UAHC) has grown substantially to this date as records indicate that it is the largest movement today, with the Conservative movement in second place.

I considered myself a friend and when he asked me not to accept the nomination for Conference Chairman, I was deeply offended. I believe he had the support particularly of Rabbi Wolfe Kelman, who was then the head of the Rabbinical Assembly and who felt strongly that a religious leader (Rabbi) should be a Conference Chairman. I did not agree to the request of Rabbi Eisendrath to not accept the nomination, or as he later suggested, split my term of office with him. A few years after I left office, Rabbi Alexander Schindler, the successor to Rabbi Eisendrath as head of the Reform movement, was elected as Chairman of the Conference and was very effective in that role. But since Rabbi Schindler completed his term in June of 1978, we have not had a rabbi as chairman of the conference.

Rabbi Eisendrath was not pleased and advised the Conference that as a result of a "reordering of priorities" by the UAHC, that body would be reducing its annual contribution to the Presidents Conference from about $3500 to $500, the minimum required for membership. The breach between the Presidents Conference and the UAHC, one of its most important constituent bodies with well over one million members, was, however short-lived. Rabbi Eisendrath was soon replaced as UAHC President by Rabbi Alexander Schindler, a younger and less rough-edged individual with whom I got along famously (we played tennis together for many years). Rabbi Alexander Schindler would himself assume the Presidents Conference chairmanship in 1976. In any event, from that point on, all opposition from within the Presidents Conference to my position as unchallenged leader of the American Jewry ceased to be a factor.

The Voice of the Community: Chairman of the Presidents Conference, 1972-74

On February 7, 1971, the day after my election as Chairman of the Presidents Conference, I gave a long telephone interview to Israel Radio in which I set forth the Conference's agenda in the year ahead. I spoke about our determination to support Israel as she grappled with security and economic problems and to marshal support for oppressed Soviet and Syrian Jewry. In addition, I said that the Presidents Conference would seek to strengthen the unity of the American Jewish community so that our concerns could be articulated effectively and persuasively to our own government in a politically sensitive election year.

I came into the chairmanship having already cemented a strong and productive relationship with the Conference's executive director, Yehuda Hellman, because of my experience as acting chairman. An Israeli citizen who had moved to New York in the 1960's and quickly rose to prominence in Jewish organizational life, Yehuda was the perfect person to serve as the Conference's top professional; an enormously talented, hard-working, politically astute and well-connected individual whose affability, old world charm and diplomatic skills served him well in the cause of maintaining unity within the councils of the Presidents Conference, even at moments of high tension when our ideologically diverse organizations found themselves pulled in different directions.

Yehuda was at my side during innumerable high-stakes encounters during the three and a half tumultuous years. His shrewd and thoughtful advice proved invaluable to me as we struggled assiduously to expand Jewish emigration from the Soviet Union, while navigating between President Nixon and Senator Jackson and their contrasting approaches to the issue. Yehuda was with me as we pressed every button we could possibly think of to get U.S. aid flowing to Israel during the darkest days of the Yom Kippur War. Yehuda was always there for the Jewish people he loved, and his tragic and much too early death of a heart attack in 1985 while he was giving a speech on behalf of the Presidents Conference, was a grievous loss for myself and many in the organized Jewish community who admired him.

Filled with anticipation about the challenges that lay ahead, I headed to Vienna, where I had a memorable visit with newly arrived Soviet Jewish émigrés at the Schoenau Castle, described in the following chapter. Jean and I then flew on to Israel aboard a flight with 80 Russian olim, and it was moving for us to watch their emotional reactions to be arriving in Israel, a place that not long before had seemed as inaccessible to them as the moon, but now would become their home.

In Schoenau Castle Jean and I had a chance to meet and sit with the new arrivals from the Soviet Union. These people were truly tired. There was a sense of relief and quiet wonderment among them as they listened to the Israeli leaders' welcome, solemnly aware of the long road both behind them and before them.

Among the highlights of that visit included a lengthy briefing I received at the Foreign Ministry on the parlous situation of Jews in Arab lands—especially the 4000 Jews of Syria—and secret diplomatic efforts being undertaken on their behalf. Also memorable were visits to the Suez Canal and the ancient, long inaccessible Santa Katarina monastery at the base of Mt. Sinai.

On March 2, I held a press conference at Bet Sokolov in Tel Aviv, where I fielded questions from Israeli print, radio and television journalists. Among the issues upon which I was questioned were the dispositions of the American Jewish voter in the upcoming presidential election; Rabbi Meir Kahane's claim that American Jews faced an impending holocaust; and the very real perils confronting Jews in the Soviet Union, Syria and other Arab lands.

The next day, I was ushered into the Prime Minister's office for a meeting with Golda Meir. I was accompanied by Yehuda Hellman, while Golda's aide Simcha Dinitz (soon to be Israeli Ambassador to the U.S.) and Michael Elizur of the Foreign Office took part in the discussion from the Israeli side. I was touched by the personal warmth Golda manifested in congratulating me on my ascension to chairmanship, and in expressing her support for the Presidents Conference and its work. I thanked her humbly and told her I hoped that the unusual and highly welcome absence of crisis and violence between Israel and her Arab neighbors that had obtained since the Suez cease-fire the previous August would continue for the foreseeable future. In the meantime, I raised several issues with her that, while less burning than the matters of war and peace Israeli prime ministers habitually deal with, nevertheless cut to the heart of the relations between Israel and American Jewry.

I urged Meir to invite the members of the Presidents Conference to Jerusalem in November for the kickoff of the observance in Israel, America and throughout the Jewish world of Israel's 25th Anniversary, a suggestion to which she responded affirmatively.

I mentioned the rather poor level of *hasbara* (public information) about Israel and asked for more television appearances and addresses to our member organizations by Israel's political figures. Then, as President of the United Synagogue, I raised the question of orthodox control of marriages and conversions. I said that our Judaism and orthodox Judaism are tied to a common past, and that we would like to see a more pluralistic understanding. I also menitoned some instances at the *kotel* when our women and men wanted to pray together and told her how badly we were treated. Although she was very friendly and heard me out, Meir did not make any definite commitments.

On my return home I sensed the need to strengthen our Conference relationship with the Reform Movement and I reached out to Rabbi David Polish, President of the Central Conference of American Rabbis. Yehuda Hellman and I made a pilgrimage to his Chicago office on March 28, 1971. Polish had been pushing for some time the idea that the Presidents Conference should hold a meeting in Chicago as a way of showing that American Jewry stretched across the country and was not only concentrated in the New York-Washington corridor. I now told Polish that I would be agreeable to his idea if he would formally invite me as the Chairman of the Conference to speak in Chicago. I informed him that the subject of my talk on that occasion would be the paramount role of the Presidents Conference in representing the American Jewish community on the issues of Israel and Soviet Jewry.

On April 18, I had the opportunity to meet in New York with General Ariel Sharon, then the commander of the Israeli Southern Command. In the course of a *tour d'horizon* of the military situation in his sector, Sharon, a noted hawk and settlement advocate even then, explained to me that "Jewish fingers" were being extended into Gaza; dividing the Strip in five places with Jewish settlements. Sharon asserted that

Gaza would have to be integrated into the totality of Israel, and not be allowed to serve as a base for future demands for Palestinian self-rule.

On that day, who could have imagined that just over 30 years later, Prime Minister Ariel Sharon would become a forceful advocate for the removal of Jewish settlements from Gaza and for allowing the Strip to become the very sort of base for Palestinian self-rule he had long abjured. Sharon, who undoubtedly did more than any other Israeli to implant Jewish settlements in the occupied territories, eventually came to the conclusion that, given the exploding Palestinian population and world hostility to the settlement enterprise, the small Gaza settlements would have to be sacrificed in order to secure permanence for the much larger settlement enterprise in the West Bank.

On April 25, I met with George Bush, our Ambassador to the United Nations requesting he arrange an early meeting with the Secretary-General of the United Nations, Kurt Waldheim to discuss problems with Syria. It was my first meeting with George Bush, who impressed me with his energy and forthrightness. Bush promised to forcefully raise Syria's oppression of its Jewish population and work to ensure that the issue of Soviet Jewry retained a high profile in deliberations of the U.N. At the end of the meeting, Bush and I exchanged phone numbers and promised to stay in touch. Neither of us had an inkling of the friendship and political collaboration that would grow between us.

Dissention in the Conference

April 26 was a red letter day. On that day I had a luncheon meeting with Rabbi Eisendrath and his soon-to-be-successor as president of the UAHC, Rabbi Alexander Schindler. Eisendrath made no effort to hide that he was angry that I had been selected chairman of the Conference instead of himself; pointing out that he had been one of the three co-founders of the Presidents Conference together with Goldmann and Klutznick. Clearly, Eisendrath felt especially chagrined because 1972 had been his last opportunity to be elected chairman since, according to the bylaws of the Presidents Conference, the body's chairman must either be president of one of the Conference's constituent organization, or have vacated that presidency during the six months preceding his or her election to the chairmanship. As noted, Eisendrath was about to turn over the presidency of the UAHC to Schindler, and I had just been elected chairman of the Presidents Conference, ending Eisendrath's longstanding hopes of attaining that position.

Eisendrath said the refusal of our membership to elect him chairman of the Presidents Conference showed how little weight the UAHC and the Reform movement carried within the Conference. Certainly, he said, it had been high time to elect a member of a denominational organization as chairman, given that three presidents of B'nai B'rith had already been elected, but that position ought to have gone to the long serving president of the UAHC, rather than the more recently arrived president of United Synagogue.

I listened carefully and respectfully to Eisendrath's statement and then replied that I did not feel guilty in having accepted the chairmanship of the Presidents Conference. I appealed to the two UAHC leaders to work with me, rather than burdening the Conference with real or imagined grievances out of the past. I ended the meeting an hour and a half later with the feeling we had cleared the air. I also felt hopeful that the situation would improve within a few months once my friend Alex Schindler took over as president of the UAHC, which, in fact, turned out to be the case.

Thankfully, I would have no further problems with Eisendrath either, who soon moved on to the status as president emeritus. It should be noted that, while keenly disappointed at his failure to secure the chairmanship of the Presidents Conference, Eisendrath always conducted himself as a gentleman. He should be remembered for the contributions he made to the Presidents Conference, the Reform movement and the entire American Jewish community during his two decades at the helm of the UAHC.

After leaving Eisendrath and Schindler, I headed uptown with Yehuda Hellman to the Columbia Club for a meeting with Dr. Joachim Prinz and Max Melamet, president and executive director of the American Section of the World Jewish Congress. I still had to resolve the conflict of interest between the World Jewish Congress and the Conference of Presidents. and in a letter Dr. Prinz he sent me the following day, he eagerly grasped it. Reaffirming that, "There is no one in the (WJC) who would think of competing with the Presidents Conference," Prinz wrote, "The World Jewish Congress represents world Jewry and not American interests, while the Presidents Conference is a purely American organization, dealing, thinking and acting in those terms." Acknowledging that the Presidents Conference had a special agreement with the National Conference on Soviet Jewry that empowered us to advocate and act on behalf of Soviet Jews, Prinz affirmed, "The Presidents Conference itself deals with matters concerning Israel in reference to the American Jewish community and the American government. The World Jewish Congress, both globally and in its American Section, deals with the problems of world Jewry. It does not concern itself with either Israel or with Soviet Jewry."

I wrote back the following day, thanking Prinz for his efforts to resolve differences between the WJC and Presidents Conference, and agreeing with his characterization of the relationship between the two bodies. Yet to erase any lingering doubts about the global reach of the Presidents Conference as the instrument of the world's most powerful Diaspora community, I wrote that not only was the Presidents Conference "the authentic body for American Jewish leadership," but that it was also empowered to "deal with issues of Jewish concern wherever they arise."

On May 2, Prinz wrote back, affirming that he accepted my formulation and concluding, "The only organization that can claim to represent the majority of American Jewry is the Presidents Conference. If the World Jewish Congress as an international organization undertakes any political intervention at all, it speaks not for American Jewry, but for world Jewry. The same is true if the American Section of the World Jewish Conference were to undertake anything.

I was relieved and gratified to have reached an amicable agreement with Prinz. He deserves great credit for an act of statesmanship. In retrospect, my agreement with Prinz had an historic quality, since not once in the 30 years since that day has another prominent figure dared to question the right of the Presidents Conference to speak on behalf of the organized American Jewish community. The Presidents Conference, an organization that Goldmann himself started 18 years earlier had been confirmed as the premiere voice of American Jewry. Goldmann was a giant figure in 20th Century Jewish history with myriad accomplishments, including helping to secure reparations for Holocaust survivors from the West German government. He should be remembered for that and many other important contributions to the Jewish people over four decades.

It proved fortuitous that I was able to put the inter-Jewish wars behind me early in my chairmanship, because the international climate became ever more stormy as 1972 progressed, and it quickly became imperative for me to focus on world events. Specifically, a string of terrorist outrages took place that summer and fall directed against Israelis and Jews—including the murder of 12 Israeli athletes at the Olympic games in Munich; ending the quiet period that ensued after the signing of the Suez cease-fire and reminding all of us anew that a full generation after the Holocaust, being Jewish remained fraught with peril.

Meanwhile, the connection I had cultivated with United States Ambassador to the United Nations George Bush was already beginning to bear fruit. Bush arranged a meeting for a Presidents Conference delegation and myself with Secretary General Kurt Waldheim on the subject of Syrian Jewry. On May 9, Bush accompanied by myself, Rabbi Israel Miller, George Gruen of the American Jewish Committee, Philip Baum of the American Jewish Congress and Rabbi Hecht of the New York Syrian Jewish community to Waldheim's office on the 38th floor of the U.N. building. Smiling and manifesting trademark bonhomie, Waldheim greeted each of us in turn. After Bush introduced me, I told the Secretary General about the Presidents Conference and its mission and then spoke about the plight of 4200 Jews remaining in Syria, many of whom were prevented from traveling abroad or emigrating, from working in their chosen professions or from passing property from father to son. I asked the Secretary General to intervene with the Syrian government to ease conditions for Jews inside Syria and allow those who wished to emigrate to do so.

Waldheim responded that he was very interested in the problem and would try to engage the Syrians on the subject. He promised to communicate with the Syrian Ambassador to the U.N., and, if that approach proved ineffective, to consider sending a special envoy to Syria. He promised to be back in touch with us on the issue. Overall, the meeting seemed to all of us to be very promising. By the end of my term as Presidents Conference chairman, I was less sanguine about Waldheim's promises to be proactive on issues of Jewish concern, but still was stunned much later, in

1986, by the news of his Nazi past and possible complicity in war crimes.

Terror

On May 31, three members of an obscure terrorist group known as the Japanese Red Army who had just arrived at Lod Airport on an Air France flight, opened indiscriminate rifle fire and tossed hand grenades at passersby at the airport, killing 26 people and wounding 76 others—many of them Puerto Ricans, who had just arrived in Israel for a religious pilgrimage. The Japanese acted at the behest of a group of pro-Palestinian Lebanese terrorists who had safe haven in Beirut, Lebanon, a country that by allowing the Palestine Liberation Organization and other terrorist groups free reign was already on a downward spiral into lawlessness that would soon lead to civil war.

One week later, the President Conference held a memorial service for the Lod Airport massacre victims at the Fifth Avenue Synagogue, to which I invited Israeli Ambassador Rabin, Japanese Consul-General Masao Sawaki, who expressed the deep shame and sorrow of the Japanese people at the massacre, and several U.S. Christian leaders, including Rev. David Hunter, deputy general secretary of the National Council of Churches of Christ in the USA and the Rev. John Sheerin, representing the U.S. Catholic Bishops Conference. Most of the victims of the massacre, after all, were Christian and I had invited the Christian leaders to let them and their constituents know that even as Israel mourned its own dead, we also felt deep sympathy for the Puerto Rican Christians who had lost their lives. This was a point made by Rabin in his powerful address that day, noting that those at the Presidents Conference that sober day were "gathered in common brotherhood to bid farewell to our brothers, Jew and Christian, who died so cruelly...The government and people of Israel mourn the pilgrims of Puerto Rico and will remember for all time the pilgrims of Puerto Rico."

In my address, I noted that the terrible event showed graphically that terrorism was an international phenomenon—here after all were Japanese killers hired by a Lebanese terror group who had boarded a French airplane that flew to Israel from Italy—and that only by working together and sharing information could the nations of the world stop the spread of terrorism and prevent international anarchy.

Pointing out that there were member states of the UN who had actually praised the Lod Airport massacre; (Egyptian Prime Minister Sidki, for example, had said in public "The operation shows that we can achieve victory in the battle with Israel)," I called upon our own government to demand that all states cease to offer hospitality to terrorists. I also expressed solidarity with Israel in its moment of grief and to support whatever retaliatory steps she felt the need to take in order to protect her people.

After powerful statements by Reverend Hunter and Reverend Sheerin, the assemblage adopted a resolution aimed at Lebanon and other Arab states that condoned terrorists operating on their territory. It affirmed that "governments must root out the cancers of terrorism which invest their body politic, [and] airlines must refuse to furnish civil aviation to those countries which ignore the basic requirements of civilized behavior by ignoring conscienceless killers. Aircraft technicians throughout the world must refuse to service the vehicles of those countries which flaunt the minimum tenets of morality."

During the first week in September, Jean and I, together with our son Stuart, traveled to London to attend an Emergency Conference on Soviet Jewry, which had been convened to build an international consensus against the abhorrent education tax that the Soviet Union had recently imposed on Jews wishing to emigrate; an exorbitant tax that really amounted to a ransom. (see next chapter, which focuses on the Soviet Jewry issue). As we were preparing to catch our flight back to New York on September 5, we heard the terrible news that 11 Israeli athletes had been accosted by armed Palestinian terrorists and were being held hostage at the Olympic Village. It was only after we arrived home in New York shortly before midnight that we received the terrible news that all 11 athletes had, after all, been murdered by their captors.

The following day at the Presidents Conference was consumed with the grim business of preparing a memorial service. I issued a statement affirming on behalf of the Conference that "The grotesque, shattering events at Olympic Village leave us sick with grief...[Yet] anguish is not enough; sorrow will not suffice. The civilized world must act—and act now. The Olympic Village massacre is part of the insane pattern reflected in the Lod horror, the attempted destruction of hundreds of aircraft...those who abet casual killing at random are known. The civilized world can no longer tolerate those who permit terrorism to cross borders, purchase weapons of mass slaughter, commit murder and hope for safety and impunity. We call upon our government and all sovereign states to demand that terrorists will be given no base and murderers no sanctuary...Concrete steps must be taken to assure than there will never be another resurgence of animalism."

The memorial service for the 11 murdered Israeli Olympic athletes was somber, heartfelt and deeply moving. Ambassador Bush was there to deliver a special message to the Presidents Conference on behalf of President Nixon. Count Harold Posadowsky, the West German Consul General, was also there to express the sorrow of his government. Those two statements of solidarity at least gave our members a reassuring feeling that we Jews were not alone in our grief—even if we remained highly skeptical that the world was prepared to punish the countries that nurtured the terrorists.

In his message to us, President Nixon affirmed that "The senseless tragedy that struck Israel's Olympic team has profoundly touched the hearts of people the world over...All men of conscience and compassion deplore this hideous perversion of the Olympic spirit and join in memorializing the innocent and courageous athletes for whom that spirit was a way of life...In tribute to them, let us reinforce, not just our aspirations, but our actions, in quest of the brotherhood that was denied to them."

Posadowsky said that all Germans mourned "this most brutal murder by Palestine extremists." Referring to the "terrible crimes done to the Jewish people" during the Nazi era, the Count said that West Germany "had wanted [during the Olympics] to make our Israeli visitors and guests feel especially welcome. But the dark pounding at the door at night again brought terror and death to Jews, to Israelis dedicated to sports, peace and human understanding." The Count contended, "All civilized nations and their governments must work together more effectively to put an end to the activities of terrorists." He specifically called on Arab governments to involve themselves in those efforts, saying that it had come as a "great shock" to many Germans "that the attempt of the German government to find a solution to the crisis with the help of the heads of Arab states proved unsuccessful."

Posadowsky's words were affecting that day, but rang terribly hollow less than two months later, after a Lufthansa airliner was hijacked on its way to Ankara, Turkey and the hijackers demanded the release of the three Palestinian killers of the Israeli Olympians. In a craven act, the West German government immediately released the three terrorists; almost, as the Jerusalem Post noted in an angry editorial, "as though they had been waiting for this to happen and to relieve themselves of the need to put their prisoners on trial." The hijackers then freed the Lufthansa passengers unharmed, but it was clear that the Germans had sent a dangerous message of appeasement of Arab terrorism and blackmail.

Upon hearing this disheartening news, I immediately fired off a telegram on behalf of the Presidents Conference to the same Count Posadowsky, as well as to the German Ambassador to Washington, expressing "shock and dismay" at Germany's "capitulation" to the hijackers; which I contended, was "an act which cannot be accepted by world public opinion as the policy of a sovereign government dedicated to law-abiding and peace-loving international relations." I predicted that Germany's act "will contribute further to the spread of Arab terrorism and place a premium on the practice of continued hijacking for which your government now must take full responsibility."

Israel's 25th Anniversary

1972 was a presidential election year; one which saw a major change in the voting habits of the American Jewish community. After voting overwhelmingly for Democratic candidates since the time of Franklin Delano Roosevelt, Jews gave more than 40 percent of their vote in 1972 to President Nixon, who was reelected over Sen. George McGovern in an enormous landslide, capturing every state except Massachusetts.

The main reason for the shift toward the GOP in 1972 was Jewish appreciation for Nixon's strong and unstinting support of Soviet Jewry and the State of Israel during his first term, and the feeling that McGovern, who campaigned for a withdrawal of U.S. troops from Vietnam, would be less staunch in defense of the Jewish state. McGovern appeared before the Conference of Presidents, but I believe many Jews could not imagine that McGovern would back Israel to the hilt if the Soviet Union became emboldened and encouraged Egypt and Syria to attack Israel. Despite my personal feelings that Nixon was by far the better choice, as Conference Chairman I did not openly advocate either candidate. No matter. Max Fisher did a magnificent job organizing the Jewish community in support of President Nixon.

Today, a generation later, our community remains predominantly Democratic, despite ongoing Jewish movement away from the left and toward the center of the political spectrum. As a long-time Republican I believe that what concerns many Jews about our party, has been the frequent embrace of hard-line social conservative positions advocated by the Christian right, and the developing new "faith-based initiatives." The concern is that such programs and attitudes might put in danger our religious freedom.

By mid-1972, I was launched upon preparations for the observation in the United States of Israel's 25th Anniversary Year in 1973. As chairman of the Presidents Conference, I was asked by Israel to serve as chairman of the Israel's 25th Anniversary Celebration Committee.

On September 8, 1972, amidst all the sadness over the Olympic massacre, I met with Mayor John Lindsay and suggested four programs that New York City could sponsor during the yearlong observance that was to begin on September 26 with a candle-lighting ceremony at the International Synagogue at John F. Kennedy International Airport. These included a Chanukah celebration at City Hall with many top Jewish leaders, a fair featuring Jerusalem as our holy city, a special night during New York's summer festival in Central Park that would be devoted to Israel's 25th, featuring top Israeli and American entertainers, and bringing an archaeology exhibition to the Metropolitan Museum of Art, including the Dead Sea Scrolls. I told Mayor Lindsay that I had held meetings in Jerusalem with the heads of the Israel Museum and government leaders and the objective was eminently realizable. Lindsay liked the whole program I suggested, but was especially enthusiastic about the museum exhibition proposal and said he would immediately contact Douglas Dillon, President of the Metropolitan Museum. The mayor felt that the proposed exhibition was a "splendid, wonderful idea."

The ceremony at JFK Airport launching the 25th Anniversary celebration came off very well and Mayor Lindsay, in particular, spoke eloquently about the strong ties binding the U.S. and Israel. He issued a proclamation honoring Israel's 25th Anniversary and there was a general consensus that the event had given the yearlong celebration a great start. Indeed, the Chanukah celebration also came off wonderfully, and those of us who organized the entire 25th Anniversary celebration felt a sense of pride and accomplishment that we were on our way to carrying off a deeply meaningful and controversy-free event that was promoting a much deeper appreciation of Israel in the American public.

Then, during March 1973, the Metropolitan Museum held a concert with a prominent Israeli musician and afterwards received a threatening letter warning it not to host Israelis and Israeli exhibitions. On March 28, after the U.S. Ambassador to Sudan was murdered in Khartoum by a Palestinian terrorist group known as Black September. Israeli musician, Museum President Dillon sent a letter to Mayor Lindsay in which he said that the horror in Khartoum and the threat the museum had received "have forced us to take another look at the proposed Israeli exhibition." Contending that "There is simply no way to protect the Museum or the contents of the exhibition…from terrorist attack", Dillon informed Lindsay that he had written to Jerusalem Mayor Teddy Kollek asking that the exhibition be postponed "until a time when it can be mounted without any danger."

Upon learning about Dillon's letter, I was chagrined that

we might not have the Exhibition, which was to have been the cultural capstone of the year long celebration. But, as was the case with the German decision to free the murderers of the Israeli Olympic athletes in Munich, I saw the violation of an even more important principle involved; one of the world's greatest cultural institutions had made a shameful surrender to terrorism. My April 11 letter to Dillon was strongly worded:

"It is inconceivable that you are prepared to sacrifice the freedom of expression which every citizen has a right to expect from the Museum on the alter of unvoiced threats and surrender to Black September terrorists. I find your letter shocking, its contents outrageous and cannot believe your decision reflects the feelings of the Board of Directors and supporters of the Metropolitan Museum. To cancel an exhibit into which so much effort and energy has been invested on the grounds of a threat to the safety of the exhibit, which threat has not been made, is to set an example which is offensive to everyone."

David Rivlin, Israeli Consul-General in New York, and a close friend who coordinated closely with me on the museum controversy—as on many other occasions during those years—dispatched a letter to Mayor Lindsay asserting that the Israeli government was deeply chagrined by Dillon's apparent decision to cancel the exhibition, which, Rivlin noted, would create an "appalling and even dangerous impression" that "even in the United States there can be no protection of cultural and civil enterprises against the terrorists." Noting that both Mayor Kollek and Foreign Minister Eban opposed Dillon's decision, Rivlin wrote trenchantly; "We can not imagine that you, dear Mayor, being one of the initiators of the idea of the exhibition, operating in coordination with the Museum and all other relevant public organizations here, would accept such a decision in New York, which would constitute an unprecedented, unjustified and unwarranted capitulation to Arab terrorism."

Lindsay must have turned up the heat on Dillon because on April 16 I received a note from Dillon offering to meet with the Presidents Conference soon to discuss the matter, and reminding me that Karl Katz, chief of the department of exhibitions of the museum, was at that moment in Israel and would also be discussing the issue with Mayor Kollek.

Teddy Kollek must have also made a strong impression on his visitor, because the following week, at a luncheon held at the office of Thomas P. Hoving, director of the Museum with Rivlin myself and Charlotte Jacobsen, then chairman of the American Section of the World Zionist Organization, Dillon said that after careful consideration, the Museum would proceed with plans for the Israeli archaeological exhibition. He insisted, however, that there was not sufficient time to prepare the exhibition—which Kollek had described as "the most important and exciting exhibit of Jerusalem's past ever sent outside Israel"—for display during 1973, and that it would therefore be held instead in 1975, in conjunction with the tenth anniversary of the Israel Museum, where most of the contents of the exhibition were permanently housed.

We were saddened that the exhibition would not take place as part of Israel's 25th Anniversary Celebration, but at least pleased that the museum had affirmed that it would be holding the exhibition and would, consequently, not, as I affirmed in a statement, "yield to terror or threats of terror." I added that the Presidents Conference was "satisfied that the exhibit will take place in 1975...We share the museum's confidence that the security needs of the Metropolitan can be fully met."

Meanwhile, I was involved in a whirlwind of events commemorating Israel's 25th Anniversary, including a gala welcome to Golda Meir held on March 6, 1973 in Madison Square Garden attended by 5000 New Yorkers; a May 2 event in City Hall Plaza, featuring an official proclamation by Mayor

Lindsey and readings by former New York City Consumer Affairs Commissioner (and former Miss America), Bess Myerson and a musical performance by actor/singer Theodore Bikel. Events culminated in a massive Salute to Israel Parade on June 10 on Fifth Avenue attended by 75,000 New Yorkers that climaxed later that day in a gala reception at Gracie Mansion hosted by Mayor Lindsay.

On March 26, 1973, the Presidents Conference, at my initiative, hosted a luncheon in honor of George Bush, who was leaving his position as U.S. Ambassador to the U.N. At the event, which in addition to Presidents Conference members, was attended by Ambassador Rivlin, Israeli Ambassador to the U.N. Yosef Tekoah, Assistant Secretary of State Joe Sisco, I pointed out that George Bush had worked closely with the Presidents Conference on many issues during his tenure at the U.N., including ongoing efforts to protect the safety and enhance the dignity of Jews in the Soviet Union, Poland, Syria, Iraq and other countries.

Turning to Bush, who was seated alongside me, I said, "Your door was always open to us. You were always willing to bring to bear the influence of the American government and your own great personal prestige on behalf of beleaguered Jews who could appeal only to the United States for desperately-needed help."

During August 1973, after a visit to Israel, I flew on to Tehran, Iran for my first ever visit to a Jewish community in an Islamic country. I found Tehran to be "a very unimpressive city, mixed styles, broad avenues lined with hovels…" but was much more impressed with the majestic ruins of Persepolis and with the ancient and exotic cities of Shiraz and Ishafan, where I visited the Jewish quarters. I noticed that the Ishafan synagogue building had no sign or outward markings on its walls to indicate its function or identity. In meetings with Iranian Jewish leaders, I learned that many of them had sent their children to the United States to be educated, and many of them, had also made substantial investments in property in the U.S. and Israel. They were clearly hedging their bets on the future of Jewish life in their country, but none of them gave the slightest inkling that they expected anything as earth-shaking as the Islamic Revolution that exploded in Iran five years later, causing the fall of the Shah of Iran, and virtual ending of Jewish life in that country.

The Yom Kippur War

Looking back today on the first nine months of 1973, I have the impression that all of us were living in a fool's paradise., True, we had to deal during those months with major challenges, including negotiating on behalf of captive Soviet Jewry with both President Nixon and Soviet leader Leonid Brezhnev. We also had to sort out the political consequences of the Watergate scandal, which was causing an escalating deterioration of the political power of President Nixon, who only months earlier had bestrode Washington like a colossus. However, our perception of Israel's strength and near invincibility vis a vis its Arab neighbors was especially comforting.

Then, during the last days of September we witnessed the shocking surrender of the government of Prime Minister Bruno Kreisky to a group of Palestinian terrorists who had taken four Austrian hostages isolated in a car on the airport runway at Vienna. Kreisky, a Jew who passed up no opportunity to criticize Israel and to prostrate himself in front of the Arabs, acceded to a number of outrageous demands from the hijackers, including that he close down Schoenau Castle as a processing center for Soviet Jews on the way to Israel. While countries like West Germany had freed terrorist killers in their custody in order to end hostage dramas, Kreisky's craven act represented the first time any country had actually changed its national policy to satisfy the demands of terrorists, and thus represented a new low in Europe's confused and timid response to the growing terrorist campaign.

Nevertheless, despite recurrent terrorist attacks against Israel, and despite the failure of U.S. and UN efforts to make any diplomatic progress in efforts to broker progress toward Israeli-Arab peace, the Jewish state's overall security position appeared strong. Israel's cease-fire lines with Egypt and Syria had been largely quiet since the Sinai cease-fire of August 1970, and no one expected either Egypt or Syria to do anything as foolhardy as to launch military attacks on an IDF that was believed to have a major military superiority over its Arab antagonists.

In presenting my account of the continuing efforts of the Presidents Conference on behalf of Israel during the 18 days of the Yom Kippur War, I have made a considerable effort to avoid distorting the story by romanticizing it. The situation Israel confronted during those bleak days was desperate enough, and our urgent efforts to help jump start the U.S. military airlift to Israel were difficult and complicated enough without the need for retroactive embellishment. Suffice to say that the organized American Jewish community rose to the enormous challenge we faced during those days by not allowing ourselves the luxury of panic. Instead, we managed throughout to keep our eye on the ball; using every resource at our disposal to overcome the resistance of powerful forces at the Pentagon and elsewhere in Washington and pushing relentlessly to get the aid flowing.

At 7AM on Yom Kippur morning, I was awakened by a phone call from Mordecai Shalev, Charge d'Affairs at the Israeli Embassy in Washington. He advised me that Egypt and Syria had just launched an attack against Israel. Stunned, I immediately called my close friend Shmuel Segev in Israel for confirmation, which I received. Segev had little information on the military situation on either front, but, in general, gave me the feeling that although it would take a few days to mobilize the IDF and bring it to wartime strength, the Israelis would still be able to hold off the coordinated attacks in the north and south.

Jean and I came to synagogue for Yom Kippur services at Temple Israel a couple of hours later, but unlike previous years, I did not join Jean in our seats in the sanctuary. Instead, I went to Rabbi Waxman's office, and, acting on the principle of *pikuah nefesh,* (saving of life) wrote and dispatched two telegrams; one to members of the Presidents Conference urging them to come to an emergency meeting in New York the following day, and another to Secretary of State Henry Kissinger appealing for U.S. support for Israel. The telegram to Kissinger read as follows:

> "PREMEDITATED CONCERTED MILITARY ATTACK BY EGYPT AND SYRIA AGAINST ISRAEL PROVIDES DRAMATIC CONFIRMATION OF ARAB DETERMINATION TO DESTROY ISRAEL STOP
>
> ARAB OFFENSIVE UNDERLINES THEIR CONTINUING COMMITTMENT TO KHARTOUM POLICY OF NO NEGOTIATIONS AND NO PEACE WITH ISRAEL STOP
>
> WE URGE OUR GOVERNMENT TO PROVIDE ALL SUPPORTIVE ASSISTANCE TO ISRAEL IN THIS CRITICAL HOUR STOP
>
> WE SUPPORT ALL YOUR EFFORTS TO RESTORE PEACE TO THE AREA AND TO BRING THE PARTIES INTO NEGOTIATION TOWARDS A PERMANENT MUTUALLY AGREED PEACE."

During the course of the day, I stayed at the synagogue, listening to a pocket radio I had brought along to keep in touch with up to the minute news reports while working the phones for a series of consultations with my friend David Rivlin, the Israeli consul-general in New York, and various

Presidents Conference members. I also reported throughout the day to members of the Temple Israel on developments in Israel. Interestingly, that report started a tradition at Temple Israel that is part of our Yom Kippur service until today; customarily during the interlude between *Musaf* and *Mincha*, I and other members report to the congregation on current events impacting the Jewish community.

That evening after breaking the fast, I spoke again to several leading members of the Presidents Conference and reconfirmed our decision to hold a meeting of the entire Conference body for the following day in Manhattan at the Plaza Hotel.

The Presidents Conference meeting that convened that Sunday at the Plaza Hotel in Manhattan, took place in an exceedingly grave atmosphere. We were addressed by Foreign Minister Abba Eban, who confirmed what had already been all over the international media; that 70,000 Egyptian troops had crossed the Suez Canal and overwhelmed 500 Israelis holding the Bar Lev Line.

As a result, the Egyptians were now firmly ensconced on the Israeli side of the Suez Canal. Eban also acknowledged the Syrians had made advances on the Golan Heights front, but relayed to us Israeli confidence that they would quickly push back the two Arab armies once the IDF was successfully mobilized. Reports on Israeli casualties were sketchy, but looked to be high, and we knew that many Israeli soldiers had been taken prisoner as well. For American Jewish leaders who had become used to thinking of the Israeli military as well-nigh invincible, these reports were indeed shocking and a cause for deep concern that the very survival of Israel might be at stake.

If we had then known the true state of things on the battlefield, we would have been even more worried and upset. In fact, during the first three days of war, Israel lost over 1000 men and about 840 tanks, almost half of its total tank corps. The massive Syrian tank assault overran the Israel northern front and, at one point, the Israeli commander in the north, Major Gen. Hoffi reported to the government, "I'm not sure I can hold out much longer." After analyzing the shocking battlefield reports, Defense Minister Dayan suggested to Prime Minister Meir that Israel might have to seek terms of surrender, adding, at one point, "This is the end of the Third Temple." With tears running down her cheeks, Meir said, "I will commit suicide before I surrender," and ordered Dayan to begin preparing, if necessary, for a nuclear Masada; assembling Israel's nuclear arsenal and loading the atomic bombs onto planes.

Those of us assembled at the Plaza had no inkling of any of this at that time, but knew that the situation was dire enough that a major effort was required on our side. We decided on a four-part course of action by the Presidents Conference. These included a major fund-raising campaign through UJA, Israel Bonds, and synagogues across the country; an effort in cooperation with United Synagogue and groups like the Anti-Defamation League, American Jewish Committee and American Jewish Congress to get non-Jewish Americans to identify with Israel; organizing volunteers for service in Israel and a blood drive on behalf of wounded Israeli soldiers, and a National Emergency Convocation in Washington by leaders of the organized American Jewish community on behalf of Israel, to be held two days hence on Tuesday October 9.

Throughout the next day, Monday, we prepared for the Tuesday's rally in Washington in a cautiously upbeat mood. Optimistic media reports from Israel fed the feeling that prospects for a quick Israeli victory seemed good. The Israeli Chief of Staff said that day; "The Egyptian and Syrian attacks have been checked and the Egyptian and Syrian forces are disintegrating," The Jewish Telegraphic Agency reported from Israel that day; "The spirit of victory seemed apparent in the country tonight. The atmosphere is almost festive." Meanwhile the U.S. Senate had passed a resolution urging a return to the cease-fire lines held before the war, although, to no one's surprise, after more than 48 hours of war there had been no meeting of the U.N. Security Council to condemn the aggressors. The Soviets, after all, were one of the five permanent members of the Security Council, and it was already clear that their military personnel in Egypt and Syria were actively involved in those countries' attacks on Israel.

Then on Monday night and early Tuesday morning, the tone of the news changed dramatically. As we were boarding flights to Washington that morning, we received word that an Israeli counterattack toward the Canal had failed and that the SAM-6 missiles the Soviets had supplied to the Egyptians were taking a heavy toll on the Israeli Air Force, which had lost 51 planes in the first few days of war, about 10 percent of its total force. As a result, Israel was in urgent need of immediate re-supply of American arms—especially Phantom and A4 Skyhawk fighter planes. Those of us who arrived in Washington early that morning quickly drafted a letter to President Nixon urgently seeking immediate resupply of aircraft and military material. I asked Max Fisher, a counselor to the President and our closest contact with Nixon, to hand-deliver the message to the President and to try to bring us back an answer in time for the rally, to be held at the Shoreham Hotel in downtown Washington.

At 2:00PM I called our Washington Conference meeting to order and delivered a speech that was to rally the American Jewish community to mobilize in Israel's defense and convince the Nixon Administration to immediately provide the military aid Israel requires. To accomplish that I sought to make clear that the Egyptian and Syrian military attack on Israel on October 6 did not come in a vacuum, but was part of a much larger Arab effort to discredit and demoralize Israel and split the Jewish State away from its erstwhile supporters in the West using a range of tactics including U.N. resolutions and terrorist attacks.

Denouncing as a "malicious lie" that Israel had started the war, I said that what had, in fact, occurred was that "At 2 PM on the Day of Atonement, the holiest of Holy days, hordes of hate-filled Arab soldiers crossed the cease-fire lines determined to bring Israel to her knees—determined that there should be no Jewish survivors of an Arab victory." I asked my listeners to consider what might have happened to Israel if the Jewish state had heeded demands from much of the world since 1967 that it withdraw to the 1967 borders despite the anti-Israel the "Four No's" the Arab nations had articulated in Khartoum.

"Again and again since 1967 the Security Council has censured Israel, deplored her acts, and has condemned her self-defense, while Arab terror finds indifference and even acquiescence," I pointed out, noting that the world had largely remained silent in the face of years of Arab terror, horrific events "were quickly glossed and forgotten as unpleasant events."

Reminding everyone how only ten days earlier the government of Austria had surrendered to the demands of Arab hijackers, I stressed that, "The civilized nations of the world must share in the responsibility for fostering a climate of opinion in Arab minds that leads them to believe they can proceed with impunity against Israel, against her athletes, her airlines, her marketplaces, her school buses and now her borders."

Only President Nixon, had commendably and forthrightly stated that the world cannot accept that governments large and small shall yield to terror—but his was a lonely voice in a world of "Hear no evil, see no evil, speak no evil," especially when it is an evil directed at Israel.

The imperative for American Jews, I said, was to "shock the world back to moral sensitivity, to an elemental awareness of conscience before the very fragile fabric of law and order...is destroyed, and the world reverts to the law of the jungle." Noting that Israel had lost in the preceding four days "huge quantities of aircraft, radar and missile installations, tanks and transport," and that I had been informed a few hours earlier by the Finance Minister of Israel, Pinchas Sapir, that the cost to date of the current battle is in excess of $1 billion, I stated, "This too is our challenge. A challenge to call on our membership to respond with cash—to redeem pledges already made—to United Israel and Israel Bonds...and to make new and enlarged commitments...to help meet the pressing immediate financial needs Israel faces." For its part, I said, the Conference of Presidents of Major American Jewish Organizations will continue and intensify its representations to our government, urging that Israel receive supportive assistance to the extent and of the nature required."

I was followed to the speaker's platform by the Rev. David R. Hunter, deputy general secretary of the National Council of Churches, who told the meeting that "desecration of the high and holy Day of Atonement is an offense before God. To desecrate Yom Kippur by armed aggression, " he said, "is an offense so great as to totally invalidate the religious sanctions of those who were responsible for it." Hunter closed his powerful oration with the words of Isaiah: "For Zion's sake I will not be silent and for Jerusalem's sake I will not rest."

The convocation then heard statements by Senators Ted Kennedy (D-Mass), Richard Schweiker (R-Pa), Charles Percy (R-Ill) and George McGovern (D-S.D.) Kennedy said, "We in the United States must remain committed to the pursuit of peace, but a peace that protects the right of Israel as a nation (and) assures Israel secure and recognized boundaries."

The most provocative address at the convocation was by Israel's Ambassador to the United States, Simcha Dinitz, who that very afternoon returned from his father's funeral in Israel. Dinitz said that the Jewish state was "paying heavily" for its decision "not to engage in a pre-emptive strike at the Egyptian and Syrian armies massed heavily along the cease-fire lines." It was one of the first official statements by a high Israeli official that Jerusalem had known an Arab attack was imminent but had deliberately decided to absorb the first blow; this decision would within weeks force the resignation of Defense Minister Moshe Dayan and within seven months that of Prime Minister Golda Meir.

Dinitz stressed two points. Despite the temporary setback, time was on Israel's side and that U.S. military equipment would be needed to replace what had been lost, and what would give Israel the capacity to turn the tide. He said that Israel was determined to push "every single Egyptian" back across the Suez Canal, to push the Syrian forces back across the northern cease-fire line and to deliver "such a devastating blow to Egypt and Syria that they will never—at least not at any time in the near future—be able to regroup for another act of aggression against Israel."

The success of Henry Siegman, then Executive-Director of the Synagogue Council of America to bring about the the attendance of many leaders of other faiths to participate in the meeting, reflected the broad level of concern and caring about the safety of Israel. Siegman well deserved the thanks for his efforts.

Shortly before the end of the meeting's program, Max Fisher returned from the White House telling us of his successful meeting. President Nixon had personally assured him "Yes, we will replenish losses in aircraft and give aid to Israel." We felt greatly heartened by Max's report as we put forward a resolution, which was unanimously adopted, that called upon "the Nixon Administration, with the support of Congress, to restore the full strength of Israel's defense capability to meet and repel the challenge of Arab aggression aimed at destroying Israel. Israel must receive the military, political and moral support she requires, to the extent and of the nature called for." We also sent a cable to Prime Minister Meir in which we affirmed:

"We representatives of American Jewry proclaim our solidarity with you and the people of Israel in the battle for survival. We share the hurt of your wounds borne in this struggle to live in peace, and freedom and dignity. With you we vow that the blood spent today in response to Arab aggression shall not be shed in vain...We salute your courage. We embrace your hopes. We share your anguish and prayers as we say together with you, Am Yisroel Chai; the people of Israel lives and shall live."

The adrenalin rush we received from the Washington Emergency Meeting brought about a massive show of solidarity with Israel by American Jews. By Thursday October 11, over 30,000 people had called the American Zionist Youth Foundation to volunteer for service in Israel. Still the news from the battlefield was considerably less encouraging. On October 10, the JTA reported, "The mood of the people of Israel has changed sharply these past 24 hours. There is uneasy concern."

For the remainder of that week, I was involved in an anxious, non-stop series of meetings and phone calls with Henry Kissinger, asking him "When is the U.S. airlift to Israel going to start?' I also forcefully asked the Secretary of State how it could be that if the President of the United States had given a commitment to re-supply Israel with the arms it needed to prevail, what could be holding up the commencement of the airlift.

The Jewish community leadership was increasingly frustrated and angry by the slow moving of the wheels at the Pentagon to get the airlift underway; especially given that on October 9, the Soviet Union had initiated its own major airlift of arms to Cairo and Damascus, while two Soviet destroyers had entered the eastern Mediterranean from the Black Sea.

I was, however, keenly aware of the need to maintain good relations with Kissinger, given that President Nixon was largely distracted because of his concentration on the rapidly worsening Watergate mess (both the resignation of Vice President Spiro Agnew and Nixon's firing of Special Prosecutor Archibald Cox and subsequent calls for his impeachment happened during the three weeks of the Yom Kippur War). Kissinger was more or less in charge of U.S. foreign policy during those fateful weeks when the fate of Israel hung in the balance, even if he did not have the authority of his boss, the President, to order the Defense Department and other recalcitrant parts of the federal bureaucracy to bend to his will.

I had established a good working relationship with Henry Kissinger thanks to our high stakes dealings on the Soviet Jewry issue over the preceding year, and the sense of mutual respect and understanding that had grown between us was vital in the very difficult circumstances in which we had to operate that week. While I and others were deeply concerned about the U.S. government's apparent delay in initiating the airlift, some in the Jewish community went further and accused Kissinger of acting with duplicity in his dealings with Israeli Ambassador Simcha Dinitz, Max Fisher and myself. The anti-Kissinger crowd claimed that while the Secretary of State presented himself as Israel's best friend and advocate in the Administration and claimed it was the Pentagon that was dragging its feet in getting the airlift started, when, in reality, it was Kissinger himself who was stringing Israel along and delaying the beginning of the airlift. Kissinger was said to be motivated in this devious course by a desire to salvage détente with the Soviets and to prevent Israel from winning a clear victory in the war; thereby placing the U.S. in position to be the principle arbiter between Jerusalem, Cairo and Damascus once the shooting ended.

These charges were fleshed out in an influential article by

Edward Luttwak and Walter Laquer that ran in *Commentary* in the summer of 1974. In response, I wrote a letter to the editor in which I absolutely rejected the authors' notion that Kissinger acted with duplicity during the Yom Kippur War toward myself, Dinitz, Fisher, or others to whom he promised the imminent beginning of the airlift and then had to backtrack. Rather, I remain convinced that Kissinger spoke to us with candor and sincerity, but that even in his strengthened position as the chief formulator of U.S. foreign policy, he was hardly in a position to dictate to the Defense Department. While Henry and I had some tough conversations during those tense days, I remain convinced that we were exceedingly fortunate that someone so able and so committed to Israel's welfare happened to be serving as Secretary of State at that historical moment. Certainly, nothing happened during those unforgettable days that caused me to personally question Kissinger's integrity or to support the thesis that he was pursuing an agenda inimical to Israel's interests.

On Wednesday, October 11, Kissinger explained to me that the Pentagon was adamantly opposed to using U.S. military planes to carry out the airlift for fear of infuriating the Arab world and causing it to begin an embargo of oil shipments to the U.S. Kissinger said the President had therefore decided that the airlift would begin using chartered civilian aircraft to fly the first leg of the trip to the Azores Island in the Atlantic Ocean off Portugal, with Israeli planes picking up the equipment from there. Yet the following day when I pressed him again, Kissinger acknowledged there was a delay; it had been determined that the civilian aircraft were not large enough to carry the military equipment in question. In addition, Portugal was dragging its feet on agreeing to the use of the Azores for refueling (Kissinger finally won their assent by threatening to come out against that country's efforts to retain its African colonies), and other European countries were telling Washington they would not allow their territories even to be overflown in the re-supply effort.

Meanwhile, strong political pressure was building on the Administration from powerful figures in Congress like Senators Henry Jackson, Hubert Humphrey, Jacob Javits, Birch Bayh and Abraham Ribicoff to get the airlift underway. Still, as Kissinger told me in a somewhat apologetic tone on Thursday, October 11 and Friday, October 12, he was having great trouble convincing Schlesinger to accept even the chartering of 20 U.S. transport planes to begin the process of flying military supplies to Israel. It was not until late Friday evening that the President overruled Schlesinger and sanctioned the dispatch of the 20 transport planes. By that time both Kissinger and Nixon were deeply alarmed by the Soviet military re-supply of Egypt and Syria, which had been going all out for three days and now seemed to offer those countries the alluring prospect of achieving a decisive military victory over Israel. Not only was the Soviet military policy blatantly in contradiction to the policy of détente with the United States that Nixon and Kissinger had worked assiduously to cultivate with the Soviet leadership for several years, but it threatened to create a situation in which a victorious Soviet Union would become the dominant force in the Middle East, thereby creating a grave strategic danger for the U.S. and the entire West.

Even though Nixon had been warned by King Faisal of Saudia Arabia that a U.S. military re-supply of Israel would trigger an Arab oil boycott of the United States, the President did not now hesitate, but on Saturday October 13 ordered an immediate and massive military re-supply effort without any restrictions and using U.S. military transport planes direct to Tel Aviv. Within hours, 67 transport planes were on their way to Lod Airport and within several days more a revitalized IDF began to push its enemy back, first on the Syrian front and later near the Suez Canal.

It would be a vast understatement to say that I was relieved and gratified to receive a call from Kissinger late on the afternoon of Saturday October 13 informing me that 76 U.S. military aircraft were in the air with top-of-the-line military supplies for Israel. It cannot be emphasized strongly enough, given President Nixon's troubled legacy and the fact that he unfortunately engaged in some thoughtless anti-Semitic banter during his White House years that was caught on his own secret taping system and thus saved for posterity, that while Kissinger spearheaded U.S. policy throughout the Yom Kippur war and pushed for the supply airlift to Israel to be green-lighted, it was Nixon who deserves the everlasting gratitude of the Jewish people for giving the order that put it into motion. As Nixon himself recalled during a meeting I held with him and Kissinger in January, 1974 when Kissinger suggested to him on October 13 that the U.S. send five aircraft to Israel right away, the president responded, "If we are going to send five, lets send 50 right away." Kissinger vigorously nodded his head in confirmation of the President's assertion.

Cease Fire

We held a massive and energetic rally in support of Israel in Manhattan on Sunday October 14 that was attended by over 100,000 people. Abba Eban spoke to the crowd, as did Mayor Lindsay and Senator Jacob Javits, who praised the President for initiating the airlift and called for it to be carried through even faster.

Meanwhile, there was a strong sense that a turning of the tide was taking place; the Israelis had by then not only pushed the Syrians back from the land on the Golan Heights they had captured during the first days of the war, but the IDF was pressing its advantage into Syrian territory ever closer to Damascus. Meanwhile, Israeli forces had decisively turned

A lunch meeting with Israeli Minister of Defense Moshe Dyan shortly after the 1973 Yom Kippur War.

At the home of Moshe Kol, signer of Israel's 1948 Declaration of Independence.

Vith David Ben Gurion at Sde Boker.

President Nixon appointing me as a member of the Task Force on International Private Enterprise.

Jean and I with Gerald Ford.

I was a White House advisor during President Ronald Reagan's administration.

The President was deeply moved as Avital Sharansky detailed the agony her husband was enduring at the hands of his KGB captors. Also attending were Vice President George H.W. Bush, Director of National Security Richard Allen, Joseph Mendelevich, and myself.
—May, 1982

Congratulating President Carter on the Egyptian-Israeli Peace.

Meeting with Secretary of Defense Caspar Weinberg and Ambassador Morris Abrams, Seymour Reich, and Malcolm Hoenlein.

Richard Allen, National Security Advisor to President Reagan, and I met with Chief Rabbi Moses Rosen of Romania, who almost single-handedly held Jewish life together in that totalitarian state.

Vice President George H.W. Bush and Barbara Bush visited newly-arrived Ethiopian children at an Israeli absorption center.

Israel's Prime Minister Golda Meir appeared before the Presidents Conference in New York, in 1970.

In Geneva, addressing the General Assembly of the United Nations as a member of the United States Delegation.

Addressing a Solomon Schechter School Affair in Roslyn, Long Island, N.Y. with Ambassador to the United States Yitzhak Rabin—March 21, 1970

I established a good working relationship and longtime friendship with Secretary of State Henry Kissinger.

With Secretary of State Al Haig and Executive Director of the Conference of Presidents, Yehudah Hellman.

Max Fisher was both a dedicated Jewish American leader and a dear friend.

back a massive Egyptian movement eastward into the Sinai and were instead now pushing back toward the Suez Canal. On October 16, General Ariel Sharon reached the southern end of the canal, thereby driving a wedge between the Egyptian Second and Third Armies, and in a daring move pressed across the canal into "Africa," as the Israeli press put it.

Seeing which way the wind was blowing, the Soviet Union, which had prevented the U.N. Security Council from passing any resolution calling for a cease-fire as long as the Arab armies appeared to be prevailing, and which had insisted that Israel must agree to withdraw all the way back to the 1967 borders, now began calling for a cease-fire "in place" so as to preserve whatever advantages the Arab armies had attained and to prevent Israeli drives closer to Damascus and Cairo. The Israelis, who were now on the offensive on both fronts and wanted to deliver a decisive defeat to the Arab armies before stopping the fighting, ignored the calls by the Soviet Union and other countries for a cease-fire; a stance which had the unspoken support of Kissinger, who dragged his heels for several days to allow Israel more time to expand its foothold on the east side of the Canal and to complete the surrounding of the Egyptian Third Army in the Sinai.

Finally on Saturday, October 20, Kissinger informed Dinitz he would be flying that day to Moscow that day for meetings with Brezhnev and his team. Even so, Kissinger told Dinitz not to worry; it was highly unlikely that the Soviets, who were still demanding that Israel would return to the 1967 lines, would propose something reasonable enough for him to agree to.

Yet just hours after Kissinger arrived in Moscow on the evening of October 21, he reached agreement with the Soviets on conditions for a cease-fire. Within 24 hours, the United States and the Soviet Union, acting together pushed the terms of the Moscow Agreement through the U.N. as Security Council Resolution 338. The resolution adopted unanimously by the Security Council, called on the combatants to terminate all military activity within 12 hours of the adoption of the resolution; to begin implementing Resolution 242, the U.N.'s famous land for peace resolution adopted in 1967 based on negotiations that were to be carried out between the parties with the support of the international community.

Mrs. Meir and her government, who thought they would be given ample time to finish off the Syrians and Egyptians, were shocked and furious by the news from Moscow, feeling that Kissinger had betrayed them. As angry as she may have been, however, Meir, a political realist, understood that Israel was in no position to reject the cease-fire and face the calumny of the entire world—including its only ally and arms supplier, the United States.

Still, Kissinger, as he boarded his plane in Moscow to fly to Israel, had to be more than a little apprehensive about the reception awaiting him in Jerusalem. When he was met at Lod Airport by Eban, Kissinger said semi-jokingly, about Meir; "I presume she is wild with anger with me,"

Kissinger explained to Golda and her team upon arrival in Jerusalem that he decided to sign the deal after the Soviets agreed to accept a ceasefire in place rather than demand Israeli withdrawal and to accept the American condition that implementation of Resolution 242 could only take place in the context of negotiations between the concerned parties. He reminded the Israelis that only a week earlier there was no way they could have achieved such a favorable agreement.

According to Israeli journalist Matti Golan in his *The Secret Conversations of Henry Kissinger* (1976), Golda and her team were somewhat mollified during the Jerusalem meeting by a suggestion from Kissinger that if they needed a few more days to improve their position, he would not prevent them. According to Golan, when Brigadier Matti Peled said that in his professional opinion it would be possible for Israel to destroy the two now-virtually trapped Egyptian armies, Kissinger responded, "Two or three days? That's all? Well, in Vietnam the cease-fire didn't go into effect at the exact time it was agreed to."

In any case, although the cease-fire officially began at 6:55PM. on October 22, fighting continued for several more days with Israeli forces moving rapidly on the city of Suez on the east bank of the Suez Canal in order to complete the encirclement of the two armies. On the following evening, I met with Kissinger at the State Department together with Max Fisher and Leonard Garment. The Secretary was under intense pressure from the Soviets at that moment to stop the Israeli forward movement, and as we shall see in the next chapter, he used that meeting to lean hard on Fisher and myself, arguing that for the sake of Israel's security, we should do something that would please the Soviets and give them evidence that détente was to their advantage.

What Kissinger asked of us was to express our opposition to the holding of an early House vote on the Trade Reform Act, which had been called for several days by supporters Sen. Jackson and Congressman Charles Vanik to place restrictions on U.S. trade with the Soviets as long as the Soviets continued to place onerous restrictions on Jewish emigration. Kissinger argued passionately and cogently that such a House vote would embitter the Soviets at the worst conceivable moment, and thereby jeopardize their cooperation in ending hostilities.

As it was, Kissinger asserted, it was only by virtue of the relationship between Brezhnev, Nixon and himself that the cease-fire had been reached, the Russians had been contained to the extent they were and there had been no major clashes between Soviet and Israeli military personnel. He needed our help now, he said.

As I will explain in detail in the next chapter, my own

energies and those of Fisher, Richard Maass of the National Conference on Soviet Jewry and my colleagues in the Jewish leadership were focused during the last days of the war and beginning of the cease-fire on a largely unsuccessful attempt to negotiate between the Administration and the forces backing Sen. Henry Jackson in Congress and the Jewish community to reach a compromise on the Soviet trade bill that would be acceptable to both sides.

In the meantime, though, we kept close touch on developments on the ground in the Middle East, including the call by Kissinger on October 25, amidst threats by the Soviets to introduce a large Soviet armed force into Egypt, of a general U.S. military alert, including the nuclear-supplied Strategic Air Command. That act of brinkmanship worked well; the Soviets backed away from their threats and the Israelis, having realized, in any case, that there was not sufficient time for the destruction of the two Egyptian armies, also accepted the cease-fire.

A few days later, top Israeli and Egyptian generals met at Kilometer 101 on the Suez-Cairo highway to discuss supplying food to the trapped Egyptian Third Army in exchange for Egypt providing Israel with solid information on several hundred Israeli prisoners in Egyptian hands. For the first time since 1948, negotiations between Israel and a major Arab adversary were underway and those negotiations would lead over the next several years to two interim agreements between the two sides brokered by Kissinger and in 1977, to President Sadat's astonishing trip to Israel and negotiations for a full peace treaty between the two sides.

As negotiations slowly picked up between Israel and both Egypt and Syria, the most pressing priority on the Israeli side was arranging the freeing of the hundreds of Israeli POW's in the hands of its two adversaries. The Israeli public's concern for its soldiers in Arab hands was heightened by credible news reports that a large number of Israelis—about 100 of the Israelis taken prisoner by Syria during the war—had been shot dead by the Syrians after being subjected to brutal torture. Despite the cease-fire however, Egypt and Syria showed no inclination to provide information on the state of the Israeli prisoners in their hands or to end breaches of the Geneva Convention of 1949, to which both Arab states were signatories, governing the treatment of prisoners of war.

The American Jewish leadership decided during the first days of November to undertake a sustained public campaign to highlight the plight of the Israeli prisoners and to demand that Syria and Egypt make clear to the world it was according the prisoners all rights due to them under the Geneva Convention. Together with the National Jewish Community Relations Advisory Council (NJCRAC) and other groups, like the newly formed American Action Committee for the Release of Israeli POW's, we at the Presidents Conference organized rallies on behalf of the Israeli POW's in New York and Washington and a protest letter writing campaign to the Egyptian and Syrian missions to the U.N. as well as to President Nixon, Secretary of State Kissinger, U.N. Secretary General Kurt Waldheim and the International Red Cross.

Our campaign had the effect of embarrassing President Sadat who was already engaged in the early stages of a PR campaign to make himself look moderate and western-oriented, and he decided to surmount the issue by agreeing to a prisoner exchange. By the end of November, Egypt had repatriated 247 Israeli POW's in exchange for 8221 Egyptians. By that time, we had learned that virtually all Israeli POW's held in Egypt had been tortured, and 28 prisoners had been shot in cold blood.

The focus now shifted to Syria, which was now believed to hold about 150 Israeli prisoners about whom it had thus far refused to provide a list or to guarantee they were being accorded basic Geneva protections.

On December 17, the father, mother and wife of three Israeli soldiers captured by the Syrians held a press conference under the aegis of the Presidents Conference to appeal for American support in their demand that Syria publish a list of POW's and permit the International Red Cross to visit them. "We ask only that Syria abide by the provisions of the Geneva Convention on the treatment of prisoners of war," They pointed out that Syria had reneged on an earlier promise to free Israeli POW's even after Israel agreed to Syrian demands that it release 360 Syrian POW's in its hands and permit the repatriation of 15,000 Syrian civilians to territory adjacent to the Golan Heights captured by Israel in the latter stages of the fighting.

During the following week, the Presidents Conference led Jewish communities throughout the country in observing Chanukah with rallies, torch light parades and other events in support of Israel and in protest to abusive treatment of Israeli POWs by Syria. On January 16, 1974, I led a three-person Presidents Conference delegation that met with U.N. Secretary General Kurt Waldheim to press the Syria-POW issue. We conveyed our deep concern about the continued failure of the Syrian government to honor the Geneva Convention concerning POW's and furnish a list of Israeli prisoners or permit visits to the prisoners by the International Red Cross. Waldheim told us of his initiatives to resolve the matter and pledged to continue his efforts.

Finally as part of an Israeli-Syrian disengagement agreement negotiated by Kissinger and signed May 31, 1974 the Syrians agreed to a prisoner exchange, which took place from June 1-6. If our campaign for the Israeli POW's had little discernable impact in convincing the Syrians to stop their barbaric violation of the Geneva Convention in their mistreatment of Israeli prisoners, we at least helped to keep the issue in the spotlight before world leaders and in the U.S. media; thereby likely helping to prevent even worse mistreatment of Israeli POW's than what actually occurred.

Aftermath of War

On November 26, 1973, Jean and I led 50 members of the Presidents Conference on a solidarity mission to Israel. It was my first visit to the Jewish state since the end of fighting in the Yom Kippur War just under a month earlier and we were one of the first large delegations of American Jews to venture back to a wartime Israel where it was still widely feared that the fighting could erupt again at any moment. Indeed, we found the country still to be in a state of shock, as Israelis mourned for 2,523 of their sons and daughters who had paid the highest price during the war, by far the largest number of Israelis killed in any war since the War of Independence. Israelis' sense of invulnerability had been shattered and the streets were filled with protests demanding an investigation as to why Israel had not been prepared for the Arab attacks and demanding the resignations of both Defense Minister Moshe Dayan and Prime Minister Meir. Both were to leave office in April 1974 even though the Agranat Commission found that the IDF leadership, rather than the political echelon, was responsible for not heeding evidence the Egyptians and Syrians were about to attack.

During our mission, we met with all the leading government figures, including Meir and Dayan and made a somewhat improvised and more than a little dangerous visit to the southern front, where I walked across one of the pontoon bridges Gen. Sharon's troops had put across the 200 yard wide Canal and briefly entered Egypt. As I put it in my diary; "I stamped my feet on Egyptian soil, did not like the sensation and quickly returned to the Israeli side of Sinai. If 4000 years ago the Jews had to fight to get out of Egypt, I had no desire now to fight to get back into Egypt." While we stood on a bluff overlooking the Canal, an Israeli Phantom jet screamed by just over our heads, and although most of the members of the Presidents Conference had no military training, we all dived to the ground so quickly in involuntary reaction to the ear-jangling noise that we won praise for correct military procedure from Gen. Jackie Evan, who was escorting us that day.

After the mission ended, Jean and I stayed on for another solidarity mission I had helped to organize, that of the United Synagogue. Israeli radio and television covered both conventions so that my name had become somewhat known among the wider Israeli public, as I found out when I went to Avis in Jerusalem to rent a car. Two women at the desk recognized me; thanking me profusely for our support for Israel in a difficult time, and then, somewhat embarrassingly, asking me for my autograph. The women spoke with tears in their eyes about the terrible losses Israel had suffered during the war and about their fears that the whole world, including the U.S., would respond to the Arab oil boycott by throwing Israel to the wolves. One of the women, an immigrant from Hungary, told me that she woke up every morning with a sense of non-existence; and wondered if she would live out the day.

On Monday December 3, I attended the funeral of Israel's elder statesman, David Ben-Gurion, who had passed away after a long illness. In accordance, with Ben-Gurion's own request, the ceremony at the Knesset was a very simple, if deeply emotional affair, with no eulogy or gun salutes. Then I was honored to share a share a helicopter ride with the U.S. Ambassador to Israel, Kenneth Keating to Ben-Gurion's kibbutz of Sde Boker in the middle of the Negev, where he was buried alongside his late wife Paula in a breathtakingly beautiful spot overlooking the arid hills and valleys beyond. The loss of Israel's founding father so soon after the trauma of the Yom Kippur War heightened the sense of deep melancholy and apprehension about the future that seemed to envelop the country like a shroud.

I returned home determined to spend my last several months as Chairman of the Presidents Conference doing everything I could to fight the Arab oil boycott and prevent the U.S. and other countries from turning against Israel as a result of it. We decided to concentrate much of our efforts on Japan, a major U.S. ally that also happened to be almost totally dependent on Arab oil. On November 23, the Japanese government announced that it might reconsider its diplomatic relations with Israel unless the Jewish state withdrew from Arab territory occupied in 1967. Hours before leaving on our mission to Israel, I had already led a delegation to meet in Washington with the Japanese Ambassador to the U.S., Takeshi Yashukawa, to express our position that Japanese surrender to Arab oil blackmail not only undercut Israel's position, but also that of the United States, Japan's closest ally, which was seeking to rally a faltering international community not to succumb to pressure from the Arab oil producers. Japanese capitulation to the oil boycott would have little impact in ensuring the continued availability of petroleum for Japan, I told the ambassador, but might instead disturb the economic and political alliance that had existed between Japan and the U.S. since the end of World War II.

As a result of that encounter, I was attacked vociferously in a November 28 nationally syndicated op-ed piece in the Washington *Star-News* by Bruce Biossat entitled *Sledgehammer Over Japan*. Biossat wrote that in our meeting with the Japanese Ambassador, I had made "one of the most disgraceful threats in recent memory...the ugly business of a consumer boycott," which Biossat said represented "the same despicable blackmail being practiced so recklessly against western nations and Japan by Saudi Arabia's King Faisal and other oil-rich Arab leaders." Biossat added, "Stein's reported position is at once shockingly arrogant and devoid of all compassion for a struggling Japan that has no energy or any other major resources of its own."

I responded in a letter to the editor of the *Star-News* that we were "not 'threatening'" Japan nor did we warn of any 'ugly business of a consumer boycott.'" Nevertheless, I wrote, Japan's adherence to the Arab oil boycott of Israel would "encourage further Arab blackmail and undercut the position of Secretary Kissinger, who said the U.S. would not be bludgeoned into changing its foreign policy by any Arab oil cutoff. This would disturb the friendly economic and political relations between the U.S. and Japan" something that I emphasized, "would surely cause many Americans to adopt a new attitude toward the purchase of Japanese goods."

Meanwhile, I received a cordial letter from Ambassador Yasukawa affirming that our meeting and exchange of views had been useful, but reiterating "the Japanese government opposes acquisition and occupation of any territories by use of force". He went on to argue, somewhat implausibly, that even though "it is true that Arab countries have put heavy pressure on Japan in various ways, the Chief Cabinet Secretary's statement [threatening to cut Japanese trade and diplomatic ties to Israel] does not by any means imply that Japan has surrendered to such Arab pressures."

On December 24, together with Yehuda Hellman and my soon-to-be successor as chairman, Rabbi Israel Miller, I met at the residence of the Japanese Consul-General in New York with a delegation of political leaders and parliamentarians of the ruling Democratic-Socialist party of Japan. The delegation members informed us that the Arab oil embargo came "like a stab in the back in the dark" and was a "great shock" to the people of Japan. Nevertheless, the delegation stressed that recent visits of Japanese leaders to the Persian Gulf states and Japanese offers to substantially invest in Arab countries "was merely a showing of greater interest in those countries which supply Japan with oil and should not be construed as any change in Japanese-Israeli relations."

I made clear to the delegation that we didn't buy that line, stating bluntly that in our opinion "Japan had surrendered the integrity of its foreign policy to the desires of Persian Gulf oil sheiks" and had "weakened the American initiative for peace in the Middle East." I let them know that the American Jewish community had shown "great restraint" in any economic reaction to Japan's pro-Arab position, but made it clear that "if further capitulation to blackmail occurred, Japan could expect a strong reaction from the American public" and with greatest intensity from the American Jewish community." In effect, we were putting Japan on notice; choose between its position as a close American ally or as a supplicant of the Arab oil sheiks."

Our unequivocal message, together with expressions of unhappiness with Japan's position by the Nixon Administration, must have been getting through, because as the weeks went by and the tumultuous year 1973 drew to a close, there was no move by Japan to carry through on its earlier threat to sever trade or diplomatic ties with Israel.

Finally, on January 10, 1974, I, together with Yehuda Hellman, Rabbi Israel Miller and Rabbi Arthur Hertzberg, had the opportunity to meet with the Deputy Prime Minister Takeo Miki in Washington. After an exchange of views that went along the lines of our previous encounters with Japanese officials, I asked Minister Miki specifically if Japan contemplated any further deterioration or further change in its relations with Israel, such as a break in diplomatic ties. Clearly having anticipated the question, Miki responded, "Not one single Arab leader pressured Japan to sever relations with Israel." In other words, we were being assured that no diplomatic break was in the offing whether or not Israel withdrew to the 1967 borders, a reversal of Japan's threats two months earlier to take exactly that action.

We continued to monitor closely the Japanese policies toward Israel until March when, having badly hurt the economies of the U.S., Western Europe and Japan, but not having succeeded in getting them to move decisively against Israel, the Arab oil states announced that they were ending the oil boycott.

It is difficult to measure how large an impact our campaign had on Japan's backing away from its threat to break relations with Israel. It may be that by the beginning of 1974, the Japanese had concluded that the Arab oil states would not push the West to the wall for fear of sparking a U.S. military response, and therefore would end the boycott within a few months in any case.

Whatever the case, I am confident that our pressure on Japan had a discernable impact in bringing about a positive result. Japan's backing down from its threat to cut relations with Israel contributed palpably to the perception among leaders of countries around the world that the American Jewish community was a powerful player on the world scene and it would not be in their interests to tangle with us. In the wake of the Yom Kippur War, at a moment when Israel's power and self-confidence had been palpably shaken, it was important that the American Jewish community remained a source of Jewish power and constancy that could help buttress Israel and world Jewry through the difficult years that lay ahead.

By November, 1973 my role as President of United Synagogue had ended, and in early February, 1974 I handed over the chairmanship of the Presidents Conference to my successor, Rabbi Israel "Iz" Miller, an Orthodox rabbi who was beloved by Jews of all streams. During my tenure as chairman I had integrated Iz more and more into some of my high level meetings and found him to be intelligent, highly respected and easy to work with. I became convinced as time went on that he would be an ideal choice for the chairmanship after my term was completed and so recommended to the membership. Happily, he turned out to be a first-rate chairman who contributed much to the work of cementing U.S.-Israel relations and strengthening Israel's position in the world in a turbulent time.

I am sometimes asked if I felt a sense of regret to be stepping down as chairman after three and a half years of running the Presidents Conference, first as acting chairman and then as chairman. I point out that leaving one's position as chairman of the Presidents Conference is very different than say, leaving office as President of the United States, or as governor or mayor. At the Presidents Conference, unlike in elected offices, past chairmen stay actively involved in the work of the organization. It is true that as past chairman, you no longer play the protagonist's role, but you have the opportunity to stay actively involved in the work of the Conference, in meeting with U.S. Presidents and foreign leaders to the extent of your energy and interest. Suffice to say that I have stayed very active in the work of the Presidents Conference until today.

I am also frequently asked how I evaluate my own and the Presidents Conference's performance during the years of my tenure. I didn't worry much about how I was doing, but instead concentrated on doing the work and tackling the difficult problems that confronted us in those days. For me, it was never about receiving credit for successes, but rather about fulfilling the responsibility I had taken on. Again, the Presidents Conference is unlike a political organization in the usual sense, but rather a collegial body of men and women committed to the same goal; cementing U.S.-Israel relations and buttressing the security and well-being of the State of Israel. The chairman of the Presidents Conference is truly the first among equals.

As the years go by, I think back to the crises we faced during my years as acting chairman and chairman of the Presidents Conference; the terrorist acts, the struggle for Soviet Jewry and, first and foremost, the Yom Kippur War, and, yes, I do feel a sense of accomplishment. I believe we faced difficult challenges and managed to surmount many of them. Israel and world Jewry suffered some hard knocks during my years at the helm of the Presidents Conference, yet despite some setbacks, we as a people continued to go from strength to strength; ultimately, coming out stronger and more secure than we had been a before. I feel some pride in having played a small part in achieving that result and a deep sense of privilege for having been given the opportunity to serve our people in a time of great challenges

During my three and a half active years of leadership, I found great strength among the Presidents of our Major Organizations. They were always available; they were always promoting new ways of accomplishing our goals, and I salute and thank the Presidents of all the organizations for their quality of leadership and their friendship.

Freedom for Soviet Jews

One of the highest priority items I dealt with during my entire term as chairman of the Presidents Conference was the issue of Soviet Jewry. A deeply complex and highly emotional issue, during my term it reached its most heated pitch and became entangled with other issues of great importance like war and peace in the Middle East and U.S.-Soviet détente. How these issues were resolved was of crucial importance to the American Jewish community, but also to both President Nixon, Israel and the Soviets as well.

As the Soviets stepped up their repression of their Jewish population during the early 1970's; denying exit visas to as many as 100,000 Jews who had applied to leave and sending a growing number of Jewish activists to the gulag, the organized Jewish community enthusiastically signed on to what became known as the Jackson-Vanik Amendment, a bill sponsored in the Senate by Henry Jackson (D-Wash), a prominent Democratic supporter of Israel, and in the House of Representatives by Represenative Charles Vanik (D-Ohio), which passed both houses of Congress by lopsided margins. The thrust of Jackson-Vanik was to deny "Most Favored Nation" trading status to the Soviet Union unless it allowed its citizens to exercise their right to emigrate.

Working in close consultation with two other key Jewish leaders, Max Fisher, then chairman of the Board of the Jewish Agency and the American Jewish leader with closest personal relationship with President Nixon and Richard Maass, chairman of the National Conference on Soviet Jewry, I faced a daily conundrum in shaping policy on the Soviet Jewry issue; namely that while the Jewish community enthusiastically supported Jackson-Vanik, President Nixon and his closest aide, National Security Advisor and soon-to-be Secretary of State Henry Kissinger, just as adamantly opposed the bill. Nixon and Kissinger considered Jackson-Vanik to be an intrusion upon their prerogative to conduct foreign policy as they saw fit and a policy initiative that could jeopardize one of Nixon's proudest achievements; the creation of détente between the two superpowers, the United States and Soviet Union.

The policy I developed and carried through in close consultation with Fisher and Maas was for the top leadership of American Jewry to simultaneously support both Jackson-Vanik and the Administration's efforts to improve our relationship with the Soviet Union, including mutual efforts to limit and control nuclear arms.

This policy, to which we stuck to doggedly during my three and a half years of Conference leadership, led some in the Soviet Jewry movement to characterize myself, Fisher and Maass, as *shdadlanim* or court Jews, supposedly ready to sell out Soviet Jews in order to do the bidding of the Administration.

At the same time, Nixon and Kissinger themselves were becoming increasingly exasperated by the Jewish leadership's support for Jackson-Vanik, with pressure from the Administration to cut back on that support reaching a crescendo during the desperate days of the Yom Kippur War. Kissinger led us to believe that continued support for Jackson-Vanik by the U.S. Jewish community might jeopardize U.S. arms and economic support for Israel in its hour of gravest danger.

Those of us in the key positions of responsibility in the Jewish community experienced some intensely difficult moments, but we persevered in maintaining support both for Jackson-Vanik and for the Administration's efforts to improve relations with the Soviets. In the end, we successfully passed through the storm without destroying either of our vital relationships with Jackson and the Administration.

By the end of my chairmanship, I concluded that passage of Jackson-Vanik in December 1973 over the objections of a President Nixon badly weakened by the Watergate scandal that would soon force his resignation, would prove counter-productive, at least in the short term. Indeed, the Soviet leadership showed their ire at the bill's passage by causing a substantial reduction in Jewish emigration during the years 1974-76 compared with the 83,000 who were able to emigrate during the years 1971-73. Yet the tide of Soviet Jewish emigration would rise again in the late 1970's, before falling in the early 1980's and finally opening wide during the Gorbachev era.

Over the long run, it became clear that Jackson-Vanik played a positive role in holding a club over the Soviets so that they would have to open their doors to Jewish emigration if they wanted continued access to the Western technology they needed so badly to keep their creaking economy from completely falling apart.

In the end, of course, the Soviet Union itself collapsed and more than a million Soviet Jews were able to leave for Israel and more than half a million to the United States. All's well that ends well, but certainly there were moments of high drama when it appeared that events related to the Jews of the Soviet Union, the Middle East and the peace of the world were taking an ominous turn and we Soviet Jewry activists might be blamed if U.S.-Soviet détente collapsed. Yet we stayed true to the course we had set on behalf of Soviet Jews, and finally triumphed; compelling proof that, in the end, we had charted the best possible course through heavy political and diplomatic seas.

To understand what prompted the long dormant Soviet Jewry issue to erupt so spectacularly at the end of the 1960's, it is important to understand the long and bitter history of the Jews in Russia.

Archeological evidence shows that Jews settled in the Crimea as far back as the First Temple period, and that 1000 years ago, the Khazar Empire, whose kings embraced Judaism, was destroyed by the princes of Kiev Rus, the first Russian state, who not long before had converted to Orthodox Christianity. Henceforth, Jews were hated and persecuted under the horrible regimes of the czars. In the late 18th Century, Catherine the Great who conquered vast territories from Poland that contained the bulk of East European Jewry, decreed that Jews would be allowed to live only in 25 restricted cantons that became known as the "Pale of Settlement" and would not be allowed to move to St. Petersburg, Moscow and the rest of central Russia. Further restrictions on Jewish life were subsequently imposed by the deeply reactionary Czar Nicolas I.

Things got even worse near the end of the 19th Century, as successive Czarist regimes sought to divert popular outrage at their oppressive rule by turning it against the Jews. They created gangs known as the 'Black Hundreds', which were allowed to roam at will through the shtetls of Pale of Settlement and unleash murderous pogroms; pillaging, raping and killing at will. The pogroms, which culminated in the Kishinev massacre of 1903, helped to stimulate the massive wave of emigration that sent millions of Russian Jews to build new lives in the United States, while a relative trickle of others went to Palestine. It was Russian Jews who founded Hovevei Zion, the Lovers of Zion—the first movement for the resettlement of Eretz Israel—which founded such settlements as Petach Tikva, Rishon Letzion and Rosh Pina nearly 20 years before the First Zionist Congress in 1897.

Nevertheless, as horrible as were conditions during Czarist times, Jews were always permitted to maintain the three essentials necessary for the survival of a nation—they were permitted to maintain a language, a religion and a culture. With the seizure of power by Vladimir Lenin's Bolshevik Party in the October Revolution of 1917 and subsequent transformation of the Russian Empire into the Soviet Union, a radical new approach obtained that threatened the very survival of Jews as a distinct people. Lenin decreed that, since Jews were the only group among Russia's 160 distinct nationalities who did not have a distinct territory, they could not be considered a nation and needed to be de-Judaized and assimilated into the great Russian mass. Lenin's regime set up a Jewish commissariat, the *Yevkom*, which translated the works of Marx, Engels and Lenin into Yiddish and espoused those doctrines in the Jewish street; declaring the entrepreneurial class, which included many Jews, to be "class enemies."

In reality, there were many Jews who believed passionately in the Revolution and deluded themselves into believing that the solution to endemic Russian anti-Semitism was for Jews to assimilate and cease to be distinctively Jewish. Many of Lenin's closest collaborators, the most prominent of whom was Leon Trotsky, were Jewish. Nearly all of these so-called "Old Bolsheviks," including Trotsky, would be murdered by Lenin's successor, Josef Stalin, who came to power in 1924, and unleashed a Reign of Terror during the 1930's.

Stalin sought to destroy all vestiges of Jewish life. He closed nearly all of the country's remaining synagogues, yeshivas, Yiddish schools and newspapers. When Hitler invaded Russia in 1941, millions of Jews were murdered by the Nazis in mass slaughters like that of Babi Yar in Kiev. After the war, the Soviets would bulldoze the site of Babi Yar and put up a memorial which said that more than 100,000 "Soviet patriots" had been killed there, without mentioning the word "Jew."

In 1948, Stalin, who apparently hoped that the Jews in Palestine might become allies of the Soviet Union against Imperial Britain, officially recognized the new State of Israel. However, the Soviet dictator was chagrined and alarmed several months later when the first Israeli ambassador to Moscow, Golda Meir was greeted with great enthusiasm by Soviet Jews, who greeted her with reverence at the Moscow Choral Synagogue and stood in silence in large numbers in front of her hotel simply to gaze at the flag of the State of Israel. Soon thereafter, a Jew, Ilya Ehrenberg, published an article in *Pravda* reminding Jews that despite the creation of Israel, they had no right to consider themselves a nation because they were economically disunited and did not have a distinct territory.

Within weeks, 431 leading Jewish intellectuals, writers, actors and authors were arrested and executed. This was followed in 1952 by the famed Doctors' Plot, in which 11 Jewish doctors were falsely accused of having plotted to poison Stalin and other Soviet leaders. It was later learned that Stalin planned to use the Doctors' Plot as a pretext to exile the entire Soviet Jewish population to Siberia. Thankfully, that plan was shelved by the dictator's successors after his sudden death in March, 1953.

Like the overall Soviet population, Jews benefited from the political thaw that followed Stalin's death. An estimated 150,000-170,000 Jews who had been held as political prisoners in Siberia were allowed to return home under a general amnesty. Yet manifestations of Jewish culture and religiosity continued to be repressed, and even the relatively liberal Nikita Khrushchev, who denounced Stalin's excesses, made Jews into scapegoats after a bad harvest in 1961; launching trials of so-called currency speculators, many of whom had conspicuously Jewish names. Then, in 1964, Khrushchev was overthrown by the harder-line Leonid Brezhnev and Alexei Kosygin, and the resultant crackdown on political dissent had a chilling effect on overt manifestations of Jewish identity and culture.

The Refuseniks

The bleak situation of the nearly three million Jews of the Soviet Union in the mid-1960's was elucidated in the West with the publication of *The Jews of Silence*, Elie Wiesel's powerful account of his visit with Jews in the Soviet Union. Yet the mental state of Soviet Jewry was fundamentally transformed by Israel's lightening victory in the 1967 Six Day War.

In cities across the Soviet Union, Jews gathered to discuss the electrifying reports on the Voice of Israel or the Voice of America, telling each other excitedly that "our" army—meaning Israel's—was pushing rapidly across the Sinai and had captured East Jerusalem. Never mind that Soviet propaganda was scurrilously comparing Israel to Nazi Germany; the fact that the Arab armies, lavishly equipped by the Soviet Union, were picked apart by Israel in a few days, had the effect of smashing the myth of Soviet invincibility in Jewish minds and emboldening Jews to directly challenge Soviet power by doing the previously unthinkable; demanding the right to emigrate to Israel.

A large underground Jewish movement began to develop, with Soviet Jewish activists communicating their ideas through an underground press known as *samizdat*. One book which was smuggled into the Soviet Union, typed page by page in Russian translation and circulated hand by hand within the underground Jewish network, was Leon Uris' stirring novel of the creation of Israel, *Exodus*. By 1969, the Soviets had begun to allow a trickle of Jews, and soon a small but steady stream—first primarily from

Georgia and later from the heartland of the country—to leave for Israel. Yet many more applications to emigrate—100,000 or more by 1972—were refused by the Soviet emigration agency OVIR. Those who were refused had already left their jobs before applying to leave, as required by law. This large and ever-growing group of people soon became known as "refuseniks," individuals and families who were forced to live on the margins of society without any income or health care and under constant threat of arrest for so-called "parasitism."

A campaign of anti-Semitic vilification was becoming a staple in the Soviet media, characterized by cartoons in which hook-nosed, bearded Jews, clad in black, bombed hapless Arabs from aircraft emblazoned with both the Star of David and the Swastika. Seized with growing desperation in the face of an escalating tide of refusals and manifestations of anti-Semitism unprecedented since Stalin's time, eight Soviet Jewish activists conspired during late 1969 to hijack a Soviet airliner from the Leningrad airport and fly to freedom in Sweden. The plot was exposed by the KGB and the planners of the hijacking were arrested. During the notorious Leningrad Trial of 1970, the group was held up for vilification as Zionist agents, with two being sentenced to death and the rest to long prison sentences. Outraged, world Jewry organized a large-scale campaign appealing for clemency, with prominent intellectuals and human rights advocates around the world pointing out that the hijacking had never actually occurred and the accused were driven to desperate measures because their innate right to emigrate, ensured under the International Declaration of Human Rights, had been violated. In the end, the two death sentences were commuted to prison sentences and the Leningrad Eight were quietly allowed to emigrate.

A Conference in Brussels

This victory taught those fighting for the well-being of

Soviet Jews an important lesson; that the Soviet government was susceptible to international pressure and might back down from particularly harsh measures if pressed hard enough by advocates of Soviet Jewry, supporters of human rights, and by Western governments.

It was to apply the lesson of Leningrad so that we could advocate even more effectively on behalf of the right of Soviet Jews to emigrate, that 700 advocates of the Soviet Jewry cause from 38 countries around the world gathered in Brussels for three days in February 1971 for an International Conference of Jewish leaders in Brussels.

I was pleased that Jean was able to travel with me to the event. We were surprised but deeply gratified upon arrival at our hotel in the Belgian capital to discover our son Stuart, whom we had not seen for several years, was there waiting for us. Stuart, who was then working in Israel as a lawyer, was in Brussels to take part in the Jurists' Workshop. That evening, Jean and I dined with Professor Hans Morganthau and then went to the opening session of the Congress at the Palais de Congres to hear Ambassador Arthur Goldberg, who resigned from his position of United States Ambassador to the United Nations and was currently President of the American Jewish Committee.

The Brussels Conference nearly dissolved from intense acrimony on several occasions due to an effort by the fire-breathing head of the Jewish Defense League, Rabbi Meir Kahane, to crash the event. It is true that Kahane, whose militant JDL had launched a sometimes violent campaign of harassment against Soviet diplomats in New York and elsewhere, had purposely not been invited to the Congress, but we certainly did nothing to prevent him from showing up if he so desired. Kahane was instead stopped from attending by the Belgian police, who, without consulting the Conference planners, arrested him at Brussels Airport when he arrived and immediately bundled him onto an outgoing flight as an "undesireable alien." Yet two high-profile conference participants, producer Otto Preminger and screenwriter Paddy Chayefsky called a press conference at which they angrily denounced the Jewish leadership for refusing to hear Kahane and for supposedly having conspired with the Belgians to have him expelled. This was patently untrue, but even more shameful was when Preminger and Chayefsky compared the action of the Conference leadership with regard to Kahane to the actions of the Nazis. This comparison naturally caused an uproar and both were soon forced to apologize. Menachem Begin, then Israel's opposition leader, also addressed the Congress and strongly criticized our decision not to invite Kahane.

Much more pleasant for me and for many others was the appearance of a very old and infirm David Ben-Gurion to address the conference. Ben-Gurion appeared worn and tired, and was assisted with walking. It was inspiring to hear the founder of the State of Israel speak out in support of freedom for Soviet Jews and to express how important Soviet Jewish emigration would be for the Jewish state.

In my own remarks to the conference, I urged international Jewry to better publicize its efforts on behalf of entrapped Soviet Jews as well as to make sure the world knew about Soviet repressive measures employed against them. I stressed the importance of expanded Jewish travel to the Soviet Union so that we could, by our presence, give strength to refuseniks and Jewish activists and demonstrate to them that they were not alone. I called on rabbis around the world to sound the alarm on behalf of Soviet Jewry, and urged all U.S. firms doing business in that country to make known to Soviet authorities their displeasure with how Jews were being treated.

The Brussels conference, which is remembered today as the event at which the slogan "Let My People Go" was popularized, issued a closing statement declaring "Our solidarity with our Jewish brothers in the Soviet Union...We are at one with them." We called upon the Soviet Union to "recognize the right of Jews to return to their historic homeland in Israel...to put an end to the defamation of the Jewish people and Zionism."

Solemnly vowing that "We will not rest until the Jews of the Soviet Union are free to choose their own destiny," we committed ourselves to a stepped-up program of action on behalf of Soviet Jews.

Throughout 1971, the number of Soviet Jews allowed to emigrate went up sharply, reaching the then-unprecedented total of 15,000 by year's end. This was compelling evidence to all of us that the Soviet government of Brezhnev and Kosygin was amenable to pressure from the West on an issue which it often claimed concerned only itself and where it would not allow foreign interference.

Several months after Brussels, the Presidents Conference, acting at the behest of the entire organized American Jewish community, responded to the heightened importance of the struggle for Soviet Jewry on the communal agenda by replacing the American Conference for Soviet Jewry, which operated under the aegis of the National Jewish Community Relations Advisory Council (NJCRAC), with a new organization, the National Conference for Soviet Jewry (NCSJ). The NCSJ was made independent of NJCRAC, given a more-than-adequate budget line and mandated to act on the Soviet Jewry issue on behalf of the entire organized community. Richard Maass, the first president of the NCSJ and Jerry Goodman, its executive director, proved a highly professional and politically astute team.

Occasionally and inevitably, there would be tactical differences between the NCSJ, which was responding to the grass-roots Soviet Jewry groups like the Union of Councils for Soviet Jews and the Student Struggle for Soviet Jewry which demanded that the American Jewish community respond as militantly as possible to the Soviet government, and the Presidents Conference, which had to take into account the larger strategic picture, including the need to maintain strong relations with the Nixon Administration. However, through all of the turbulence, I was able to work together fruitfully with Richard Maass, who became a good friend, and with whom I shared a common commitment both to freedom for Soviet Jews and to the larger communal agenda. Together, we managed to maintain a communal consensus in our dealings with the Nixon Administration and with Congress, which, as we shall see, took a decidedly harder line position on Soviet Jewry issues than the Administration, and with the Soviets themselves.

That year, I paid a visit to Vienna, where I met and spoke at length with Soviet Jewish refugees who had arrived in the West only a few days earlier. At that time, the refugees were being housed by the Austrian government in the Schoenau Castle, a medieval structure outside Vienna where they were debriefed by the Jewish Agency and HIAS while preparing to catch flights to their new homes in Israel and America. I found my discussions with these Jewish brothers and sisters who were experiencing their first days of freedom after living all of their lives under a totalitarian anti-Semitic regime to be both inspiring and illuminating. Again and again they told me that they had felt comforted and encouraged to persevere in their persistent efforts to emigrate against apparently daunting odds thanks to Russian-language short wave radio broadcasts on Kol Yisrael (the Voice of Israel) reporting that Jews and human rights activists in the free world were demonstrating and pressuring the Soviet government on their behalf. Jean and I wished the Soviet Jews well and assured them they would be welcomed in Israel and able to build a good life.

Exactly one year after the Brussels conference, in March

1972, I attended a follow-up International Conference on Soviet Jewry in London as chairman of the Presidents Conference and led the final session that stated, in part, "We call on the Soviet government. Halt the persecution. Free the prisoners of conscience. Hear the voice of Soviet Jewry. Let my people go."

Still, in the Soviet Union, there were continuing arrests of Jewish activists. These people, who came to be known as "Prisoners of Zion," typically received onerous prison sentences of 2-3 years.

Despite this, the London Conference reiterated the policy guidelines of the Brussels Conference, which seemed appropriate at that moment because, despite many individual setbacks, there were positive signs of improvement.

President Nixon and National Security Advisor Henry Kissinger raised the issue forcefully with the Soviet leadership in advance of the Nixon-Brezhnev Summit in Moscow in June, 1972, and many individual refuseniks on lists prepared by Soviet Jewry organizations in the West were given permission to emigrate.

Exit Taxes

Any good feeling on the Soviet Jewry issue abruptly ended as soon as the summit was over. On August 3, the Soviet Council of Minister stunned both Soviet Jews and their legions of supporters in the West by adopting a decree requiring would-be emigrants who had acquired higher education—the great majority of Soviet Jews—to pay a so-called "exit tax" or "diploma tax," supposedly to compensate the Soviet state for the loss of their skills. On August 14, the Soviets established a scale of fees that were so exorbitantly high that payment by those holding advanced degrees would be all but impossible. Even before the adoption of the Exit Tax, emigrants were required to pay a head tax of 940 rubles per person, a large amount in a society where the average salary was 120 rubles a month (about $150). Now, under the new regulations, said to be based on value of their higher education, teachers would have to pay an additional 4500 rubles, holders of technological diplomas, 7700 rubles, pharmacists 8300 rubles, all the way up to doctors of science who would have to pay a tax of 19,400 rubles. For world renowned scientists, apparently, the sky was the limit; Benjamin Levich, a world authority on electro-chemistry, was informed he would have to pay 150,000 rubles to receive permission to leave for Israel.

Soviet Jewish activists responded to this dismaying news by bravely assembling before the Western media in Moscow on August 15 and holding a press conference, expressing contempt for what they termed the "Ransom Tax," which, they said, would create "a new category of human beings, the slaves of the 20th Century." Fortunately, it quickly became evident that the Soviet Jews were not alone in their revulsion for the tax. Especially shocked were the international scientific and academic communities. 21 Nobel laureates soon issued a public statement expressing "dismay" at the "massive violation of human rights" by the imposition of "exorbitant head taxes." The Exit Tax was widely denounced by the U.S., British and other European governments and even by western socialist leaders like France's Francois Mitterand.

Naturally, it was the Jewish community that took the lead in fighting the Exit Tax. On September 4, leaders of the Soviet Jewry movement from around the world gathered again in London for an emergency conference. At the conclusion of our deliberations, we demanded revocation of the "cruel and inhumane tax," which we called a "virtual reversion to Stalinism". We rejected "the right of any government to turn its people into chattel to be bought and sold..." and vowed that world Jewry would "resist, oppose and combat this decree with our utmost capacity and with the anger and indignation of a people not willing to stand by while our brethren are afflicted by cruel and tyrannical acts of persecution."

The Jackson Amendment

Meanwhile, a new strategy was emerging in Congress to resist the Exit Tax and to tie the Administration's pledge to extend Most Favored Nation status to the Soviet Union to that country's according its citizens the right to free emigration. (Nixon and Brezhnev had agreed at the Moscow Summit that the Soviets would receive MFN status, which would allow it access to the American market at the lowest possible tariff rates in exchange for Soviet agreement to pay the U.S. in several installments a fixed portion of the enormous debt it owed for the Lend-Lease help it received from Washington during World War II). The idea of making the linkage between MFN status for the Soviets and free emigration was first developed by a group of Capitol Hill aides, especially Morris Amitay, an aide to Senator Abraham Ribicoff (D-Conn), who later became the head of AIPAC, and Richard Perle, an aide to Senator Henry Jackson (D-Wash). The idea was taken up avidly by Jackson, a hawkish Democrat and old friend of the Jewish community, who had presidential ambitions (By this time it was obvious that Nixon would be handily re-elected in November over George McGovern and Democrats like Jackson were already looking to 1976).

The Jackson Amendment, as it emerged from consultations by mid-September, 1972, would refuse MFN treatment, as well as credits, credit guarantees, and investment guarantees, to a non-market economy country if that country denied its citizens the right to emigrate, or imposed more than a nominal tax on emigration or exit visas. The President of the U.S. would be responsible for determining a country's eligibility for MFN and would have to have to make a report of compliance to

Congress at the time MFN was grated to a particular country and semiannually afterward.

Once Jackson announced he would sponsor the Amendment in the Senate, it immediately attracted almost universal support in the Jewish community. On September 27, the Board of Governors of the NCSJ unequivocally endorsed the Jackson Amendment, as did NJCRAC two days later. At the same time both the Israeli government and the World Zionist Organization denounced the exit tax and refused to sanction payments to the Soviet for what they called "blackmail."

Also on the 27th, Richard Maass and I met with one of Nixon's top aides, Leonard Garment, to inform the Administration that the Jewish community was determined "not to recognize MFN treatment of the Soviet Union" and not to support that country receiving "large scale loans and credits" until it changed its policy on the exit tax in particular and on emigration in general. After cataloging for Garment the string of negative developments on the Soviet Jewry front in the three months since the Nixon-Brezhnev Summit; including Soviet jamming of Israeli Russian-language broadcasts, stepped-up arrests of Jewish activists, with sentences increased from two and a half years to three and a half years, an intensified campaign in the Soviet media against those seeking to emigrate to Israel and, above all, the imposition of the exit tax, we handed him a memo that made clear that the Jewish leadership was deeply upset with the Administration's failure to address adequately the deterioration in the position of Soviet Jews, and, consequently, we were strongly in support of the Jackson Amendment.

The memo read, in part, "We felt confident that the plight of Soviet Jewry was understood to be an issue of such compelling urgency that it would be high on your agenda. Instead during the last four months we have witnessed with growing anguish a steady increase in incidents of harassment and oppression of Soviet Jews, culminating in the imposition of an extortionate and inhuman emigration tax...During these months of mounting peril for Soviet Jews, the American Jewish community has awaited a firm response by you as our president. We believe that the worsening condition of Soviet Jewry makes your response imperative. We ask you therefore to make known to the Soviet leaders our country's inability to enter into a new and close trade relationship until these practices are stopped. We ask you at this time to make known to us, to all the American people and to the Soviet leadership your determination not to recommend MFN treatment for the Soviet Union, nor to qualify the Soviet Union for large scale loans or credits so long as it continues its unconscionable demands upon a defenseless minority."

On October 2, Maass, Fisher and I met with Kissinger. We made a point in our statement after the meeting to affirm; "We wholeheartedly support the President, Secretary of State, and Dr. Kissinger in their diplomatic efforts to resolve [the] difficult problems" of the ransom tax and harsh Soviet discriminatory practices against Jews." Nevertheless, we called upon "the American Jewish community and all Americans to participate in a concurrent effort urging Congress to act in such a way that the benefits of détente will be conditioned on the removal of the immoral education exit fees recently imposed by the Soviet Union." In short, while we were deeply appreciative of Administration efforts on the issue, we would no longer leave it in their hands alone.

Jackson had no difficulty lining up support for his legislation; on October 17, he announced that he had 76 co-sponsors in the Senate. In December, Jackson and Ribicoff formally introduced the Jackson Amendment in the Senate and by the following month, Rep. Charles Vanik (D-Ohio), acting in concert with House Ways and Means Committee chairman Wilbur Mills, has assembled a list of 144 representatives who agreed to sponsor in the House legislation similar to the Jackson Amendment that became known as the Mills-Vanik Bill. As the Jewish community stepped up a massive letter-writing campaign, support for the Jackson Amendment came from different parts of American society, including the union movement and various religious groups.

While Administration officials continued to insist that negotiations and behind-the-scenes personal diplomacy with the Soviets offered the best hope of free emigration for Soviet Jews, we soon began to see signs that the Jackson Amendment was forcing the Soviets to retreat from their hard-line on the Exit Tax. Already on October 18, a group of Moscow Jews were called to a special review committee of the emigration agency OVIR and informed that if they left the Soviet Union within 10 days, they would not have to pay the Exit Tax. Nearly 200 families were allowed to leave without paying the tax, although others continued to be told that they would have to pay. Deputy Minister of Interior Boris Shumalin acknowledged in a meeting with Jewish scientists that the waiving of the tax in this case, "was not a change in the authorities' approach to the emigration problem, but a gesture toward a certain foreign power with which the Soviet Union is seeking to develop commercial and economic relations." This was encouraging evidence our campaign was working.

In any case, between August and March, of the 20,000 Jews who were allowed to emigrate, only 900 actually were compelled to pay the tax. Finally after months of conflicting signals, the Soviets stopped collecting the tax altogether. On March 30, an official communiqué of the Soviet government unambiguously confirmed that, "Soviet citizens who receive permission to emigrate can be exempted fully from refunding the expenses mentioned above." The Administration hailed the Soviet decision, and on April 10 submitted to Congress a Comprehensive Trade Reform Act, which would authorize the President to lower and raise tariffs to facilitate the expansion of trade and enabled him to grant MFN to the USSR and other non-market countries, provided neither the House nor Senate vetoed the bill within 90 days. Meanwhile in an apparent harbinger of things to come, Occidental Petroleum signed the largest business deal with the Soviet Union in the history of U.S.-Soviet trade.

Yet Jackson insisted that he would not withdraw his bill despite the abrogation of the Exit Tax, noting that the issue was not only about trade, but rather that "We ought to use our vast economic power to help bring freedom and dignity to thousands of individuals who have been willing to stand up and fight for their right to leave Russia." Realizing that a solid majority of senators continued to support the Jackson Amendment, President Nixon decided to make his case on the issue to the Jewish leadership. He invited 14 top Jewish leaders, including myself, to a 90-minute meeting at the White House on April 19. It was the first such meeting Nixon had held at his own initiative with the Jewish leadership.

The President, under great Watergate scandal pressure which his mood reflected, remained cordial, emphasizing his long-standing support for Soviet Jewish emigration. After about an hour and twenty minutes we had spelled out our concerns that 100,000 Jews had still not been granted visas, that activists continued to be harassed, and that the broad use of the security designation limited emigration. The President finally realized that we were concerned with far more than the emigration tax. He worried that the Jackson Amendment, which he understood would easily pass both Houses of Congress if voted on at that time, threatened to destroy his effort to give the Soviet Union MFN treatment, something he said was an integral part of his efforts to achieve détente. At one point he became exasperated, telling us testily, "You gentlemen have more faith in your senators than you do in me, and that is a mistake. You'll save more Jews my way."

The President informed us that he would set up a meeting for us with Kissinger in 10 days time. Meanwhile, Max Fisher, Charlotte Jacobson (then vice chairman of the National Conference on Soviet Jewry) and I issued a statement on behalf of all the Jewish participants:

"We reaffirmed the commitment to Soviet Jews and our determination to continue maximum efforts in their behalf. We expressed our sincere appreciation to the President for the meeting which we regarded as a historic event. The President reaffirmed his concern for the plight of Soviet Jews and pledged his continuing personal efforts on their behalf."

I felt strongly that the Jewish community should endeavor not to alienate either the Administration or Congress. After all, both the President and Jackson were striving to help Soviet Jews acquire their freedom, and it seemed to me that both approaches were needed in order to help them. Shortly after the meeting, I wrote a memo to myself, expressing my belief that "We should at this time address ourselves to the possibility of effecting a resolution which would be acceptable to the White House and to the co-sponsoring senators which would, on one hand, give the President the power to bargain for further concessions and on the other hand, would pass the Senate and House. I therefore propose we begin a series of meetings with Senators Javits, Ribicoff and Jackson, to this end."

Unfortunately, our efforts to find a formula that would accommodate both the Administration and Jackson camps were undercut by grassroots activists and supporters of Senator Jackson who insisted that the Jewish leadership must take an uncompromising stand in favor of the Jackson Amendment. The fact that the President had been weakened politically by the escalating Watergate scandal made opponents of Administration policy less willing to compromise. The pressure on those of us in the leadership grew worse after April 23, 1973, when 100 leading Soviet Jew activists in Moscow sent an open letter to American Jewish leaders supporting the Jackson Amendment and appealing to us not to support any compromises with the Soviets that would cause themselves and their families to be "sacrificed."

Under the circumstances, I realized that we would lose all credibility in the Jewish community if we appeared to be ambiguous about the Jackson Amendment and too close to the Administration. Max Fisher also presented an acute perception problem since he was not only the President's close friend, but also a major fund-raiser in the Jewish community.

On the morning of May 1, hours before Max, Richard Maass and I were scheduled to meet with Kissinger, I went to Max's office and presented him with a resolution in support of the Jackson Amendment that I proposed to sign together with Maass even if Fisher himself felt he could not sign. Max read it and told me he believed it would be taken to be a slap in the face to the President. I told Max that he should not allow himself to be put in a position in which the Administration could use him as a wedge against the Jewish community. In order for his credentials with the community to remain viable it was necessary that he identify both with the Jackson Amendment and with support of the President's initiative. Finally, Max relented and agreed.

The three of us then went to meet Kissinger. We gave him a list of 42 Prisoners of Conscience and over 900 activists unable to get visas. He promised that he would present these names to Brezhnev in Moscow later that month, when he would be there to plan the upcoming summit in Washington in mid-June. Overall, our meeting with Kissinger turned out to be a fairly hard-nosed encounter. Kissinger said he had been under the impression that, with the Soviets' removal of the education tax, the problem of the legislation withholding MFN status from the Soviets would be resolved. Max insisted that the problem went beyond the education tax, and I detailed for Kissinger our concerns over the procedure of visas that allow for the harassment and humiliation of Soviet Jews, the 100,000 whose visa applications are pending and who are living under difficult conditions and the 42 prisoners whose only crime as far as we knew was to apply for an exit visa. Kissinger wanted to know whether if this "shopping list" was met, we would then come up with another shopping list. I pointed out that that since the last Nixon-Brezhnev Summit the previous June, mainly negative signals had come out of the Soviet Union, but if there were meaningful gains, we were prepared to recognize those gains in an appropriate fashion.

Kissinger emphasized that the U.S. had already received important benefits from the promise of the President to get "MFN" status for the Soviet Union. He wondered whether the Jewish community was really prepared to take the risk of blocking MFN status for the Soviets, with all of the issues involved in American-Russian relations. He acknowledged that for the time being we had to hold to our position of support for the Jackson Amendment, but that the time might come when some formula for giving MFN status to the Russians would have to be worked out.

Afterwards, Maass, Fisher and I issued a joint statement in which we "acknowledged with appreciation the initiative of President Nixon" in helping to secure the Soviet annulment of the education tax, while stating that we continued to "believe that the Jackson Amendment and the Mills-Vanik bill have contributed and will continue to contribute to the effort to alleviate the plight of Soviet Jews."

Several days later I gave an interview to the Jewish Telegraphic Agency in which I argued that there was "nothing contradictory" in the Jewish leadership supporting both the President and the Jackson Amendment, especially given that the Amendment would not come up for a vote before the fall at the earliest. By that time, I said, Nixon and Kissinger might be able to accomplish important results for Soviet Jews through their continued diplomatic efforts.

Soviet Encounters

Certainly the President's appreciation for our efforts to prevent an open breach between the organized Jewish community and the Administration must have played a role in the the decision to invite Max and I to a State Dinner the President would be giving in the White House in honor of Brezhnev on June 18. When the invitation became public, we were subjected to bitter invective from some in the movement for accepting the invitation. One local Soviet Jewry chapter threatened to picket my home in Great Neck if I went ahead with plans to attend the dinner. I defended myself, pointing out that the dinner represented an important opportunity to bring our message face to face to the highest Soviet leaders, a more effective way to communicate than addressing them over a telephone when they are 6000 miles away.

In any case, I said, the Jewish community would have had better cause to complain if the President had failed to invite Jewish leadership to the historic dinner. By doing so, I felt, Nixon was demonstrating to Brezhnev that ours was a country where all religions were respected and had a place at the table.

I am often asked whether I took personally the charges I was subjected to during those heated days that I was somehow betraying Soviet Jews by maintaining a conciliatory position toward the Administration. The answer is that I never let those critics get me angry, even on the occasion when a group of activists disrupted a meeting of the Presidents Conference. Those of us in the leadership were serious adults negotiating on behalf of the Jewish community. We weren't going to be diverted from our serious work by what I felt were a few young people raising a little hell.

I have always sought to maintain a civil dialogue with those with whom I disagree, and certainly stayed with that approach throughout my tenure at the helm of the Presidents Conference. On the Soviet Jewry issue, I always sought to incorporate the concerns of the various parties involved until arriving at a solution which I believed offered the most effective answer to a specific situation and the greatest hope of moving things forward. Despite how heated things got during those months, I remained cool because I have always been an unemotional sort of guy who has simply been in business too long to get carried away by a lot of heated rhetoric. Let them call me whatever they wanted. I had a job to do.

At a reception before the Brezhnev dinner, President Nixon introduced me to the Soviet leader; very clearly identifying me as "a leader of the American Jewish community."Brezhnev motioned to Foreign Minister Andrei Gromyko to seek me out, and during the reception before dinner I had the opportunity to discuss the Soviet Jewry issue with him and with Soviet Ambassador to Washington, Anatoly Dobrynin, who told Gromyko that I was a "reasonable Jewish leader." After listening as I briefly laid out the points of special concern to the American Jewish community about Soviet mistreatment of Jews wishing to emigrate or openly espouse their Jewishness, Gromyko, who was given to Delphic expressions, predicted with regard to Soviet Jewry that "Everything will be all right. The road will be wider." That seemed to me a hopeful portent because the term "wider road" seemed to imply there would be more traffic. Dobrynin invited me to continue the discussion in a more substantive way and scheduled a meeting for Max Fisher and myself for a luncheon at the Soviet Embassy on July 25.

Although Brezhnev intensely lobbied Congress during his visit to Washington on behalf of the U.S.-Soviet Trade Agreement and MFN status for the Soviets, he made little discernable progress in moving either the Senate or House away from overwhelming support for the Jackson Amendment. We in the American Jewish community also made clear that we would stand firm.

Preparations for lunch with Dobrynin were continuing apace. Aware of the meeting, Kissinger encouraged us to raise whatever issues we wanted, pointing out, "You can say things the Administration can't say. You can raise issues we can't raise. Go ahead and raise them." On the other hand, Dobrynin himself urged us to bring our wives, which seemed a way to turn what we hoped would be a substantive encounter into a social one. In the end, Jean came to the luncheon, as did Mrs. Dobrynin, although Marjorie Fisher did not.

After an exchange of pleasantries, I took the floor and, determined to ensure the meeting would be more than fluff, I spoke forcefully about the humiliations would-be Soviet Jewish emigrants were forced to endure, such as the need to obtain a "*karakteristika*," a reference from an applicant's Worker's Council, an encounter from which flowed the loss of jobs, social ostracism and even physical abuse. I pointed out that "security sensitive" was being used in an arbitrary and unfair fashion as a reason for visa refusal, and said that the ongoing publication of anti-Semitic material by official Soviet publishing houses, thinly disguised as anti-Israel material, was creating a deep suspicion of Jews by their fellow Soviet citizens. Finally, I stressed the hardships placed on people who wanted to live in the Soviet Union as observant Jews, protesting the lack of kosher slaughtering, of Jewish cemeteries, and seminaries to train rabbis.

When I finished, Mrs. Dobrynin, clearly annoyed by my presentation of the situation of Soviet Jews, turned to her husband and asked in a demonstrative tone, "Why don't we put all of our Jews on a TWA plane and send them to the United States?" Before Dobrynin could reply, Max sought to defuse the situation by asking her, slightly tongue in cheek, "Could you do that? We would be happy to pay their way."

For his part, Dobrynin, an extremely polished diplomat, heard me out and then replied that the Soviet Union would not allow the problem of Jewish emigration to stand in the way of achieving détente with the United States. At the same time, he said, repeating the phrase three times for emphasis, the Soviet Union was "a great power" that "would not be pressured."

I gave Dobrynin a list of some 20 specific names I said we wanted to see action on, some of whom would indeed be allowed to leave within a reasonable amount of time. Overall, I felt that both the Brezhnev dinner and Dobrynin lunch were very positive meetings and that much was accomplished during those face-to-face encounters that might otherwise not have happened.

During September, Kissinger, who had just been appointed Secretary of State and, as virtually the only major Administration figure untouched by Watergate, became, de facto, the most powerful man in the country, began a major push for passage of the trade bill in both Houses of Congress. On September 19, the House Ways and Means Committee affirmed by voice vote its denial of MFN status to non-market countries that restricted emigration, but the Administration managed by a trick maneuver to get a section of the bill barring credits and credit guarantees dropped from the bill. The excised section of the bill came to be known as Title IV and henceforth the forces led by Mills and Vanik and supported by the organized Jewish community worked to restore Title IV and thereby ban credits and credit guarantees to the Soviets. Despite equally frenzied efforts in the other direction by the Administration, every indication was that the votes were there to pass Mills-Vanik, including a restoration of Title IV.

At the end of September, just as Rosh Hashanah was about to arrive, Palestinian terrorists invaded the Schoenau Castle in Austria, held several Soviet Jews hostage; agreeing to free them and leave the country only after the appeasement-oriented Austrian government of Dr. Bruno Kreisky, agreed to close the Castle to Soviet Jewish refugees. During the week between Rosh Hashana and Yom Kippur, I and the Presidents Conference were focused on events in Austria; denouncing Kreisky's action in closing the castle and scrambling to find other accommodations for the refugees. Like most of the rest of the world, including the government of Israel, we had no inkling of the blow that was about to land in the Middle East.

I described in detail in the previous chapter of this book my extensive efforts during the first two weeks of the Yom Kippur War to pressure the Administration to begin its promised emergency airlift of war supplies to Israel. As I noted, during the five days before the airlift commenced in earnest, I was on the phone with Kissinger every few hours demanding to know where things stood. Throughout that difficult time, I was constantly receiving calls from agitated officials at the Israeli Embassy informing me that Israel's initial reverses had been more severe than officially acknowledged, and that unless the U.S. airlift started promptly, the very survival of the Jewish state hung in the balance. In such a desperate situation, which would have been unimaginable only a couple of weeks earlier, all other Jewish communal priorities, including passage of an intact version Jackson-Vanik, suddenly became lower priorities for the American Jewish leadership.

Title IV

Even as he struggled to shake down the Pentagon bureaucracy to get the aid pipeline flowing to Israel, Kissinger was not adverse to forcefully making the point to us that the

Administration would soon need the Soviet Union to lean hard on its Egyptian and Syrian allies to achieve a cease-fire and for this reason an early House vote on the Trade Reform Act with the restoration of Title IV could jeopardize Soviet cooperation in ending hostilities.

The vote on the bill had been scheduled for October 24 or 25. On the evening of October 23, Kissinger, who had just returned from a whirlwind trip to Moscow and Tel Aviv during which he had nearly pinned down a cease-fire only to see it come unstuck, summoned me with Max Fisher and Richard Maass to the State Department. Kissinger gave us an overview of the U.S. re-supply effort to Israel, which by then had helped the IDF to turn the tide of battle on both fronts and advance within striking distance of Cairo and Damascus. He pointed out that he had personally intervened to ensure that the supply to Israel of a critically needed type of ammunition was expedited, even prior to the onset of the general airlift.

Boasting of how critical his own role had been in succoring Israel during the days of its greatest peril since 1948, Kissinger said he remained deeply concerned about Soviet intentions in the crisis, especially the very real possibility that the Soviets might attempt to re-supply the 5th Egyptian Army that had been trapped by the Israelis on the east side of the Suez Canal in Sinai. He then told us that as part of its effort to convince the Soviets to agree to a cease-fire in place between the two sides, the Administration urgently wanted to delete Title IV of Trade Bill from consideration by House. In that context, he pledged to us that, no matter what happened, the Administration would not enter into any new credits or loan guarantees with the Soviet Union until the Trade bill passed by both houses of Congress.

Kissinger acknowledged to us that the Soviets' aggressive actions in support of Egypt and Syria certainly meant that they didn't deserve a trade bill at all, but that Soviet-American relations had become so fragile over the Middle East crisis that it would make his job of stabilizing the area much more difficult if the House voted to support Mills-Vanik Amendment. He pressed us as to reveal what would be the attitude of the Jewish community if the Administration moved to have Title IV removed. We were caught off guard and needed to caucus among ourselves and with the rest of the top communal leadership. We contented ourselves at that moment by urging the Secretary to discuss the issue with Senator Jackson.

The following morning, Maass and I convened a meeting of the Joint Policy Committee of Presidents Conference and the NCSJ to discuss fast moving events and, especially, our meeting with Kissinger the evening before. We were all seized with the gravity of the Middle East situation, and after much heartfelt discussion, came to an agreement what our policy would be. We decided that if any congressmen called us about the upcoming vote in the House, we would advise them that in view of the crisis in U.S.-Soviet relations, we would have no opposition to the Administration delaying a vote on MFN and credits and loan guarantees by withdrawing Title IV from the Trade Bill before the House. We then communicated this to Kissinger by phone, while reminding him of our continued support of the Jackson Amendment and urging him again to meet with Jackson to see if they could work out a solution acceptable to both sides.

Later that day, however, we were advised by Leonard Garment that it would be necessary for us to actively inform congressmen of this position in order for the Administration to be successful in its attempts to withdraw Title IV. It was immediately clear to us that we could not go that far—we would face open revolt in much of the Jewish community if we tried to further accommodate the Administration. We advised Garment categorically that we were not prepared to take that step and again urged the pressing importance of a Kissinger-

Jackson meeting. Yet the Administration remained adamantly opposed. Given that reality, our Joint Policy Committee decided that we ourselves should meet with Jackson as soon as possible in order to review the matter of the Jackson Amendment and where things stood on Title IV a few days later. A meeting was scheduled with Jackson for November 5.

In the meantime, the grass roots organizations for Soviet Jewry swung into action, flooding the Presidents Conference, NCSJ and Jackson's own office with telegrams demanding that both the senator and the Jewish leadership should stand firm in support of Jackson-Vanik and in support of the restoration of Title IV.

I went up to Jackson's Capitol Hill office on November 5 together with Maass and Charlotte Jacobson. We had expected to have a detailed and private review of the situation with the senator, but were chagrined when we arrived at Jackson's office to find that he had invited an additional 6-8 people, including Senator Ribicoff and the aides to both men who first proposedthe Jackson Amendment, Richard Perle, Morris Amitay and Mark Talisman. Also there were David Blumberg and Herman Edelsberg, respectively president and executive vice president of B'nai Brith. The presence of these people in the room seriously inhibited the frankness of the exchange and ensured that Jackson would content himself to repeat his positions in the most inflexible terms. That, together with an effort to intimidate us into quiescence, was, no doubt, exactly the reason these people had been invited. I listened to everybody but only addressed my comments to Senator Jackson, though they were often reponded to by his guests—all members of his "troop."

I stuck to my guns, telling Jackson that concern for Israel's safety was the top priority for the Jewish community, and that therefore we took Kissinger seriously when he told us that his hand would be strengthened in his dealings with the Soviets on the Middle East situation if Title IV to the Trade Bill were deleted in the House of Representatives. Jackson replied somewhat scornfully that the Administration is "always using you" and insisted that the only way to get Jews out of the Soviet Union was to stand firm on all aspects of the Amendment, including Title IV. Ribicoff attacked us in even harsher terms; asserting that we were ready to sell Soviet Jews down the river at the first threatening sounds from the Administration.

I calmly answered both men that I deemed it critically important as a Jewish leader that the Jewish community should not become involved in a conflict between the Administration and Senator Jackson. We were deeply concerned for the welfare of Soviet Jews, but to protect their interests, we needed the help of *both* Jackson and the Administration. I told Jackson I was deeply concerned that the passage of the amendment might hurt Soviet Jews by causing the Soviets to limit the number of emigrants in retribution. Jackson appeared to dismiss that possibility and seemed more upset that Kissinger declined to meet him, asking us why it was possible for Kissinger to meet Brezhnev and Chairman Mao, but not himself. There hardly seemed a point to pressing us on that question, since we ourselves had repeatedly urged Kissinger to meet with Jackson. However, there was no shouting in our discussion—the tone was civil but tough.

My experience with politics over the years led me to I understand that Jackson's uncompromising tenor meant he had successfully lined up his troops in Congress and in the Jewish community, and therefore was not prepared to be flexible on the Jackson and Mills-Vanik bills. Rather, he had called the meeting only to inform us that he would insist on the inclusion of Title IV to the Trade Bill before the House. It was clear to all concerned that the we had lost control of the issue of Soviet Jewry, and it was now completely and totally in the hands of Jackson, with the "troops" being directed by the senator's aide, Richard Perle.

After the meeting, Maass and I stopped by at the White House to advise the President's Congressional liaison, Peter Flanagan, and Helmut Sonnenfeld, an aide to Secretary Kissinger, that we would be continuing our support of the Jackson Amendment in the Senate and the Mills-Vanik version in the House. We again strongly advised Kissinger to meet with Jackson on any matters relating to his Amendment, making clear that our conclusion that Jackson alone was in control of the situation.

The House passed the Trade Bill including Title IV in December 1973. Even though the cease-fire in the Middle East was clearly holding and Kissinger was engaged in negotiating between Israel and Egypt; lessening concern about possible Soviet military intervention, several responsible Jewish leaders, including myself, expressed renewed concern during the debate over the bill that the Jackson Amendment could backfire and result in reduced emigration. Even after the House vote, we continued to press for compromise well into the following year as the Senate geared up to consider Jackson's own version of the bill.

On March 17, 1974, shortly after stepping down as chairman I attended a meeting of the Conference at which I called for a compromise on the Jackson Amendment. I argued that rather than imperil all the gains that had been achieved in Soviet Jewish emigration "by an all or nothing demand," there should be a reformulation of the Jackson Amendment that would offer Soviet Russia an incentive to increase the number of exit visas granted.

"Let us open channels of trade between our two countries," I declared, "but make continuation of the United States grant of trade benefits conditional on further progress in the USSR toward the principle of unrestricted emigration, free of harassment. If emigration statistics continue to show an increase and if harassment of would be emigrants ceases, the trade benefits to the Soviets should continue without interruption. But if the Soviets cut back on emigration and continue their campaign of intimidation against those who ask to leave, American trade benefits should be halted."

I was not alone in urging such a compromise. By early 1974, it was clear most Jewish leaders were unable to speak out due to internal pressure from Soviet Jewry 'activists' within their own organizations. In the meantime, with President Nixon in full meltdown and about to be impeached, Kissinger alone was unable to prevent passage of Jackson-Vanik, including inclusion of Title IV. Once the Jackson Amendment became law—as I predicted— the Soviets indeed retaliated by cutting back sharply on the number of Jews allowed to emigrate.

Looking back on the entire drama over Soviet Jewry that played such a central role during my chairmanship of the Presidents Conference, I want to make clear that the Jewish community certainly owes a vote of appreciation to the late Senator Jackson and to all the legislators who supported his amendment. By their actions, they set forth clearly the Soviet mistreatment of Jews and denial of basic human rights in violation of the United Nations Declaration of Human Rights. Certainly, the Jackson Amendment gave President Nixon the muscle necessary to bring about an end to the Soviet education tax.

Yet I also feel that there were profound problems with the approach encapsulated in the Jackson Amendment of seeking to advance human rights and freedom through Congressional legislation that undercut all efforts at quiet diplomacy. Walking a fine line between supporting the Nixon policy and supporting the Jackson Amendment was a trying time.

In the end, the Soviet Union collapsed, one million Jews were able to leave and the approach encapsulated in Jackson-

Vanik seemed to have been fully justified. Yet given the underlying rottenness of Soviet society which became so evident by the 1980's, it seems to me possible that these processes might have played out more rapidly if the Soviet leadership had not felt pressed to the wall. We will never know for sure, of course, whether that would have been the case. I remain convinced that the nuanced course toward the Nixon Administration, the pro-Jackson forces and the Soviet Union itself that I struggled to maintain during my years at the helm of the Presidents Conference was the right way to go.

Israel and America: Bridging Troubled Waters

After completing my concurrent terms as chairman of the Presidents Conference and president of United Synagogue, I remained somewhat active in communal affairs, but re-focused my energies on my real estate business. I have endeavored since my early adulthood to be simultaneously involved in the life of my synagogue, in the political life of the Jewish community and in the world of business. Now, with Jimmy Carter and the Democrats in Washington, it was time for me to focus on my business life before thinking about rejoining the political fray.

I have known over the years businessmen and women that drifted into politics and never looked back, leaving business far behind. For me, the enjoyment of the business process was never supplanted by the excitement and glamor of the political world. Even during my years at the helm of the Presidents Conference, when I was directly involved in world politics at the very highest levels, I never lost my taste for the more prosaic, but every bit as fascinating, real estate business. I have always enjoyed searching for properties in diverse localities that appear likely to yield the best return on investment, and making the best possible case for development of these properties to local officials who are responsible to sign off on the needed zoning permits. The process of taking a real estate deal from conception to realization is long and arduous, but I have always relished the challenges involved and enjoyed the personal relationships I have formed along the way.

Back to the Community

One of the reasons, I was able to devote so much of my time to my communal activities, was that during the mid-1960's I formed a business partnership with a top rate Suffolk county based realtor named Max Staller. We named ourselves Emjay Properties (MJ stood for Max and Jack). We then took on another partner, a Long Island realtor named Ben Kasper, although we kept the Emjay Properties banner. Thus, although I was unable to give Emjay Properties my primary attention during the five or so years I was at the helm of United Synagogue and the Presidents Conference, the company continued to thrive in part because of the understanding of my two wonderful partners and their willingness to work harder in my absence. They were fully supportive of me throughout this period, and never complained even when world travel kept me away for weeks at a time.

In addition, my wife Jean stepped up her own hands-on involvement in the business during those years, taking over many of my functions. In 1981, when I took my position at the Reagan White House and moved to Washington, Jean would spend 2-3 days a week at my office in Hicksville, Long Island.

During the mid to late 1970's, however—the period between my leadership of the Presidents Conference and my joining the Reagan Administration—I focused the lion's share of my energy on the real estate business; expanding the geographical range of our holdings throughout Long Island, as well as in adjoining areas like New York City and Connecticut. In addition to continuing to develop new residential housing during that period, we also invested heavily in commercial real estate, including shopping centers. Among other big-tickets items, we were involved in the construction of a chain of food stores known as Bohacks.

I eventually left Staller and Kasper during the 1980's, and went back to using my old name for the business, Jacob Stein Realty. We decided to split the business, not because of any disagreements, but because all of us were getting older and our personal interests were pulling us in different directions. We made a very fair distribution of our developed properties and undeveloped land. We remained close personally and at one point Jean and I were joined by Max, Ben and their wives on a trip to Israel. Both of my wonderful partners passed away in recent years. I was privileged to deliver a eulogy at Ben's funeral. Their deaths were a great personal loss.

During the mid-1970's, I was invited to join the Board of Directors of Key Corp, a banking and financial firm with branches on Long Island. I had established a relationship with Key Corp thanks to our need to secure mortgages on many of our properties, but sitting on the board put the relationship in a different light and gave me valuable "big picture" insights into how a financial firm operates. I stayed on the Key Corp board for 25 years before retiring.

At the same time I joined the Board of the Stony Brook Foundation, which raised money and helped set policy for the State University of New York at Stony Brook, a relatively obscure member of the SUNY family that grew by leaps and bounds during my tenure to become the premiere institution of higher learning on Long Island. I have always been a great believer in the importance of finding ways to deliver quality public education to as wide a spectrum of society as possible, and was able to make a contribution to turning Stony Brook into a university that Long Island could truly be proud of. One area upon which I focused was on the building of a childcare center at Stony Brook, so that the school's growing faculty would have quality place to leave their children during their working hours. A second major effort was to invite a hotel chain to build a hotel with ample meeting facilities to house the growing number of meetings and seminars and conferences which the growing Stony Brook University was developing. Unfortunately the effort failed.

Throughout the mid and late 1970's, I remained active in the affairs of the Presidents Conference. As I have noted, one of the best features of that organization is that former chairmen can remain prominently involved in the work of the Presidents Conference for the rest of their lives if they so desire, taking part in missions to the White House and the State Department, to Israel and countries around the world. The late 1970's were the years of President Anwar Sadat's astonishing trip to Jerusalem and the ensuing negotiations that finally led to an Egyptian-Israeli peace treaty. I was on the first mission of American Jewish leaders to Cairo to meet with Sadat soon after his epochal visit to Israel, and he received us with great warmth and enthusiasm (My personal letter of invitation from Sadat through the Egyptian Embassy was mistakenly addressed to "Rabbi Stein").

Upon arrival in Cairo early in 1978, I reflected how close, but how far away, I had been to that city when I crossed the Suez Canal and stood on African soil while visiting General Ariel Sharon's army during the Yom Kippur War. It was unimaginable that less than five years later I would be visiting the Pyramids and being warmly received by the President of Egypt as a member of a delegation of American Jewish leaders. It was exhilarating to play a role, in helping to facilitate peace between Israel and its largest Arab neighbor, one with which Israel had fought five deadly wars.

One of the joys of serving in the ranks of American Jewish leadership was not only to meet and discuss issues with some of Israel's top leaders, but also to form personal friendships with some of them. I was fortunate to form such friendships with two of Israel's most compelling political personalities, Menachem Begin and Shimon Peres.

Begin, who was prime minister from 1977-1983, was a warm Jew who did not stand on ceremony or position, but reached out to someone he liked as an equal. Begin somehow found the time during those tumultuous years to be in frequent touch with me by phone or via the mail. On ocassions he would turn to me and discuss political dynamics in Washington and within the American Jewish leadership. He was always kind and thoughtful; always asking about the well-being of Jean and our children. Having been the leader of the pre-independence underground group *Etzel* or Irgun, Begin was one of the founding fathers of the State of Israel and the first leader of the Likud Party to come to power. Having the opportunity to meet and discourse with an important historical figure was a real privilege.

Shimon Peres, who remains a dear friend has a fertile and creative mind, which he continually put to use developing plans to jump start negotiations between Israel and her Arab foes. It was Peres as Israel's foreign minister in the early 1990's who initiated the Oslo process between Israel and the Palestinians, and I know he was heartbroken by its eventual collapse and the return of violent conflict between the two sides. I have remained in communication with Shimon in good times and bad and retain enormous respect for his ongoing efforts to find a formula for peace; even when doing so has hurt his own personal popularity. Jean and I during our visits to Jerusalem always visited with Shimon and his friendly wife, Sonya, who frequently had prepared a meal for us together in their apartment.

It was during this time that I also grew closer to an American political leader, George H.W. Bush, who was U.S. Ambassador to the U.N. Bush envinced an easy informality, an openness to people of diverse backgrounds and a disinclination to pull rank. Bush was a networker par excellence who had a huge rolodex of friends that stretched from top world leaders to people of all walks of life. In our own case, from the beginning we were on a "Jack" and "George" basis, something that remained the case even after he became president. George made a point to ensure that our wives were often included when we got together, something that added to the feeling of warmth and informality.

As time went by, I felt more and more respect for his intelligence, knowledge and loyalty, his calm reasoning and composure. I was also convinced that he was a strong friend of Israel and of the cause of Soviet Jewry. His moderate conservative views on most issues closely mirrored my own. Max Fisher was similarly impressed by Bush and at one point in 1978 came to me with an affirmation of something I was already pretty sure of; that Bush intended to run for president in 1980. Fisher also had a question for me; "Would I be willing to work together with him inside the Jewish community on behalf of Bush?" I unhesitatingly agreed and during the ensuing year I traveled widely, speaking before Jewish audiences in a variety of settings to talk up Bush's candidacy.

Although Ronald Reagan, who had an adoring base in the conservative wing of the party, was the favorite in a crowded Republican field that included Senator Bob Dole, Senator Howard Baker, Representative John Anderson and former Texas Governor John Connally, Bush quickly moved into the position of the main alternative to Reagan. In January 1980, Bush won the "first in the nation" Iowa Caucuses; causing him to announce that he had the "Big Mo," his shortcut description for momentum. Everything looked possible for a short ten days, but then Reagan defeated Bush decisively in the New Hampshire primary, and from that point on, Reagan surged into an insurmountable lead (although Bush later won primaries in Pennsylvania, Michigan and a few other states). By early may, Bush had acceded to the inevitable and dropped out of the race. That seemed to be that.

Yet it wasn't. Having sewn up the nomination, Reagan realized he needed to select a younger and more moderate running mate to appeal to millions of middle of the road voters who were paying heed to Democratic claims that he was an extreme right-winger. At the Republican Convention in Detroit that July, Reagan announced that he was choosing Bush for the vice presidential spot on the ticket. The Reagan-Bush ticket quickly moved into a small but steady lead over the incumbent President Jimmy Carter and Vice President Walter Mondale, who were beset by recession, high inflation and the never-ending Iran hostage crisis. Reagan won the final presidential debate by asking Americans his famous question 'Are you better off today than you were four years ago?' and then he and Bush rolled to a landslide victory on Election Day, capturing all but six states.

Not long after the election, Bush let me know he would be recommending me for a position as advisor to the Reagan White House. No doubt I had addtional support from Max Fisher, who had a close political ties with Reagan.

Several weeks before the inauguration I was invited by Attorney-General Designate Ed Meese to meet with him, at his club, to discuss a position in the Administration. He asked me, as I had been led to expect, to take on the Jewish portfolio. I replied that while I would be happy to do that, I did not want it to be my sole area of involvement. I also wanted to handle responsibilities in other policy areas in which I thought my knowledge, expertise and skills would be useful. After a considerable discussion covering a broad range of issues, Meese informed me that I would be engaged as a special advisor to the White House, dealing with all matters.

After I decided to take the position, Jean and I sub-leased an apartment at the Watergate Apartments, a stone's throw from the Kennedy Center and a short taxi ride from my office at the Old Executive Office Building.

Jean and I were frequently able to attend theater and dance productions at the Kennedy Center, and, on several memorable occasions, were able to invite friends to join us as guests in the presidential box.

Another wonderful perk of the job was the privilege to enjoy the superb cuisine in the Executive Dining Room of the White House, a mixed blessing as it turned out as I soon found myself on the losing end of a battle to maintain my optimum weight. Despite the perks, the White House job was far from a joyride. The hours were long and the pressure great. Much of the pressure I felt was self-imposed; I was acutely conscious that my ideas and proposals might have an impact on the entire nation in a way they had not in any previous position I had held, including Presidents Conference chairman.

My new position was in the Department of Public Liaison, a sprawling agency then headed by Elizabeth Dole that included several counselors like myself who were charged with the job of reaching out to key ethnic and religious communities. Down the hall from my office was that of Gary Bauer, who was the Administration's liaison to the Evangelical Christian community. I found Gary to be a delightful person and animated conversationalist.

There were sometimes turf and communications issues within the department. At first, I communicated my thoughts and ideas directly to Mrs. Dole, until for reasons never explained, I was asked to communicate with Mrs. Dole through her assistant Red Caveney, who, to put it mildly, was not too familiar with the Jewish-related topics with which I was dealing. So things got a little sticky before being straightened out.

I had arranged a meeting with Elizabeth Dole and Richard Allen, head of the National Security Council. The Conference of Presidents was then chaired by Harold Squadron, President of the American Jewish Congress. The meeting was to be an "off the record" discussion of the proposed Awacs sale to Saudi Arabia. The meeting was held, the dialogue was completed. A day later the essence of the meeting became public in the Jewish community.

I received a call from Elizabeth and went to her office. She started to blast me for allowing the "off the record" conversation to become public. I realized from her tone and words that she thought she was talking to a youngster, the age of most personnel working with her. I advised her that she was not talking to this type of personnel and to cool it, but told her that I share her unease that the meeting went public, and that we would suspend for a time further meetings with the Conference. She settled down and all ended smoothly.

Fortunately, even at difficult moments, I had fairly easy access to Attorney General Ed Meese, who clearly valued my counsel about how the Administration could prevent its ties to the Jewish communal leadership from collapsing in mutual acrimony amidst what turned out to be an unexpectedly rough ride in 1981. Ed never pressured me to publicly support Administration positions that were unpopular in the Jewish community, a move which he understood would destroy my credibility in the community. I would then no longer be of use to the Administration.

It turned out that the great majority of my time during my year in the White House was indeed spent on issues of Jewish concern, but I did have input on a number of other policy issues. I took part in meetings of the National Security

Council and had a direct line to National Security Adviser Richard Allen, with whom I enjoyed a cordial relationship.

I was also assigned to study the question of whether the U.S. government should accede to a request from West Germany, first communicated in October 1977, that we return some 6342 paintings, lithographs, sculptures and drawings seized during our invasion and occupation of Nazi Germany and held for more than three decades in a warehouse in Alexandria, Virginia. Congressman William Whitehurst, who had been pushing to return the art to Germany, sent a memo to the President asserting that a decision not to return the paintings "could only be regarded as an unfriendly gesture toward one its strongest allies."

After visiting the facility and looking through the paintings, I recommended a limited return of the works of art. While I found most of the collection to be relatively non-controversial, I opposed the return of any art that contained Nazi emblems or could be seen as a glorification of Nazism. That certainly included any of Hitler's own works. Four paintings were the work of Adolf Hitler himself and signed by him. I marked those four Hitler pictures as "not returnable." I was thinking of the six million of my people who were murdered on the orders of Adolf Hitler as well as the memory of our soldiers who lost their lives during the war, but there was another factor in my recommendation. It seemed dangerous to return works of art that might conceivably become relics that would be inspirational to Germany's small, but growing neo-Nazi fringe. In the event, the U.S. government largely followed my advice in how it later disposed of the so-called "Nazi art."

While I understood that there were bound to be disagreements and misunderstandings between White House and the organized Jewish community, I had expected a relatively harmonious relationship, at least compared to the poisonous atmosphere that had developed between the community and the Carter Administration.

Certainly, the portents looked good in the wake of the 1980 elections for a sharp upturn in U.S.-Israeli relations. During the 1980 presidential campaign Reagan had criticized President Carter for pressuring Prime Minister Begin not to build settlements in the West Bank and Gaza and to negotiate a turnover of those territories to the Palestinians, whose leadership in the Palestine Liberation Organization openly called for the destruction of Israel.

Top Reagan foreign policy advisors like Richard Allen and Jeanne Kirkpatrick, in vivid contrast to their counterparts in the Carter Administration, advocated disentangling the U.S. from the Israeli-Palestinian issue and instead focusing on America's rivalry with the Soviet Union to win influence in the Middle East. They placed special emphasis on maintaining American influence in the Persian Gulf region, which was severely shaken by the Iraq-Iran War that had commenced in September 1980.

In addition, signals from the Reagan White House in its first few weeks in office seemed very much in sync with the policy positions of Begin, who had clashed bitterly with Carter. Begin himself was involved in an uphill battle to win in elections set for June (In the end Begin would prevail over Labor Party leader Shimon Peres by a paper-thin margin). For example, top Reaganites left the distinct impression that they viewed Syria as a largely irredeemable Soviet client state, and agreed with Begin's emphasis on terrorism as a major international threat.

AWACS

As it turned out, however, expectations that I would have a relatively smooth tenure in my position as the Administration's official liaison to the Jewish community were shattered by a series of explosive events throughout 1981 that tended to bring Arab-Israeli conflict issues to center-stage and provoke tension in US-Israel relations. These included the Syrian Missile crisis, the PLO's rocket offensive along the Lebanese-Israeli border, the June 7 Israeli raid destroying the Iraqi nuclear reactor outside of Baghdad, the July 17 Israeli bombing of Beirut and the Israeli annexation of the Golan Heights in December. Of course, throughout the year, the roiling battle between the Administration and the Jewish community over U.S. plans to sell five AWACS spy planes to Saudi Arabia.

I will deal with all of these issues in this account, but it was the AWACS controversy, that came to define that period and took up the lion's share of my time, that I will turn to first. The sale had first been proposed by President Jimmy Carter, who had sent AWAC planes to a Saudi airbase in 1979 to monitor developments in the nearby Iran-Iraq war, but kept them under U.S. control. Yet after his decisive reelection defeat reelection, Carter went back on an earlier promise to Israel not to sell the planes to the Saudis, and instead suddenly proposed to do so. Nevertheless, the incoming Reagan Administration made clear that the arms sale would be put on hold until it completed a Middle East policy review.

Many in the Jewish community were optimistic that the pro-Israel Reaganists would quietly kill the AWACS sale. So they were dismayed to find out by early spring of 1981 that the same Administration officials who appeared so solicitous of Begin and Israel were now leaning in favor of the AWACS sale. Their reasoning, it turned out, had little to do with the Arab-Israeli conflict. Rather, advocates of the AWACS sale argued it would enhance Saudi security amidst the regional turbulence set off by the Iran-Iraq War, and would help to protect the Saudi oilfields and the Persian Gulf area against aggression by Soviet or local radical forces. Realization of these goals would, in turn, strengthen American military and intelligence-gathering efforts and buttress US-Saudi relations. Conversely, failure to deliver the AWACS to the Saudis, the Administration argued, would severely undermine American credibility in the Gulf.

Opponents of the arms package saw the proposed AWACS sale as endangering America's most secret technology by placing it in the hands of a country whose security, stability and friendship to the West was questionable. Entangling U.S. interests with a regime whose fall might be encouraged by excessive military transfers would leave Washington in a situation similar to that which followed the Shah's overthrow. Pro-Israel forces, spearheaded by AIPAC, feared the planes in the hands of the Saudis would directly imperil Israel's security. The reason was the super sophisticated nature of the AWACS aircraft, a modified Boeing 707 with a 30-foot wide revolving radar dome mounted on top of the fuselage. An AWACS aircraft essentially serves as a flying radar station providing surveillance and the basis of battle management. At an altitude of 30,000 feet, the aircraft's radar can see into enemy territory, and spot enemy aircraft 360 miles away, which meant that AWACS aircraft in the northwestern part of Saudi Arabia could observe all of Israel.

Until that time the U.S. had sold only one AWACS, and that was to its close European allies in NATO. To place one of these ultra-sophisticated planes in the hands of Saudi Arabia, from which it could monitor the movement of all planes inside Israel, seemed, to much of the Jewish community, to be the height of irresponsibility. Saudi Arabia after all, was a sworn enemy of Israel, had a policy forbidding entry to all Jews and which had broken diplomatic relations with Egypt for signing a peace agreement with Israel.

I had been in my position in the White House only a couple of months when the news the pro-Israel community had long dreaded was announced. On a lovely April day, with the cherry blossoms in full bloom around the Jefferson Memorial and the President still recovering rapidly from the attempt on his life a month earlier, the Administration announced that it was planning to sell eight and a half billion dollars of military might to Saudi Arabia. The sale included five ultra-sophisticated AWACS aircraft, together with Sidewinder air-to-air missiles, auxiliary fuel tanks, and bomb racks for US-built F-15s already purchased by Saudi Arabia.

Israel quickly made known its strong opposition to the proposed sale, with Prime Minister Begin declaring that the AWACs in Saudi hands would represent, "a grave threat to Israel's security…the AWAC's intelligence-gathering aircraft will make our country with it's airfields and even it's other weapons systems absolutely transparent."

Begin's opposition, backed by virtually every major American Jewish organization, all but guaranteed that a fierce battle between the White House and Israel's staunch advocates in the U.S. Senate and House of Representatives was sure to erupt. Much of the Congress made clear its opposition to the proposal, including Republicans like Senator Rudy Boschwitz (R-Minn) and Senator Roger Jepsen (R-Iowa) both of whom vowed to fight against it in the Senate Foreign Relations Committee. In the House of Representatives, another influential Administration ally, Rep. Jack Kemp (R-NY) quickly declared his opposition to the Saudi Arms deal.

The Jewish organizations moved quickly on the offensive, directing a letter-writing campaign to the White House demanding that the AWACS sale be cancelled. As the Jewish community liaison in the White House, I became the target of much of the opposition—and more than a little of the invective—from many in the Jewish community who were bitterly opposed to the AWACS sale. Howard Squadron, who was Presidents Conference Chairman at the time of the AWACS imbroglio, brought a delegation to the White House to inform me and high-ranking Administration officials, off the record, that the Presidents Conference would be "obliged to vigorously oppose the proposed sale."

Howard expressed his opposition to the sale in gentlemanly terms, but there were others who were far more vehement both toward the sale and toward my own position in trying to strengthen ties between the community and Administration in the midst of a political whirlwind. Many called outright for me to resign to protest the proposed AWACS sale. On one occasion I received a package that had a bullet inside the envelope. I promptly turned the material over to the FBI. On another occasion I accepted an invitation to speak before a meeting of the Women's League for Conservative Judaism and was subjected to a cascade of boos and catcalls that made it all but impossible for me to speak. I was shocked and ashamed for the organization's leadership for allowing such a breakdown of civility. It was especially painful for me given that the incident took place at a meeting of an organization representing the Conservative movement, my own spiritual home.

I believed I was doing the right thing by staying in my position inside the Administration and working to cancel or at least modify elements of the sale; location of the basing of the plane and a role for U.S. to receive information received in the AWACS. Despite the AWACS decision, I continued to believe that President Reagan's Mideast policy was good for Israel and the American Jewish community. That policy was shaped by three imperatives: providing for the security of Israel and other nations in the region from Soviet threats; protecting America's oil supplies and fighting terrorism. In addition, the Jewish community was well aware of President Reagan's active support of our campaign to gain freedom of emigration for the Soviet Jews and his sensitivity to the Holocaust.

As for the AWACS decision itself, I pressed the issue again and again with Attorney General Ed Meese and other top Administration officials, explaining why it had elicited such a negative reaction in the Jewish community. Meese patiently heard me out, understanding that I could be much more effective in explaining the President's policy to the Jewish community if I was not compelled to express personal support for the AWACS sale, something that would have all but discredited me in the eyes of the leadership of the organized Jewish community.

I have always believed that when one is confronted by the kind of challenge I faced in striving to maintain good relations between the Administration and the Jewish community at a time of great strain, walking away from the table amounts to an admission of failure. I believed that my resignation at such a moment would have been bad for both of the constituencies I served. On the other hand, if I stayed in the White House, I saw the opportunity to limit the damage already done and prepare the way for the reconciliation that would need to be effected by both sides no matter how the AWACS vote came out.

As it turned out, I was actually able to bring about some changes in the arms package itself that made it less threatening to Israel. For example, as the Administration struggled to bring a number of Republicans on line for the vote, it changed its position and agreed that the communications system on the aircraft would be designed in such a way that they would only be able to contact Saudi jet fighters, effectively preventing the AWACS from being used to launch a multi-national attack on Israel. The Saudis also eventually promised to base the AWACS planes at air bases in the eastern part of the country that were too far away from Israel to allow them to spy on IAF movements. In addition, the United States would retain the right of on-site-inspection of the aircraft.

Within two months of the Administration's proposal of the sale of AWACS to Saudi Arabia, it became clear that

In Jerusalem, the Conference of Presidents was greeted by Mayor Teddy Kollek.

I played the sensitive role of urging Prime Minister Shamir to reconsider positions President Bush thought were unhelpful to the cause of peace.

I often met with Arik Sharon in his various capacities of Major General, Defense Minister, and finally Prime Minister of Israel.

In Cairo with Hosni
Mubarak of Egypt.

One of several meetings
with King Hussein
of Jordan following
the peace agreement
with Israel.

In Cairo with Hosni Mubarak of Egypt.

Visiting with the Prime Minister of Israel, Ehud Barak.

Jean and I were invited to the home of former Prime Minister of Israel Shimon Peres and his wife Sonya on a Shabbat afternoon.

I was presented to Pope John Paul II at a Jewish-Catholic summit meeting in Miami, Florida.

Major General Yigal Allon, Deputy Prime Minister of Israel, called for Israeli protective presence on the West side of the Jordan River.

Addressing the Israeli Knesset with Prime Minister Golda Meir.

Vice President George H.W. Bush bowed his head in prayer as he touched the ancient stones of the Western Wall in Jerusalem.—July, 1986

At the Jewish Theological Seminary with Rabbi Mordecai Kaplan (left) and Rabbi Louis Finkelstein (right) Seminary Chancellor.

Jean and I at the Suez Canal following the 1973 Yom Kippur War.

My wife Jean touring Cairo with Jehan Sadat, wife of President Anwar Sadat.

Jean Stein received a certificate from the Jewish Theological Seminary in recognition of her many social efforts to aid the blind. The award was presented by Rabbi Mordecai Waxman of Temple Israel of Great Neck, New York.

My wife Jean Stein with Mother Teresa.

Making conversation with
President Bill Clinton.

President George W. Bush has
always greeted me warmly.

Meeting with Presidential
candidate Bob Dole in 1986.

Madeline Albright, Secretary
of State for President Clinton.

a majority of members of the U.S. Senate, including many Republicans, were opposed to the sale. In June 1981, Senator Bob Packwood, a Republican from Oregon, let it be known that fifty-four Senators had signed a letter to the President opposing his commitment to sell the AWACS package to the Saudis, and urging the President not to send the proposal to Congress. The House of Representatives on the same day put forth a resolution opposing the sale signed by 224 House members. Yet the Administration made clear it planned to go ahead and bring the plan to a vote. The administration began a campaign involving the application of intense pressure on a number of Republican senators to change their positions.

In early July, I thought I could play a more educated role in discussing the AWACS issue if I had a better feel for the aircraft. I decided that taking a flight aboard an AWACS would be instructive. A quick call to the Secretary of Defense, Caspar "Cap" Weinberger and it was all arranged. At 7:15 A.M. on July 30, I board an AWACS aircraft at Langley Air Force Base in Virginia. It had the feeling of a large office with rows of narrow seats with radar screens in front of each seat occupied by trained airmen. From the airspace in Virginia, I marveled at being able to see aircraft in the New York airspace on the radar screens.

Two events that took place in early August heightened pressure on Congress to authorize the AWACS sale. The first event, on August 6, was the assassination of Egyptian President Anwar Sadat, the only Arab leader to have signed a peace agreement with Israel. Sadat was gunned down as he reviewed a military parade by radical Islamists in the Egyptian military who opposed his recognition of Israel.

The day after Sadat's assassination, Secretary of State Al Haig declared that a defeat of the arms sale would "make a mockery of all that President Sadat stood for." Several Senators moved to a more positive position on the AWACS sale, feeling that to fail to support the President in a time of crisis would be wrong.

The following day, August 7, Crown Prince Fahd of Saudi Arabia, the highest-ranking figure in that country, unexpectedly presented a Middle East peace plan during an interview on Riyadh radio. The timing of the initiative was certainly meant to impress Congress as it prepared to vote on the AWACS as to the supposed moderation of "peace-seeking" Saudi Arabia. Despite some expressions of support in certain corners of Congress, for the most part the Fahd Plan did not fly. After all, the Saudi initiative, which called for complete Israeli withdrawal from all Arab territory occupied in 1967,dismantling of all settlements; right of Palestinian return, or compensation, and a Palestinian state with Jerusalem as it's capital, clearly did nothing to address Israel's legitimate security concerns and move the peace process forward.

The U.S. House of Representatives, voted 301 against the AWACS sale and only 111 in favor. A 1974 amendment to the Arms Export Control Act empowered Congress to block a proposed arms sale to a foreign state, but only if both Houses of Congress passed resolutions of disapproval. So all forces pro and con including the Administration, the Saudi Embassy, the Israeli Embassy and the pro-Israel community, went to work trying to win over a majority of senators.

On October 1, the debate began in the Senate on the multi-billion dollar package including AWACS (Airborne Warning and Command System) and other advanced military equipment to Saudi Arabia. The American Israel Public Affairs Committee (AIPAC) took a strong and uncompromising stand against the sale, affirming; "We are unalterably opposed to the sale of AWACS and F-15 enhancements to Saudi Arabia. The sale contradicts the declared objective of the administration and jeopardizes American interests in the Middle East." Rabbi Sol Roth, President of the Rabbinical Council of America announced that more than 1000 Rabbis would deliver sermons during the following weeks against the sale of the military hardware to Saudi Arabia.

At the same time, my friend, Abe Foxman, who was then assistant executive vice president of the Anti-Defamation League (he would ascend to the top position there in 1986), distributed a sheaf of paper with editorial commentary on the AWACS sale from forty newspapers across the country. Of these, 34 newspapers were critical of the arms sale, five were generally in favor and one took no position. These newspapers, which were distributed to rank and file ADL members in all regions of the country, stimulating a flood of anti-AWACS letters directly to the President.

Feeling under intense pressure from the Jewish community, some supporters of the Administration responded with ever-nastier rhetoric of their own. A suggestion was made in some quarters that American Jewish opposition to the sale was Israel-instigated, and American Jews opposing the arms sale were therefore guilty of dual loyalty. The *New York Daily News* ran black headlines on its cover page: "Ron to Israel: BUTT OUT. President Raps Jewish anti-AWACS lobby." Arab supporters of the sale were not quiet. The Federation of Islamic Associations in the U.S. and Canada sent a telegram to President Reagan opening with the words; "Scandal on the Hill...Who runs America; Reagan or Begin, Americans or Israelis? Is it our country or theirs?" Naturally, many of us were fearful that all of this would lead to a rise in anti-Semitism.

I received clearance to participate in meetings of the National Security Council, and I welcomed the opportunity to relate to and work with Richard Allen, National Security Advisor to the President. I found that use of the "Reagan or Begin" slogan was not limited to Arab-Americans. It came to my attention that several members of the National Security Council staff had 'Reagan or Begin' bumper stickers on their cars. At the next meeting of the NSC, I took the floor to express my dismay over the slogan, pointing out that it was a direct appeal to anti-Semitism. I was informed later that most of those bumper stickers came off.

Despite all of the opposition, Congress finally voted in favor of selling AWACS to the Saudis. The package narrowly made it through the Senate by a 52-48 vote on October 28, 1981. This represented quite a turnaround, as the *New York Times* had reported in a survey only a few days before the vote that only 38 senators were in favor of the sale and 53 opposed. Yet the Administration pulled out all the stops to pass the package and, in the end, it is very difficult for members of Congress to challenge a President on matters of foreign policy.

Immediately after the Senate vote approving the sale of AWACS President Reagan made some remarks of great importance. After thanking the Senate for passing the measure, the President said, "Our support for the security of Israel is undiminished by today's vote. The United States will maintain its unshakable commitment to the security and welfare of the State of Israel. We recognize that a strong Israel is essential to our basic goals in that area."

Nevertheless, it was clear that Reagan felt let down by Begin's high-pressure opposition to the AWAC's sale. Secretary Al Haig believed that Begin misled him about the extent of Israeli opposition to the sale. In his biography of Reagan entitled President Reagan, veteran newsman Lou Cannon wrote vividly of the behind the scenes tensions surrounding the battle over the AWACS sale. "Israel adamantly opposed the sale and exercised its political clout in the U. S. Senate where a bipartisan coalition opposed the deal. Begin paid a state visit to Washington on September 9. In his conversations with Haig and Reagan, he left the impression that he would oppose the sale but make no attempt to mount a major campaign against it. Then, Begin denounced the AWACS sale in a speech to

Congress and in several television interviews. Reagan was sensitive to what he saw on television. Encouraged by White House Chief of Staff, James Baker, Reagan made the AWAC's deal a test of his personal prestige.

In the aftermath of the AWACS vote, I helped to arrange two important meetings aimed at promoting reconciliation; the first for top Administration members with a group of Jewish supporters of the President led by Max Fisher, and the second, a meeting with members of the President's Conference and leaders of member organizations. The President, Attorney General Ed Meese, National Security Advisor Richard Allen, and Elizabeth Dole participated in both meetings; Vice President George Bush joined the meeting arranged by Max Fisher. At both meetings, the President spoke reassuringly and repeatedly expressed America's undiminished support for Israel. Nevertheless, he again emphasized; "It is not the business of other nations to make American foreign policy."

If the AWACS sale had been the only irritant that year in U.S.-Israel relations it might not have become such a huge issue. Yet as noted there were many other difficult moments, including the Israeli bombing of the Osirak nuclear reactor, and Reagan's tough reaction which involved delaying a promised delivery of weapons to Israel. In one memo to Ed Meese, I sought to explain the intensely negative Israeli-American Jewish reaction to the AWACS sale by pointing out that our community felt a sense of frustration augmented by U.S. "support for parts of the Fahd (peace) plan and by the perceived failure of U.S. Ambassador Philip Habib to effect the removal of Syrian missiles from Lebanon." In short, there were a lot of elements in the mix.

Not everything dominated by contentious issues brought the Administration and the Jewish community into conflict. Shortly after assuming my new office, I decided we needed to take a new and fresh approach to the observance of Yom

Hashoah in official Washington. In previous years, the annual observance of that solemn day had been held in the Rotunda of the Capitol Building with speeches and a lighting of candles. I pushed successfully to upgrade the nation's observance of the day by having the event transferred to the White House with a special address by the President for the first time. Everyone involved in the annual commemoration, including Ben Meed, the head of the largest Holocaust survivors organization and Elie Wiesel, who was the Chairman of the President's Commission on the Holocaust thanked me being able to make the change and secure the President's personal participation. Then the problems began; involving scheduling, security, the guest list and White House insistence on the right to pre-approve Elie Wiesel's remarks, and the latter's equally obdurate refusal to submit them in advance.

In the end, thankfully, all of the issues were worked out and Yom Hashoah was observed with great solemnity in the East Room of the White House. Only as the ceremony was unfolding did I feel a sense of certainty that my efforts had paid off; that despite all the problems it had all been worthwhile. The bottom line was that here was the President of the United States embracing Holocaust survivors in the White House, making Jewry's most terrible tragedy America's own. I commenced the event with brief opening remarks and was followed by speeches by Elie Wiesel and the President. Congressman Sidney Yates of Illinois directed the candle lighting ceremony of an exquisite seven-branch menorah. Participants at the ceremony included such prominent survivors of the Nazi death camps as Sigmund Strochlitz, Sol Goldstein, Miles Lerman, Benjamin Meed, Hadassah Rosensaft, Siggi Wilzig and Eli Zborowski. Cantor Goodfriend of Congregation Ahavat Achim in Atlanta Georgia said the *El Moleh Rachamim,* and the President of the Hebrew Union College, Alfred Gottschalk led us all in the *Kaddish*. Closing remarks were by Monroe

Freedman, director of the United States Holocaust Memorial Council.

In late May, I received a report from Jerry Goodman, chairman of the National Conference of Soviet Jewry that Mrs. Avital Sharansky was in the United States to raise awareness as to the desperate situation of Anatoly Sharansky, who had been held in Soviet prisons for four years. There were reliable reports that Sharansky, the most celebrated Prisoner of Zion and greatest hero of the Soviet Jewry movement, was losing his sight and memory and his weight was down to 92 pounds. Feeling the urgent need to intercede, I met with National Security Council director Richard Allen, and urged him to arrange a meeting for Avital Sharansky with the President. I was elated to hear that the request was approved and a meeting scheduled to take place in the Oval Office on Thursday, May 28.

Mrs. Sharansky arrived at the meeting with Josef Mendelevich, another Prisoner of Zion who had been released and allowed to leave the Soviet Union three months earlier after surviving eleven brutal years in the gulag. Among those taking part in the meeting with the two visitors were President Reagan, Vice President Bush, Richard Allen, and myself. It was the first time a U.S. President had received Soviet dissidents in the White House. Realizing that the meeting would draw heavy fire from Moscow, the White House did not announce that the meeting had taken place at all until two hours after it ended.

Mrs. Sharansky detailed to the President the agony her husband was enduring at the hands of his KGB captors in a labor camp near the city of Perm. The President was clearly deeply moved and at one moment I saw that tears had come to his eyes. He assured Mrs. Sharansky and Mendelevich that his Administration would forcefully raise the issue of the treatment and condition of Anatoly Sharansky with Soviet authorities and do everything it could to convince them to free

Sharansky and the all the other Prisoners of Zion. Following the meeting, Mrs. Sharansky met the press and reported that her meeting with Reagan and Bush had made her more hopeful that her husband might be saved. She told reporters she was convinced by the meeting that the President "understands that the life of my husband is in danger" and he would do all he could to help him.

Several weeks later, I was told that a number of Soviet Jewish couples living in the Washington area who had been married in atheist ceremonies (those were the only kind available in the USSR), now desired to be married according to Jewish law. Rabbi Stanley Rabinowitz of Adas Israel Synagogue in Washington, together with other local rabbis brought together several couples and invited me to attend on behalf of the White House in what was called, "the first Jewish wedding celebration for Russian resettlers." The event, held on July 1 at Adas Israel, was a joyous event that was deeply moving both to the participating couples and to a large crowd of Russian and American Jews who attended. I read a letter of greetings and congratulations that I had secured from President Reagan.

In the White House, I worked with Congressman Tom Lantos (D-Calif), originally from Hungary and the only Holocaust survivor in Congress, to secure White House approval for granting Honorary U.S. Citizenship to Raoul Wallenberg, the Swedish representative in Budapest, Hungary during the closing months of World War II, who was said to have saved the lives of more than 100,000 Jews. Of course, missing at the Rose Garden ceremony, held on October 5, was Wallenberg himself, who was been imprisoned by the Soviets after they conquered Budapest in 1945, and vanished into the Gulag, never to be seen or heard from again.

Raoul Wallenberg was in the full sense of the word the "Righteous Gentile." He was a thirty-one year old architect who offered to go to Hungary to help the Jews there, and the Swedish government gave him the position of the attache. Wallenberg addressed most of his efforts to bringing Jews under Swedish protection. He rented a large building and applied Swedish extraterritorial status to it, and it became a safe place for hundreds of Jewish religious leaders. He issued protective Swedish passports and bought several more "safe haven" buildings, all of which resulted in Wallenberg saving at least 20,000 to 30,000 Jews. One estimate of Jewish lives saved reached 100,000 Jews. The Russian Army took Wallenberg for "protection" on January 17, 1945, and he has never since been heard from. A Russian statement declared that Wallenberg had died of a heart attack in a Russian prison in 1947.

While signing citizenship papers on behalf of Wallenberg, President Reagan stated solemnly, "What he did, what he accomplished, was of Biblical proportions." The President termed Wallenberg's arrest by the Soviets, "a violation of diplomatic immunity and international law;" adding there was evidence that the diplomat might still be alive in a prison camp. (Sadly, no evidence of Wallenberg was ever found and after the collapse of the Soviet Union, former KGB sources said it was likely he had died in imprisonment several years after the war.)

In my own remarks on the occasion, I commented that it was fitting that this event was taking place between Rosh Hashanah and Yom Kippur which is a time "to rededicate ourselves to all things good and true." Among those attending the ceremony and a reception I held in my office before the main event were Congressman Lantos and his wife, Nina Lagergren, Wallenberg's sister, Guy von Dardel, Wallenberg's brother, Nazi hunter Simon Wiesenthal, and Mrs. Nina Kaplan an active member of the New York Wallenberg committee. In addition, I welcomed my dear friend Max Fisher, Rabbi Marvin Hier, executive vice president of the Simon Wiesenthal Center, Gordon Zacks, Wallenberg biographer John Bierman and Tibor

Baranski, an associate of Wallenberg. Wallenberg was only the second person awarded with honorary U.S. citizenship, with the first having been Winston Churchill.

Later that month, with U.S.-Israel tensions high in advance of the AWACS vote, Moshe Dayan, the great Israeli military hero and former Defense Minister passed away. The President asked Jean and I to attend the funeral as part of an official U.S. delegation that included Attorney General William French Smith, Representative and Mrs. Dick Cheney, Senators Roger Jepsen, Edward Zorinsky and their wives. Israel's Ambassador to the United States, Eppy Evron flew with our delegation. We left Washington Saturday night, October 17th, aboard an Air Force plane; stopped in Madrid for refueling and on to Ben-Gurion airport, arriving Sunday shortly after noon. An Israel plane took us to Ramat David and we immediately motored to the funeral services in the village of Nahalal. The services lasted an hour and we were taken to the King David Hotel.

The following morning we were received by Prime Minister Begin in his office with no discussion on the pending Senate approval of the AWACS. A brief visit to Foreign Minister Yitzhak Shamir, a collective sympathy call to Mrs. Rachel Dayan, and then on to Ben-Gurion airport. We stopped again at Madrid for refueling-and some free port shopping-and on to Washington, and were back home at 10PM Monday the 19th and back to the AWACS tensions. Still, it was a symbolic affirmation that despite that disagreement, ties of solidarity between the U.S. and Israel remained strong.

President Reagan made a series of conciliatory gestures towards Israel after the AWACS vote. Yet the still-fresh wounds between the two countries were exacerbated on December 14 when Minister Begin announced the Knesset had voted to extend it's "law jurisdiction and administration" to the occupied Golan Heights. The world overwhelmingly condemned Israel's assertion of sovereignty over the strategic plateau and the U.S. promptly signed on to a Security Council resolution opposing Israel's action. In addition, the President showed his displeasure by postponing indefinitely a scheduled meeting between U.S. and Israeli military officials to implement a Memorandum of Understanding signed two week earlier. This memorandum provided for joint naval and air exercises in the eastern Mediterranean, and called for working groups to address specific military issues.

Begin, who was never known for being overly diplomatic, reacted defiantly to the U.S. action: "Are we a vassal of yours? Are we a banana republic?"

Top U.S. Jewish leaders leaped to Begin's defense. Chairman of the Presidents Conference Howard Squadron stated, "No self-respecting leader of any country would react differently." Rabbi Alexander Schindler, head of the Reform Movement, who was generally seen as dovish, defended Israel's annexation of the Golan, which it had already controlled for 14 years, and said, "It was wrong of our Government to impose sanctions against our friend and ally, Israel."

Amidst this latest U.S.-Israel crisis, I was again being deluged with angry mail as I prepared to hold a Chanukah Party—the first ever in the White House.

I requested my Temple Israel of Great Neck, Rabbi Mordecai Waxman, to prepare for me an essay explaining Chanukah and its meanings. He wrote an excellent explanation, and copies of the paper were taken by many of the guests.

The United States Navy had some records of Jewish Chanukah songs and forwarded about a dozen to me. I carefully handed them out to guests. I was satisfied that between 30 and 40 guests attended. The White House kitchen was helpful in preparing some light kosher foods.

Among those who attended the event, held on December 21, 1981 were Vice President George Bush, Elizabeth Dole and her deputy Red Caveney, my secretary Beth Barnes, Richard

Schifter, and Hy Bookbinder, the longtime Washington representative of the American Jewish Committee. It was a wonderful experience, one that reminded everyone who attended that despite several policy disputes with Israel, the Reagan Administration was attuned to Jewish Americans and their observances and celebrations.

Battle-scarred but unbowed, I expected to continue my work in the White House, building bridges between the Reagan White House and the organized Jewish community. Yet it was not to be. I had not been feeling well physically for some time and my waistline had been expanding with overeating and stress. Home in Great Neck for the holidays, I realized that my blood pressure was much too high and decided to undergo an extensive medical exam by my son Richard, who was by then Chief of Cardiology at Downstate Medical Center.

After giving me a thorough checkup and a stress test, Richard said "Dad, I think you have had enough White House." He warned me that keeping my White House position and continuing with the lifestyle I had been living during the previous year might well lead to a full-scale heart attack.

It was difficult for me to leave, especially at a time of continuing policy disputes between the U.S. and Israel, yet I felt that I had no choice. I had developed warm friendships with many in government positions and I found each day in the office a day of challenge that tested me. But my physical well being clearly came before other considerations. I drafted a letter of resignation, which I read and re-read before submitting it to Department of Public Liasion Elizabeth Dole. Certainly, I was not leaving under any pressure from the White House.

I requested a meeting with the President to express my appreciation for the opportunity to serve him and was pleased when he agreed to meet with Jean and myself.

President Reagan received us in the Oval Office and thanked me for my efforts. I mentioned the tensions of dealing with the sale of the AWACS aircraft to Saudi Arabia. It must have shown on my face. The President smiled. "Don't look so sad Jack. You can use a little vacation." Then he asked me to go to Geneva, Switzerland as a member of the United States delegation to the United Nations Human Rights Commission.

I turned to look at Jean, then said, "Thank you, Mr. President. It will be an honor to accept." After a year in the White House, I felt gratified that I would still have an opportunity to serve our country. Rather than leaving the Administration, it appeared that I was simply changing positions.

GEORGE H.W. BUSH: A FRIEND IN THE WHITE HOUSE

The stately old city of Geneva was certainly a much more peaceful scene than the whirlwind of Washington, although Jean and I found that the French cuisine there more than rivalled the culinary glories of the White House mess. I don't recall whether I had much success in losing weight during the six weeks I spent as a member of the U.S. delegation to the United Nations Conference on Human Rights between February 2 and March 14, 1982, yet my raised blood pressure did retreat as I regained my inner calm.

I was lucky to be serving with two old-timers. Ambassador Richard Schifter was a soft-spoken but tough-minded veteran Washington hand. Schifter would later handle many of the negotiations with the Soviets that led to freeing the long-term refuseniks and human rights activists. There was also Dr. Michael Novak, a brilliant Catholic philosopher, who been involved in previous negotiations on behalf of the U.S.

Geneva is a tidy little city set on beautiful Lake Geneva, with alpine peaks soaring in the distance. Jean and I enjoyed the international diplomatic life, which we found quite broadening, although the basics of amiable socializing do not vary all that much whether among the good people of Temple Israel in Great Neck or among the U.N. upper crust. On one memorable occasion Jean and I hosted a dinner, which came off very well. It was a warm, friendly event, held to say farewell to the colleagues who worked with me as we pressed for our human rights goals. My wife and I decided that, all things considered, we could get used to living in the heart of Europe.

One issue was paramount during the U.N. session: the repression of the Solidarity labor union in Poland by that county's Communist government, which had declared martial law and arrested the top leadership of the opposition. The U.S. delegation, naturally, took the lead in denouncing the wholesale violation of human rights by the Communist regime of General Jaruzelski. Yet even as Poland carted away hundreds of union activists whose only crime was a call for democracy in their country, the opprobrium of many of the nations represented at the conference was not on the Polish government, but rather on Israel, which was condemned for locking up Palestinians who sought not to achieve democratic rights, but to murder Jews.

Promptly each morning I headed for my office in the International Organizations building. As a United States Advisor to the 38th session of the UN commission of Human Rights, I received information sheets from the American Embassy listing important telephone numbers and providing Embassy background. Among these sheets was one interesting memo written by deputy Secretary of State William B. Clark. It was a reminder that "Human Rights is at the core of our foreign policy because it is central to what America stands for."

I also received administrative instructions from our Mission with the first papers outlining procedures and actions required in connection with a bomb threat. I was told to familiarize myself with these instructions. The opening line was, "The threat of bombs in today's atmosphere of unrest is ever present in every country in the world." A second sheet of instruction told me how to discharge my security obligations and secure the private and classified papers I would be working with. Its opening instruction was, "rotate the dials of combination locks at least four times in one direction. This is required to clear the tumblers."

One of my more interesting challenges was addressing groups of students from the United States visiting the American Mission building. One such group of 55 students from Kent University was particularly alert and responsive.

In its March 11, 1982 issue, the *International Herald Tribune* reported on a paper that I presented to the Commission in which I accused the Soviet Union of "virtually eliminating Jewish institutional life in the country and preventing up to three million Jews from emigrating."

Fridays were non-action days for the Commission, and Jean always planned excellent weekend trips to such places as Paris and Swiss resorts. We once visited Budapest, Hungary, where we took a taxi first to Miskolc and then to the town of Edeleny, the home of my grandfather and grandmother. It was exciting. We introduced ourselves to the current occupant, and with the taxi driver as our interpreter I explained our interest in the house. We were shown around and then went outside. The owners took us to a shaft in the ground and explained that they had a coal mine. This was just as my grandfather had told me. We went back to Budapest, and then back to Geneva.

The hypocrisy and cynicism of Israel's many critics was deeply disheartening to those of us who had come to the conference with a genuine commitment to improving human rights around the world. Yet, I reflected, it was nevertheless important that we supporters of Israel involve ourselves in the work of the U.N. to counter the vicious anti-Israel propaganda and provide solid information about Israel's efforts to maintain correct human rights standards in its occupied territories, even as it stood vigilant against those who plotted the destruction of the Jewish state.

Honors and Protest

Shortly after returning from Geneva to Great Neck, and returning my professional focus to my real estate business, I was informed by Rabbi Mordecai Waxman that Temple Israel wished to honor me for my decades of service to the synagogue as well as for my recently-completed work as Jewish liaison in the Reagan White House. I sent an invitation to Vice President Bush, asking him to attend the event and present remarks, and to my delight, he immediately accepted.

My family and I looked forward to the big day, but what I hadn't counted on was the lingering resentment among many Jews at the Reagan Administration for the AWACS sale, and at my not accepting calls to resign in protest. This would lead to a public protest at the event by a number of people from synagogue. Angered because the synagogue bulletin did not include a statement they made denouncing the upcoming event honouring Jacob Stein, the small band of protesters retaliated on the day of the event by standing with picket signs outside the synagogue. They also released a statement to the media which read in part:

> "Because the minutes [of the synagogue bulletin] did not include our stated views, we would like to go on record as opposing the forthcoming event honoring Jack Stein. We believe the handling of his position with the current Administration has been detrimental to the American Jewish community, as well as to the security of the State of Israel. Further we believe a luncheon in his honor involving a high Administration official,

> can only send the wrong message to Washington from our important Jewish congregation that we understand and condone Washington's Middle East policy."

I had developed a thick skin about such protests directed at me from within the Jewish community. However, I would not be honest if I did not acknowledge that this one stung quite a bit. Here were people from within my own own synagogue community, including several with whom I had been friendly with for many years, who apparently felt comfortable seeking to humiliate me on a day of such special significance to myself, my family and others in the community. Whatever the political motivations of the protestors, the sale of the AWACS included, their action seemed to many of us a major breach of acceptable civil behavior. I was also worried that the vice president might feel affronted. As it turned out, with all of the security at the event provided by the Secret Service and the local police, I'm not even sure if George Bush was aware that anything unusual was going on outside the synagogue.

The event came off well. For those of us inside the sanctuary, the protest that was taking place down the block from the synagogue was out of sight, out of mind. For my part, I was deeply moved by the words of deep affection and appreciation for my role at Temple Israel delivered by my friend and spiritual mentor, Rabbi Waxman. Then the vice president gave a speech filled with kind, words about the importance of my work at the White House. Bush went on to speak warmly about the U.S.-Israel relationship, stressing that despite occasional differences—a clear reference to the recently concluded battle over the AWACS— the fundamentals of the alliance between the two societies, built on shared values and common interests, remained strong and vibrant.

Bush's speech received wide coverage in the Jewish media and was seen as a significant moment in the process of rebuilding trust between the Administration and the Jewish community in the aftermath of the AWACS fight.

Despite the behavior of a few congregants who ought to have known better, the event gave my family and myself considerable pleasure. I felt both proud and humble to be honored by the synagogue I had served for so long, and my efforts to be acknowledged by the vice president of the United States. I found myself wishing my parents were still alive to have been with me that day.

The Bene Israel

Despite efforts to restore U.S.-Israel relations to a smoother course, there was a good deal more turbulence in the coming months. On June 3, 1982, Israeli Ambassador Shlomo Argov was severely injured when a Palestinian opened fire against him as he was leaving the Dorchester Hotel in London. The Ambassador was rushed to the hospital, and although his life was saved, he was left paralyzed. The attack was considered in Israel a part of the continuing Palestinian attacks on Israel, particularly the PLO militants in Southern Lebanon. They were nightly shelling the Jewish communities on the upper Galilee and the residents were forced to spend many nights in their shelters. Three days later on June 6th, Minister of Defense Ariel Sharon led Israel's army into Lebanon; what was planned was a limited action to destroy the PLO settlements there. But Israeli forces continued north into Beirut and established their presence there well into September.

The Palestinians were concentrated in two refugee camps, Sabra and Shtila, both in Beruit. Israeli forces sealed the two camps and two days later, on September 17th, Phalangist forces entered the two camps, with Israeli permission, and massacred the inhabitants, militants and non-militants alike. An Israeli Army report said that 474 Muslims were killed, including women and children. When the camps were opened to the press the next day, they reported finding 2,300 bodies in the camps.

Defense Minister Sharon's decision to push the Israeli troop entry into Lebanon right up to the gates of Beirut was an effort to capture or kill PLO leader Yasir Arafat and deny Lebanon to the PLO as a sanctuary. Ultimately, the Reagan Administration, acting through Ambassador Philip Habib, convinced Prime Minister Begin to allow Arafat and his fighters to board ships that would take them to a new place of refuge in Tunisia.

After the terrible massacre in the Sabra and Shatila refugee camps, carried out by Lebanese Christian militias but predictably, blamed on Israel by much of the world, the IDF pulled back to southern Lebanon and the U.S. Marines took up positions around Beirut—until the fall of 1983 when a suicide bomber killed more than 200 marines and caused the President to pull all U.S. forces out of Lebanon.

Yet through all this, the Administration, spearheaded by Vice President Bush, was quietly doing much to be helpful to Israel. On the world Jewry front, the gathering of a new group of Jewish olim to Israel, the Beta Israel, or Falashas—the exotic black Jewish tribe from the highlands of northern Ethiopia, were brought in significant numbers to Israel.

The Beta Israel (House of Israel) had lived in Ethiopia's Gondar province, perhaps since the visit of the Queen of Sheba to King Solomon in Jerusalem 3000 years ago. For a long time, they had a powerful independent kingdom, but that ended in the year 1624 when they were defeated in battle by an Ethiopian army aided by the Portuguese. Those Jews captured alive were sold into slavery, forced to be baptized and denied the right to own land. Their oppressors, the Ethiopian Christians, henceforth referred to the community as Falashas (the alien one, the invaders).

The Beta Israel survived the ensuing centuries in the rugged mountains of Gondar, although their estimated numbers in the early 20th century of about 100,000, was far less than the half a million that had existed at the time they lost their independence. By the 1960's those numbers dropped even further to about 40,000. And even for a community used to existing in extreme poverty, conditions became unbearable during the late 1970's as the new Marxist regime of Colonel Mengistu Haile Mariam pursued a policy of forced collectivization in the countryside that led to mass starvation among the rural population of the country.

During the early 1980's, Ethiopia forbade the practice of Judaism and the teaching of Hebrew and numerous members of the Beta Israel were arrested as Zionist spies. For a long time, Israel was lukewarm to aliyah by the Beta Israel, since much of the Orthodox rabbinate refused to accept the community as authentically Jewish. Eventually these barriers were overcome and over 8000 Beta Israel managed to come to Israel between 1977 and 1984.

With the support of the Reagan Administration, the Israeli government and Jewish Agency conducted "Operation Moses" from November 18, 1984 to January 5, 1985. Thye managed during, under a news blackout, to move 8000 more Falashas out of Ethiopia to camps across the border in Sudan, from which they were whisked by planes to Israel. It was a wonderful accomplishment, but thanks to the publicity from an ill-timed article about the airlift in the *Washington Jewish Week*, Arab nations began to pressure the Sudanese government to prevent any more Jews from using Sudan as a way-station to Israel. The mission ended prematurely with about 15,000 Beta Israel, about two thirds of the community, still stuck in Ethiopia. In addition, close to 1000 Falashas, who had already left home to take part in Operation Moses were stranded in Sudan, where there was great hostility toward them from the predominantly Arab Muslim population.

Clearly, the Falashas in Sudan were the ones who needed help most urgently and it was to succor them that George Bush now involved himself directly in the drama. During the first week of March 1985, Bush visited the Sudanese capital of Khartoum and met with the country's strongman, President Jafaar Numeiri, who was desperate for the release of $100 million in U.S. aid to Sudan withheld by the Reagan Administration because Numeiri's failure to follow through on a promised economic reform package. The two leaders quickly reached an understanding. Within a few days of the Bush-Numeieri meeting, the U.S. released $15 million of suspended aid to Khartoum and Numeiri gave his agreement in principle to a further airlift of Falashas out of Sudanese territory. The Sudanese dictator placed three conditions; the Israelis were to have nothing to do with the airlift; it was to be kept a secret and the flights should not go directly from Sudan to Israel.

The U.S. moved quickly to carry out the operation which was now named "Operation Joshua." On the night of March 28, 481 Falashas were trucked under the cover of darkness from their refugee camp to a remote site where they were met by six U.S. Air Force Turbo-prop C130 transport planes painted in desert camouflage, which had flown there from a U.S. base in Germany. Although the refugees were issued with visas for European destinations in order to comply with Numeiri's condition that there should be no direct flights from Sudan to Israel, in reality the planes flew directly to an Israeli air force base in the Negev desert. The secret of the airlift was blown soon thereafter. The rest of the Falashas trapped in Sudan were flown out on regular international flights.

The American Jewish community was deeply appreciative of Vice President Bush's personal role in making the rescue possible. That was hardly the end of his hands-on involvement in the deliverance of the Beta Israel; over the next five years, both as vice president and president, Bush stayed abreast of developments concerning the remaining 18,000 Falashas in Gondar. After the overthrow of the Marxist Mengistu regime in early 1991, the Bush Administration pressed the new Ethiopian regime to allow the Falashas to depart. Former Senator Rudy Boschwitz was dispatched to Addis Ababa on April 26-27 with that appeal. In exchange, Bush promised desperately needed aid and help in arranging a cease-fire between Ethiopia and Eritrea.

The Ethiopians quickly gave their assent. President Bush sent an official letter to Ethiopia's Acting President, Tesfaye Gebre-Kidan, on May 22, asking for the release of the Falashas. Two days later, an emergency Israeli airlift, known as "Operation Solomon," commenced. Over the next 36 hours, a total of 34 El Al jumbo jets and Hercules C-130s—seats removed to accommodate the maximum number of people, flew the rest of Beta Israel community to Israel. Thanks in large part to the patient work and unrelenting commitment of George Bush, a 3000 year-old exiled community seemingly lost in the wilds of Africa had come home to Israel at last.

Bush Goes to Israel

By early 1986, with George Bush clearly gearing up for his own run for president in 1988, there was a strong feeling among his supporters in the Jewish community that an official visit to Israel would help a great deal in strengthening his position in the upcoming election among Jewish voters. Bush and his political advisers agreed with that analysis, and planned the itinerary of a Bush visit to Israel that was set for late July 1986. It was decided that Bush would fly on his first official visit to Israel together with a group of friends and supporters in the Jewish community who came to be known as the Gang of Eight. In addition to myself, the gang included Paul Borman of Detroit, Joe Gilderhorn of Washington, D.C., Barbara Gold of Chicago, Richard Goldman of San Francisco, Jay Kislak of Miami, Ivan Novick of Pittsburgh, Gordon Zacks of Columbus, Ohio, national co-chairperson of the National Jewish Coalition, a body closely identified with the Republican Party. A television crew joined to film moments of Bush at places like the Western Wall and Yad Vashem that could be during the campaign.

During the flight across the Atlantic to the Rhine Main Air Force Base in Germany, a number of us had a candid talk with the Vice President about the up-coming campaign. Our purpose was to signal to Bush that while we understood his need to reach out to the Christian Right as part of his coalition building efforts in 1988, a too-ardent embrace of their agenda, including prayer in the schools and a ban on abortion, would hurt his efforts to build support for his upcoming campaign. Bush clearly had to walk a fine line in terms of what he could say, yet he made clear to us that he was a pragmatic politician who held centrist positions.

Bush's visit was filled with both substantive events and others that had a more photo-op character. First up was a meeting with Prime Minister Shimon Peres, at which Bush assured the Israeli leader that the affair of Jonathan Pollard, the American Jew arrested in Washington several months earlier and accused of spying for Israel, did not presage deterioration in "the strong, intimate relationship" between the United States and Israel. Obviously pleased, Peres responded with praise of Bush as "an outstanding person who has demonstrated great sensitivity through his actions on behalf of Soviet and Ethiopian Jews."

Bush followed that meeting with another with Foreign Minister Shamir, who was scheduled several months later to switch positions with Peres in a power sharing arrangement worked out between the two main parties. Bush delivered an address to the Knesset, met with Soviet and Ethiopian immigrants at an absorption center near Jerusalem and toured the Old City on foot with then-Mayor Teddy Kollek (the first time such a high ranking U.S. official agreed to go to the Old City in an official capacity since Israel's annexation of East Jerusalem in 1967). He met with Natan and Avital Sharansky (Natan had only been liberated from the gulag a few months before), and with a group called Mothers of Freedom—women whose children had been refused permission to leave the USSR. We travelled to Ben-Gurion's home and gravesite near Sde Boker in the heart of the Negev, where Bush and Peres discomfited the Vice President's staff by sitting on the ground and conversing with local high school students. Bush met in Jerusalem with a group of up and coming young Israel leaders and also with a delegation of Palestinian leaders from the West Bank and Gaza to whom he emphasized there would be no U.S. negotiation with the PLO until that body recognized Israel.

One of the most memorable moments of the trip was a visit to the Hatzerim Air Force base in the Negev, where, after receiving an intelligence briefing from Defense Minister Yitzhak Rabin and viewing Israeli made weapons such as the Kfir fighter plane and the Merkava tank, Bush witnessed a spectacular airshow which climaxed when a parachutist from an aerial acrobatic team dropping from a plane, landed directly in front of the vice president and presented Bush with a copy of the Old Testament in Hebrew.

For me, the most emotionally powerful moment of the trip came as I stood alongside George Bush at the Western Wall and watched my friend, one of the most powerful men in the world, bow his head in prayer as he touched the ancient stones. It meant a lot to me as a Jew to see this good man, a Christian, praying with deep evident emotion in front of the most sacred site in Judaism. To me at that moment, Bush represented all that is good and decent in the United States of America, the only Diaspora country in history where Jews have been made to feel fully at home and have truly been accepted as full citizens.

That afternoon, at a reception at the King David Hotel, I took the podium to say to my friend George Bush that just as the high priests of ancient Judea had once blessed visitors to the Temple Site, I felt inspired after our visit to the last remnant of the Second Temple to offer the priestly blessing to him, his wife Barbara, and his family as he grappled with all the troubles of the world. First in Hebrew then in English, I intoned solemnly:

> "May the Lord Bless You and guard you.
> May the Lord show you favor
> And be gracious to you.
> May the Lord show you kindness
> And grant you peace."

I had known George Bush quite a long time, but I think that for both of us the trip to Israel resonated with unexpected power and had the desired impact. In the ensuing years, he would often remind me of that trip to Israel and say that seeing the Jewish state up-close gave him a much richer appreciation of the place and its tenacious struggle for survival. The trip left me with the realization that in my entire life I have rarely had a non-Jewish friend whom I came to trust and believe in as much as George Bush. I vowed to do all I could to help him become President.

The further strengthening of my relationship with George Bush made me feel comfortable faxing him memos with my thoughts on the issues of the day, both related to Israel and the Jewish community as well as to other foreign and domestic issues. This was a practice I would continue throughout the four years of his presidency. I would open each letter with the salutation "Dear Mr. Vice President" (later "Dear Mr. President"), followed on the next line with "Dear George." No matter how busy he was, George almost invariably sent me a brief acknowledgement of receipt and would sometimes write back with a brief reaction to my thoughts.

Obviously, my letters received his prompt attention because my high profile leadership over decades in American Jewish life gave me credibility as someone who could accurately reflect the opinion of that community. Yet Bush also related to me as a loyal personal friend who believed in him and who wanted to help him succeed. Even when, during the height of the loan guarantee crisis of 1991, when I felt compelled to criticize his actions toward Israel and the Jewish community, he accepted that criticism graciously and expressed appreciation to me for telling him the truth as I saw it.

That same trust and mutual respect led him to send me on several occasions to meet with Prime Minister Shamir to urge him to reconsider positions Bush thought were unhelpful to the cause of peace. Overall, I was proud to play such a sensitive role for a U.S. president I considered a truly great man, and I am only sorry that Bush's efforts to bring peace closer between Israel and the Arab world did not come to a happier end.

A year after the trip to Israel, on October 3, 1987, just before the onset of the 1988 campaign season, George penned a note from aboard Air Force Two, the vice presidential plane, as he jetted home from a trip to Europe during which he had toured the Auschwitz death camp. He wrote, "I just wanted to let you know what a profound effect our visit to Auschwitz had on both Barbara and me. I don't think I have ever been so moved and so disturbed."

Only a week later, I received another note from Bush in which he wrote that he was "delighted that you have accepted my invitation to serve on the National Steering Committee of the George Bush for President Campaign. It means a great deal to Barbara and me to have your active support in my bid for the presidency. I want to bring the American people a message of hope for the future. Together, we can build a stronger, more prosperous America."

The 1988 Campaign for President

On April 12, 1988, with the primary campaign effectively over, and with the Bush for President campaign refocusing its attention on the soon-to-come general election, I faxed the vice president a long memo in which I sketched out my ideas as to how he could run a successful campaign in the Jewish community. First, I proposed Max Fisher to head our Jewish Campaign Outreach, with co-chairs Gordy Zacks, Marshall Breger, and myself, and a committee consisting of Jay Kislak, Richard Fox, Alma and Joe Gildenhorn, Ivan Novick and Leonard Greenberg. That suggestion was accepted and implemented. I myself would work in the area of Jewish organizations and Jewish leadership. I also promised to recommend key Jewish groups that Bush should consider meeting with and urged him to give timely interviews to the American-Jewish press.

I then presented Bush with a "wish list" of positions the Jewish community would like him to take in relation to the Arab-Israeli conflict, including maintaining Israel's quantitative and qualitative military superiority over any combination of adversaries. Also opposition to an independent Palestinian state, support for a united Jerusalem under Israeli sovereignty, support for Israel in the United Nations and its agencies, opposition to the sale of sophisticated offensive weapons systems to any Arab state at war with Israel, opposition to any American effort to impose a settlement on Israel. I also stressed that the Soviet

Union, by now rapidly changing under Gorbachev's glasnost regime, should be brought into Middle East negotiations.

Of course, I did not expect Bush to support our position on every one of those points, especially my affirmation united Jerusalem, given that the U.S. had consistently refused to recognize Israel's annexation of the eastern part of the city in 1967. Still I considered it important to lay down some markers for Bush as to the American Jewish consensus vis a vis Israel, and to and let him know what kind of approach would help win the maximum Jewish support.

In August, Jean and I traveled to New Orleans to attended the Republican National Convention as one of the leaders of the National Jewish Coalition. Bush's performance was first rate there, including his brilliant acceptance speech during which he spoke of "1000 Points of Light" and a "kinder, gentler" version of conservatism.

I felt some chagrin at the lack of preparatory work by Bush's staff that led to the selection of Senator Dan Quayle (R-Ind.) as the vice presidential candidate. The first public impression of Quayle was that he lacked seriousness and was too inexperienced. Revelations about his draft deferment during the Vietnam War, that his parents were long time members of the John Birch Society contributed to the idea that he was a bad choice.

I wrote to George Bush on September 2nd:

> "There is concern in the Jewish community about the 'hard right' positions of Dan Quayle [who] should schedule some synagogue events on his next visit to New York and meet with a group of Jewish leaders. Dan Quayle is considered to represent 'rightist' positions on many issues. I think George Bush should begin to address the center of the electorate by dealing with environment, housing, heath care and AIDS."

Bush evidently disregarded my advice on that occasion, running his campaign markedly to the right of center and savaging his Democratic opponent Gov. Michael Dukakis of Massachusetts on his membership in the American Civil Liberties Union and disinclination to mandate the recitation of the Pledge of Allegiance in classrooms in his state. The broader American public clearly didn't mind that campaign strategy; they elected Bush comfortably in a 40-state-landslide. The percentage of Jewish votes for Bush dropped considerably from the percentage that had supported Reagan four years before. I consoled myself that election campaigns are, by their very definition, nasty; and as Bush himself said at one point, a campaign team must sometimes do "whatever it takes" in order to elect its candidate. Once he was elected, I told myself, the kindlier, gentler George Bush would emerge.

In fact, he did so, but not always in ways that pleased the Jewish community. As part of his commitment to leaving a better world behind after finishing his presidency, Bush was determined to push harder than Reagan had done to achieve a breakthrough to peace between Israelis and Palestinians. The time seemed propitious for such an effort; at the Palestine National Congress in Algiers in November, 1988, the PLO had signalled that it was at last ready to recognize Israel within its 1967 borders. As a result, the outgoing Secretary of State, George Shultz, reversed a long-standing U.S. policy to have no contact with the PLO, and opened a dialogue with them.

Bush's choice as Secretary of State, James Baker III, clearly understood that if he were to make progress toward getting Israeli-Palestinian negotiations up and running, he would have to exert considerable pressure on the Israeli side to stop building settlements in the West Bank. This was especially the case given that Israeli Prime Minister Yitzhak Shamir was a tough-minded Likudnik who considered the settlements a holy cause.

Yet as we shall see, Baker often needlessly alienated influential American Jews with a gruff Texas oilman manner.

The first big crisis in this regard came in late May 1989 when Baker gave a speech to AIPAC in which he laid down markers to the Shamir government, stating bluntly, "For Israel, now is the time to lay aside, once and for all, the unrealistic vision of a Greater Israel [and] stop settlement activity." Laying out the goal of creating Palestinian self-government in the West Bank and Gaza, Baker stressed that this needed to be done in a way that would provide ample protection for Israel's security and also would be acceptable to Jordan.

I wrote to the President on June 5, 1989. I allowed that I personally thought Baker's speech to AIPAC was "a well-balanced call to all parties to deal with the issues," but then gave the President the bad news that "many in the community felt it was too even-handed and did not take note of Israel's 41 year search for peace in contrast to the 41 years of Arab war, violence and terror. There is concern that the call to abandon the dream of a Greater Israel did not at same time restate the American position of 'no return to the June 1967 borders' and the position that Jerusalem remain an undivided city. Perhaps at the appropriate time, these concerns can be addressed by you or Jim Baker."

Concerned that Baker's speech indicated a tone deafness to Jewish concerns that might lead to politically damaging collisions between the Administration and the community, I proposed to the President in that same memo that I should "continue my practice of meeting with you from time to time, every three or four months for a brief period, to discuss my view on the current issues; sometimes general issues, most frequently issues of particular interest to the Jewish community. If this is useful to you, I would like to continue it and await your guidance as to how to proceed." I did not receive a formal response, but heard from Bush's office that he highly valued my advice and would be happy to meet me at regular intervals.

On July 19, I sent the President a memo in which I pointed out that Israel was going through something of a political upheaval, with both Prime Minister Shamir and Finance Minister Peres, the leaders, respectively, of Likud and Labor, being challenged by "Young Turks" within their respective parties. Both challenges were being "fuelled by a mixture of the hope of, and the fear of, peace with the Palestinians. Under the circumstances, the best approach for the Bush Administration would be a show of "patience and understanding as the Israeli political battle is played out...During these difficult days for Israel, we should be supportive, repeating our commitments to Israel's security and the lasting nature of our friendship and alliance."

On Sept 14, I again wrote to the President on several matters related to Israel. First, I thanked him for the "realistic and compassionate proposals the Administration is putting forward in connection with Soviet Jewish refugees." With the floodgates of massive Soviet Jewish emigration about to open, the Administration, in close consultation with the Jewish community leadership had set forth new guidelines, which channelled most Soviet refugees to Israel, but reserved a generous number of U.S. refugee slots for those Soviet refugees who already had relatives here. Meanwhile, in the preceding several weeks, Shamir had finally come out of his perpetual box as 'Mr. No' and was proposing to allow the holding of Palestinian elections in the West Bank and Gaza. I urged the President to embrace the Shamir proposals, which, as I noted, had the support of a vast majority of Israelis.

I also reminded the President that although the first Palestinian Intifada or uprising, then in its second year, was "very troublesome", in reality the major military threat confronting Israel was "external, with (special) concern about Syria's missile capacity, combined with chemical warheads." I urged him to press America's "moderate" Arab allies, like Saudia Arabia, Kuwait and Jordan to enter into a dialogue with Israel and to end their economic boycott. Even Egypt I pointed out, which had a peace treaty with Israel, had not fully normalized its relations with the Jewish state. "A key helpful move," I wrote, that might cause the Arab states to realize that Israel could not be delegitimized and eventually wiped off the map "would be the decision (sic) of the United Nations General Assembly 'Zionism is racism' resolution. Another forward step would be to have our liaison to the Vatican urge Vatican recognition of Israel."

Offering a bit of not insincere flattery, I concluded, "It will take the wisdom of Solomon and the skills of George Bush to break the present impasse and start the process of peace already 41 years too late. I know you have the wisdom and patience to deal with this problem."

Several weeks later, I was in a position to do some damage control on behalf of the Administration. An American solider in Lebanon, Colonel William Higgins, was abducted and murdered by the fundamentalist movement Hezbollah, who claimed it was in retaliation for Sheikh Abd al-Karim Obeid, abducted by an Israeli elite force. The Sheikh was a Senior cleric Hezbollah leader and was the military commander of the Islamic Jihad in Lebanon. Senate Minority Leader Bob Dole (R-Kansas) took the Senate floor to say, "Perhaps a little more responsibility on the part of the Israelis one of these days would be refreshing." There was criticism of Dole by Jewish leaders and the suggestion that his comment was reflective of a growing Republican antipathy toward Israel. I decided to take the initiative and clean up the Dole problem and address that inaccurate perception without compelling the President and his political team to deal with it.

I arranged a meeting for Dole with 40 leaders of Jewish

organizations. As I reported to the President in a memo dated October 4: "The senator's reaction to the Israeli capture of Sheikh Obeid and video of Colonel Higgins was discussed at the meeting in a spirited fashion, but the air is cleared and the issue is now behind us." I also pointed out that the Jewish leaders had discussed with Dole prospects for pressing the Saudis "to become more active in support of our peace initiatives." I noted that Max Fisher raised the question of congressional support to allow Israel to obtain U.S. guarantees for housing for the expected large numbers of Soviet Jews choosing to go to Israel. (This was the first mention in my correspondence with Bush of an issue that would soon become a major source of contention between the Administration and the Jewish community: the need for settlement growth and expansion to accommodate the expected large immigration from Russia.) In any event, I concluded, "The many expressions of friendship by the organizational leaders indicated that relations are on sound and friendly footing with Bob Dole. I'm pleased."

The following month I served on a six member presidential delegation headed by former Senator Edmund Muskie to observe the maiden elections for the new nation of Namibia, a former German colony on the southwest coast of Africa, which had languished for nearly 70 years under the rule of the apartheid regime of South Africa. Beset by a stubborn guerilla war in the colony headed by Sam Nujoma of the South West Africa Peoples Organization (SWAPO), the new reformist South African regime of F.W. De Clerk had decided to allow Namibia to go its own way. Nujoma, formerly a radical Marxist, was rapidly transforming himself into a moderate and pro-Western figure as independence approached. Yet while Nujoma was a shoo-in to win the elections, President Bush was determined to make sure they should be run impartially, with all sectors of society able to take part.

Our delegation landed in the capital city of Windhoek and

immediately transferred to a small prop plane to the north of the country. There we dealt with complaints by native Africans who were kept virtually as serfs on vast white-owned farms that they were not being given time off from work to register to vote or take part in the political process. Considering the feudal conditions, desperate poverty and bitter memories of being exploited by the white minority, the overwhelming majority black population behaved with great dignity, eschewing the temptation for violence and revenge. After many years of war, there was a palpable sense among the people of hope for the future. On the actual day of voting, our delegation visited many polling stations. There was a celebratory flavor to the occasion and, for us observers, it was an uplifting experience to see the enthusiasm with which people went to the polls.

Afterwards, it was time for some relaxation and in the huge nature reserve in the Kalahari Desert, we had the incredible experience of driving alongside vast herds of wildlife; elephants, giraffes, and some lions.

Before we returned to Washington we returned to the capital, Windhoek, for a day. I had the opportunity to visit the synagogue there. I spoke with a present member, who complained about being separated from international Jewish activity. I promised to add the Synagogue to the mailing list of the United Synagogue of America, and quickly did so on my return home.

Within a few days of my return to the U.S., I left on another journey, this time to Poland and Czechoslovakia. Only weeks earlier they had thrown off their Communist regimes. Amidst the tumult in Warsaw, I met with Prime Minister Mazowiecki to whom I transmitted the greetings of President Bush and expressed the pleasure of the American Jewish community to see at last a free and independent Poland. The prime minister told me that the economic situation confronting his newly freed nation was desperate. Poland urgently needed fuel and energy so that longer range economic planning, which could lead to positive changes, could be developed.

In Prague, I walked in Wenceslaus Square and spoke to many who were dazed and exulted at their success in having suddenly swept away the Communist regime that had oppressed them for decades. They told me they were determined to achieve democracy through free elections that seemed almost certain to bring the dissident hero, Vaclav Havel to power.

Havel was a dramatist and wrote a large collection of esays. He was a leading spokesman against the Communist regime in Czechoslovakia; his plays were banned and he was imprisioned for four years for leading Charter 77, a dissident group. Following the collapse of communism in 1990, he was elected President of Czechoslovakia. He resigned in 1992 in response to the pending dissolution of the Czech and Slovak federation.

The good news for the Czechs is that their infrastructure is in relatively good shape, and that combined with their memory of having a genuine democracy between the two world wars, should help them to re-establish democracy and economic self-sufficiency relatively quickly.

Upon my return to New York, I sent the President a note about the results of both trips. Considering the fact that Nambia had an illiteracy rate of 60 percent and given the endemic tensions between the white landowners and the tribes, the elections had been both free and fair. "The vote was heavily tribal and I hope that tribal legalities can mature into a sense of national loyalty," I noted.

As for Eastern Europe, I was content to pass along Mazowiecki's plea for economic help and to transmit my own sense of wonder at the transformation of Eastern Europe. Thanks in part to the strength and constancy that the Reagan and Bush Administrations had shown in standing down the

"Evil Empire" I witnessed in Warsaw and Prague a world truly turned upside down.

The following month I met briefly with President Bush and took the opportunity to stress that a distinction should be made by the Administration between the Occupied Territories and East Jerusalem.

I followed it up with a letter to him. I referred to Senator Moynihan, who had just introduced a bill calling for U.S. recognition of united Jerusalem as Israel's capital. I explained that within the Jewish community "There is unanimity in regarding Jerusalem as united and as Israel's capital, and efforts will be made to secure your backing and the backing of Congress for this position...I suggest a way be found to separate the issue of Jerusalem when referring to the West bank and Gaza Strip and when using the term "settlements." This may not be the moment with delicate negotiations between Israel and the Palestinians yet to commence, but it may not be too soon to study the possibility of our developing a new policy for Jerusalem."

Meanwhile I pressed another issue that was growing as a source of contention between the two governments—that of loan guarantees for housing for Soviet Jews. I suggested to the President a way to deal with that issue and Jerusalem at the same time: "We trust that the request for $400 million of loan guarantees for housing for Soviet Jews in Israel will be quickly approved. The community is aware of and generally accepts the limitations that these funds not be used for settling immigrants in the territories. However all believe that this restriction would not apply to united Jerusalem."

I didn't have to wait long for a reply to my letter, and I was disappointed but not terribly surprised to see it was negative. On March 26, Bush wrote, "Jack, in my view, this is not the time to change the policy of the U.S.," although he softened the blow adding, "I am grateful to you for your advice, counsel and most important, your friendship."

I understood the President's perception of the need to pressure both sides so as to create the conditions for negotiations. Yet I feared that Baker and others in the U.S. foreign policy apparatus were leading the President to believe that a somewhat confrontational attitude toward Israel and her supporters in the U.S. was needed to push the process along.

I felt very much the opposite; that the only hope to get Shamir to move was to reassure the Israeli public and the American Jewish community that it was safe to make concessions for peace. Public pressure of the sort Baker was placing on the Israelis would only push them in the other direction and strengthen the hand of the hard liners. What was especially frustrating to me was that I knew the President to be a rock-solid friend of Israel. Yet a very different impression was being created.

Given the impasse between the Bush Administration and the firm policies of the government of Yitzhak Shamir, I decided to propose a new path. On July 9, 1990, I wrote the President, "We have thus far been unsuccessful in making meaningful progress through the route of Israel-Palestinian talks. I am concerned that further efforts along this path will create added U.S.-Israel tensions without any possibility of beneficial results. I believe there is little likelihood that the present Shamir government will negotiate with the Palestinians. "

Bush gave evidence of his continued confidence in me, appointing me as an alternate United States delegate to the United States Mission to the United Nations for the year beginning in September, 1991. I was warmly welcomed to that position by the U.S. Ambassador to the U.N., Thomas Pickering, who made it clear from the outset that I would be a high profile delegate with plenty of responsibilities. One of the issues Pickering and I agreed I should focus on would be an ongoing U.S. effort to bring about the revocation of the notorious 1975 "Zionism is racism" resolution. Pickering's astute political antennae, honed by decades of international diplomacy, told him that, with the ongoing implosion of the Soviet Union, it was likely that many third world and former Eastern bloc countries would be ready to reverse their earlier votes.

The Gulf War

In a flash, however, Iraq's blitzkrieg conquest of Kuwait on August 2, 1990, transformed the entire Mideast and world panorama and forced all other issues onto the back burner. Thus, my early months at the U.N. were spent working with Pickering and the rest of the U.S. team rounding up votes for a series of resolutions condemning the invasion of Kuwait and imposing an economic boycott on Iraq. The U.N.'s relatively strong stance on the issue was precipitated by George Bush's immediate answer to the Iraqi aggression against a U.S. ally in a region from which the U.S. gets significant share of its oil. Bush said simply and resolutely, "This shall not stand." As the Iraqis commenced the looting of Kuwait, the Administration began moving U.S. troops to the Gulf and deftly putting together an international coalition that almost totally isolated Saddam. President Bush first learned of Saddam's intention to invade Kuwait in August of 1990, and the next morning heard that Iraqi troops had entered Kuwait. One month later he still sought a non-military answer in a directive: "Normal relations between the United States and Iraq would serve our longer-term interests and promote stability in the Gulf and in the Middle East." The President had already alerted our warships in the Indian Ocean to head for the Persian Gulf. On August 2nd the United Nations Security Council warned of an "Arab solution" to the Iraqi invasion, fearing that it might be resolved by a compromise.

Ambassador Pickering, our superb Ambassador to the United Nations whom I enjoyed working under, was busy circulating draft resolutions on sanctions to members of the UN Security Coucil. At a press conference the President said, "I view very seriously our determination to reverse this awful aggression...this will not stand, this aggression against Kuwait." There were intense efforts by Jim Baker to bring the problem to a negotiated end - with no success.

On January 15, 1992, our attack against Iraq started and our television screen was filled with bomb bursts. On Friday, February 15th, the television news early in the evening reported that Iraqis announced that they would comply with UN Resolution 660, including the withdrawal from Kuwait. About ten days later Iraq started to withdraw. On February 27th, the President said on national television, "Kuwait is liberated. Iraq's army is defeated. Our military objectives are met."

I greatly admired Bush's determined stand against Saddam and his sure-handed diplomacy and took the occasion of the High Holy Days to tell him. On Sept 19, 1990. I wrote, "You are a man of destiny, one whose actions are shaping the direction of relations among states. Historic failures of the past to check nationalist expansionist aggressions are not being repeated. All mankind stands to gain from your leadership."

By the following month, though, Bush's success at building an international coalition against Iraq that appeared likely to include several Arab states that remained bitter enemies of Israel, such as Saudia Arabia and Syria, was causing jitters among the Israelis. On October 23, I wrote Bush that it would be wise to allay those concerns by sending "a high-ranking administration figure to visit Israel and explain our relationship with the Gulf States and the sensitivity of the Gulf Coalition. Israel should be reassured as to America's commitment to its security..." I added, "We should reach out, difficult though it is, to Shamir and also try to develop relations with members of the Shamir cabinet. I believe that the strongest and most influential member is Arik Sharon. Sharon would understand the military situation in the Gulf and the need for us to address that issue as a priority matter."

Lawrence Eagleburger turned out to be the high administration official sent to Israel to hold Shamir's hand if Scud Missiles were used against the Jewish state, and use his influence to control any Israeli repsonse to the Scuds.

Clearly, in asking Israel not to launch a pre-emptive attack or even if it was hit with Iraqi missiles, Bush was asking Israel to do something that went against its defense doctrine. It meant Israel would have to absorb a first strike and almost certainly suffer casualties that might be avoided by pre-emptive action. The Israelis' experience had taught them two things over the decades: one, that it was far better to pre-empt than to wait to be attacked; and two, the failure to respond to an assault would be interpreted by their enemies as weakness.

Israelis were deeply worried because Saddam's SCUD's were capable of delivering chemical weapons into the heart of Israel. In preparation for a possible missile attack, Israelis were given gas masks and told to prepare sealed rooms in their homes to stay in during a possible assault. Special enclosures had to be used for cribs to protect infants. Hotels acquired gas masks for their guests.

The word coming back from several high level U.S. envoys who met with Shamir was that Israel would likely hold off responding militarily to Iraq as long as Iraqi missile attacks on Israel did not contain chemical or nuclear warheads and did not kill a large number of Israelis. In the event of large-scale damage, all bets were off.

On January 17, 1991, the U.S. began its aerial bombardment of Iraq, and two days later, on January 19, Iraq fired its first Scud missiles at Israel. Initial reports seemed to confirm Israel's worst fears, that Saddam had indeed used his chemical warheads. This proved untrue, but the possibility of future attacks remained.

In response to Israeli pleas to be allowed to take out the Iraqi missile sites, Bush responded sternly that such a course by Israel might have grave consequences including for the future of U.S.-Israel relations. As more missiles hit Israel in the ensuing days, causing only a few deaths but widespread damage, Bush promised Shamir that U.S. and coalition would make destruction of the Iraqi missile launchers their top priority.

To partially compensate Israel for its decision to hold its fire, Bush offered to send Patriot missiles to Israel. The first batteries arrived on January 20. These proved only marginally effective, however, because Patriots that did intercept incoming Scuds (and fewer than half did) caused them to explode over population centers, sending debris that caused extensive damage.

During those days, knowing that I planned to be in Israel on a solidarity mission, the President asked me to meet with Shamir on his behalf to thank him for his restraint and to promise to work with him constructively in the post-war period. As I wrote to the President in a January 30, 1991 letter to convey the results of my encounter with Shamir:

"I returned home a few hours ago from a short visit to Israel. At a four eyes meeting with Prime Minister Shamir, I conveyed your good wishes and advised that you welcomed Israel's restraint in responding to Iraqi missile attacks, while understanding Israel's right to respond. The Prime Minister said many voices are calling for independent military action against Iraq, but repeated that everything done would be coordinated with the US. He pressed me as to why the 400 million dollar mortgage loan guarantee program was not finalized, indicating that all requested documentation had been provided, and he specifically requested me to raise this issue with you."

I suggested to Bush that he ought to "consider ways

to help sustain Israeli morale while they remain under the threat of missile attack. Your supportive statements on Israeli restraint are welcomed... It would be helpful in many ways if you would send a ranking personal representative to Israel during these days of civilian trial by missile. The presence of such a person would be very reassuring of American concern and support to a terrorized population, and could avoid a serious miscalculation by the Israeli government."

I also urged Bush that in order to build upon the wave of good will among Israelis at seeing U.S. anti-missile crews helping to defend Israel, "We should expedite the final approval of 400 million loan guarantee program, even if some problems remain to be worked out..." The President did not respond to that part of my letter, which indicated to me that he had no intention of acceding to it. Clearly, Bush and Baker saw the loan guarantees as their best available dangling carrot to get Shamir to ease up on the expansion of settlements.

As I wrote to Bush, on the evening of January 28, the last night of our stay in Israel, Jean and I had received a vivid and unforgettable taste of what all Israelis were going through those days. "The night before last, during dinner at the Hyatt Hotel in Jerusalem, the alert for an incoming missile sounded," I wrote. "With outward calm, Jean and I proceeded to the sealed shelter. The gas masks we carried with us at all times since our arrival, were hastily and clumsily put on. We heard BOOMS, not knowing what they were. With our gas masks in place, Jean and I turned toward each other and squeezed hands until the All Clear sounded."

"Zionism is Racism"

The war ended in a complete victory for the U.S-led coalition and without serious damage to Israel. George Bush's approval rating hit a phenomenal 91 percent and he looked to be a shoo-in for re-election. In the months after the end of the war I spent much of my time back in the corridors of the United Nations, trying to build support for revoking "Zionism is Racism" and other U.S. priorities. In my networking with U.N. ambassadors from around the world, I dropped in at missions and met with delegates in Delegates Dining Room. I invited many who I got to know to meet top leaders of the American Jewish community or to address my Temple Israel of Great Neck, and a number accepted; including Amr Moussa, then Egypt's Ambassador to the U.N. and later to be Foreign Minister and then Secretary General of the Arab League. Moussa obviously had strong differences with many of my positions, but he was extremely gracious and made a lasting impression with his appearance at Temple Israel. Here was an Arab leader with whom it was possible to dialogue.

Yuli Vorontsov, the last ambassador of the Soviet Union to the U.N. and the first ambassador of independent Russia, was similarly warm and animated during his Temple Israel visit. Without specifically apologizing for long-standing Soviet anti-Semitism, he assured our congregation that such practices had been consigned to the dustbin of history. Free Jewish emigration was assured and Jews who chose to stay in Russia would be treated as full citizens, he said.

I wasn't successful in reaching out to Dai-Allah El-Fattal, the Syrian Ambassador to the U.N. I shook hands with him in the U.N. Delegates Lounge and after some small talk invited him to come to lunch with a group of informed and influential United States citizens who happened to be Jewish. When the ambassador heard that he turned pale and shook his head forcefully. "What are you trying to do to me?" he asked me accusingly. "Do you want me to lose my pension?"

One person with whom I coordinated closely in my campaign against "Zionism is Racism" was Ambassador Yoram Aridor of Israel. Often I had coffees and lunches in the delegates lounge alone with Yoram because so many delegates were boycotting him and would turn ostentatiously and walk in the other direction whenever he would appear. Such behavior made my blood boil, and gave me a greater personal impetus to defeat "Zionism is Racism."

Ambassador Pickering and I strategized a lot about the best way to introduce a resolution for revocation. For a while, we toyed with the idea of having Britain or France propose rescinding it, figuring that more nations would go along with such a sponsor than if it came from the United States itself. Yet the Europeans seemed ambivalent about spearheading the proposal, and finally Pickering and I decided that the most effective way to go about overturning the resolution was head-on. The plan was to have President Bush himself advocate doing so in his speech to the new session of the U.N. General Assembly on September 23, 1991.

Pickering wrote Bush a memo advocating that he include such an appeal high up in his address to the General Assembly and affirming that according to his head counting, it appeared a majority of the U.N. members were ready to dump the resolution. I also lobbied the President to use his speech to call for getting rid of "Zionism is Racism."

I had already left the U.N. My term ended at the end of August. I was delighted when the President informed me shortly before the speech that he had decided to issue a strong statement but was electrified when Bush stated unequivocally during his speech; "to equate Zionism with the intolerable sin of racism is to twist history and forget the terrible plight of Jews in World War II and indeed throughout history."

The U.S. began a full court press to get the resolution revoked and Israel helped the cause by making revocation a condition of its participation in the Madrid Peace Conference that took place that November. Shamir eventually decided to come to Madrid because it had become obvious that "Zionism is Racism" would be voted on within a few weeks and would almost certainly go down.

Yet I think all of us who were veterans of that fight still couldn't quite believe it when the culmination of our long struggle came on December 16, 1991. On that historic day, the U.N. General Assembly voted to revoke Resolution 3379, the "Zionism is Racism" resolution by a vote of 111 to 25 with 13 abstentions, a greater margin than the 72-35 with 32 abstentions by which it had originally passed.

This overwhelming overturning of an international libel of the good name of the Jewish people was a testament to the sustained efforts of many good people, in the Jewish community and beyond, who worked patiently to overturn the vile resolution for more than 15 years, even during long stretches when it appeared an immutable part of the international order. "Zionism is Racism" of course, soiled the reputation of the U.N. far more than it did Israel, and with the revocation the world body started the process of reclaiming its lost honor.

Loan Guarantees for Israel

The role of President George H.W. Bush in achieving long deferred justice on this issue should not be forgotten, even though it is usually overlooked by those who charge Bush was anti-Israel. At the height of a political battle with the Israeli government and its American supporters over the loan guarantees issue, Bush did not lose sight of the importance of reversing the "Zionism" resolution and took a principled stand in his General Assembly speech that was the defining element in winning revocation. It was a victory for human decency that will forever stand as a memorable part of Bush's presidential legacy.

However, the fight over the loan guarantees was surely the most painful part of George Bush's legacy concerning Israel and the Jewish community. Shamir and Bush had taken adamant stands on opposite sides of this issue throughout 1990, a year during which 200,000 Soviet Jews flooded into Israel. That aliyah which brought in about three-quarters of a million people in less than five years between 1989 and 1994, was a huge demographic bonanza for Israel, although it presented immediate difficulties that stretched even Israel's vaunted ability to absorb large number of new immigrants. New housing was vitally needed, and the loan guarantees offered by Congress and the Bush Administration would greatly facilitate its building. Yet for Shamir and much of his Likud Party, deeply committed to the cause of the Greater Land of Israel, the temptation was to strengthen Israel's hold on the West Bank by channelling as many newly arrived Russian Jews as possible to new settlements there. George Bush and Jim Baker were convinced that Israel had to stop building settlements if they were ever to get peace talks going. They therefore sought to use one of the few points of leverage they had available, and informed Shamir he would not get the loan guarantees unless he stopped settling new immigrants in the occupied Territories.

In the aftermath of the Gulf War, the confrontation between Bush and Shamir began to feel like unstoppable force against immovable object. Shamir, having shown enormous forbearance in not launching military strikes against Iraq in retaliation for the missile strikes out of deference to the Bush Administration, now insisted that Bush and Baker owed him one and ought to drop their opposition to the loan guarantees. Now, it felt, was the time to move boldly to achieve a breakthrough to Middle East peace.

I saw the way things were moving when Bush asked me to go and talk to Shamir and carry the message that "the United States is opposed to settlements in the occupied territories." Shamir listened and then advised that settlements would continue. I returned and so advised the President. About six weeks later. President Bush dispatched me to Israel with a second message for Shamir; "The continuation of the settlement policy will cause problems with your relations with the United States." Shamir exploded banging his fist on his desk and shouting at me "Whose land is it? Is it British land? No! It's our land and no one can tell us what we can do in our own land!"

I returned to my hotel and found a message to contact General Sharon. Sharon asked me to come early the next morning to the airport at Sde Dov and he wanted me to visit some of the settlements on the West Bank and Gaza. We met and his helicopter took off and landed at a high point. Sharon and I got out of the helicopter and he said to me, "Look, we are over the 'green line.' You can see Ben-Gurion Airport from here, and according to the President this would be in Arab territory." We made a few more stops like that and a visit to Gaza, and were impressed by the beauty of the land with direct Mediterranean Sea frontage. We lunched at a settler's attractive home, then inspected some of the farm developments and back to Sde Dov. I flew back to Washington with my report of the Shamir meeting and my day-trip with Sharon.

I spoke to the President with a full report of my Shamir meeting and that Gaza visit with Sharon. He told me to meet with General Scowcroft (head of the National Security Council) and advise him of my report. And I did so raising the Ben-Gurion view from the first stop on territory claimed by the Palestinians. I said, "Israel's security must be taken into account."

The Jewish community was split on the issue. There were quite a few influential Jewish leaders, like myself, who had supported Israel all our lives and would continue to do so, but who understood that, in the end, Israel would have to trade all or most most of the occupied territories to get peace.

Many of us were convinced that George Bush was a good and true friend of Israel and what he was pushing for was really in Israel's best interests.

In fact, seeing the intensity with which AIPAC, the Presidents Conference and other Jewish groups were fighting on the issue, and realizing that Congress would likely go against him on the issue, the President had already backed away from his early insistence that he would prevent Israel from receiving the loan guarantees as long as Shamir refused to explicitly agree that none of the new olim would be settled in the Territories. Instead, in early September, 1991, Bush put forward a new position, calling upon Congress not to debate or vote on the loan guarantees issue until after a 120 day period. The 120 day delay tactic seemed especially wise because Bush and Baker were making good progress towards getting up and running a first-ever Middle East conference that would include Israel, the main Arab states and a delegation, linked to Jordan, representing the Palestinians, but not the PLO. It seemed likely that the historic event would take place within a month, although the venue and many other issues were still to be determined (the conference would eventually be held in Madrid during early November). Under the circumstances, therefore, putting off consideration of the contentious loan guarantees issue made a great deal of sense from many vantage points.

A Bush Misstep

Shamir refused to consider compromise. AIPAC brought to the Congress on September 11 and 12 about 1000 pro-Israel activists from around the country to urge Congess to approve of loan guarantees. This infuriated the President, who suddenly saw his very right to direct U.S. foreign policy as he saw fit as being at risk. He abruptly called a press conference that very day to make his case on the loan guarantees issue over the heads of AIPAC and Congress directly to the American people. And during that press conference, with a few poorly chosen words, the President managed to give to his opponents in the Jewish community all the ammunition they would need to credibly paint him as hostile to Israel.

As it happened, I was in the White House that day, having come for previously scheduled meetings with senior officials and hopefully, if time would allow, a brief conversation with the President. Two weeks earlier, concerned about the declining state of the economy, including a sharp drop off in consumer spending and a rise in unemployment, I had offered some advice about steps that he might take to encourage banks to give easier credit, especially to ease their classification of loans to real estate operators. I had gone to the White House that day with the intention of talking economics and also to brainstorm with the President how to deal with the loan guarantees situation. Yet when I arrived, I learned that the President had decided suddenly to hold his press conference. All I could do was sit in the reception room and watch on TV as the press conference commenced and problems arose.

Bush started out with quite a reasonable opening statement, noting that, "A few days ago I asked Congress to defer consideration for 120 days of Israel's request for $10 billion in additional U.S. loan guarantees meant to help Israel absorb its many new immigrants. I did so because we must avoid a contentious debate that would raise a host of controversial issues, issues so sensitive that a debate now could well destroy our ability to bring one or more parties to the peace table."

Bush emphasized, "It's not about the strength of my or this country's support for immigration to Israel. Both as Vice President and as President, I've tried my hardest to liberate Jews living in Ethiopia and the Soviet Union so they could emigrate to Israel…Nor should our request for delay be viewed as an indication that there exists any question in my mind about the need for a strong and secure Israel...Just months ago, American men and women in uniform risked their lives to defend Israel in the face of Iraqi SCUD missiles."

The key issues, Bush said, was that there was now a chance for Israeli-Arab peace and "nothing should be done that might interfere with that prospect." Then the President said something that caused alarm bells to start ringing in my head. After affirming that "The Constitution charges the President with the conduct of foreign policy," he went on to say, "And now again, there is an attempt by some in Congress to prevent the President from taking steps central to our nation's security. But too much is at stake for domestic politics to take precedence over peace. This I know is something the bulk of the American people understand."

That comment felt uncomfortably close to saying that the loan guarantee supporters were putting Israeli or Jewish interests over the very security of America. Then, responding to a reporter's question, the President said something that made things a great deal worse. Asked why his argument that the loan guarantees should be delayed 120 days to allow the peace process to work was not selling with congressional supporters of the loan guarantees, Bush responded, "I think it will sell, but its taking a little time. And I'm up against some powerful political forces, but I owe the American people to tell them how strongly I feel about deferral...I heard today there were something like 1000 lobbyists on the Hill working the other side of the question. We've got one lonely little guy down here doing it."

I quickly suggested to the President that he explain his words. I suggested that I ask Shoshana Cardin, the current Chairman of the Conference of Presidents, to write him a letter relating the Jewish concerns, which the President would answer with words of clarification. Shoshana would go public with the letter and the issue would be calmed. The President agreed.

Cardin agreed and wrote the President a letter, noting that "more than 1200 Americans representing Jewish communities in 40 states and numerous Christian leaders came to Washington to meet with their senators and congressmen" to express support for the loan guarantees, and in doing so "they were exercising their right—even obligation—as American citizens, consistent with the democratic process, to advocate their position on this vital humanitarian issue.

"Therefore, I found some of your comments at your press conference on Thursday to be disturbing and subject to misinterpretation. In particular the references to "1000 lobbyists on the Hill working the other side of the question" and to "powerful political forces" trouble me and many others."

The following day, September 17, the President sent Cardin a letter, almost immediately released to the media, which showed he understood the political damage his language at the press conference had caused. "I am concerned that some of my comments at the Thursday press conference caused apprehension within the American Jewish community. My references to lobbyists and powerful political forces were never meant to be pejorative in any sense," he wrote. "I have great respect for free expression in the democratic process...Politically organized groups and individuals are a legitimate and valued part of the decision-making process in a democracy."

However, President Bush made clear that he still intended to make a stand on his call for a delay in considering the loan guarantees: "We obviously disagree on the question of the 120-day delay in the submission of the loan guarantees. I believe, as you do, that we can have honest disagreements on the issues...[but] we are committed to the same principles and our areas of agreement far outweigh our areas of disagreement."

The President's letter said all the right things but didn't have the effect of calming the outrage in the Jewish community. Some of this was due to the fact that said outrage was being hyped by people who wanted to keep it alive, people who were furious at Bush for sidelining the loan guarantees for at least four months. The hard-liners were also not happy that the Administration stood on the verge of arranging its historic Middle East conference, which would soon be scheduled for early November in Madrid. Thus, they continued a drumbeat of attacks on Bush as though he hadn't written that letter to Cardin at all."

For the time being, I told the President, "Your 'quiet' policy as regards response statements from the White House is correct despite the barrage of critical reactions from Israel and from a large portion of the American Jewish community. The response I urged was an 'active' policy of meetings of various members of the Administration with Jewish organizations, the Jewish press and importantly with the religious leadership...The theme of these meetings should be the Bush administration efforts to secure peace for Israel."

On October 21, after receiving word that the Madrid conference had been arranged, I wrote a congratulatory note to the President, affirming that "At last, after 43 years of seeking a direct dialogue with her Arab neighbors, your persevering efforts hold out that probability, nearing reality, of such talks. Peace is in the interests of all parties and will require your continuing persuasion. The necessary compromises will not be volunteered by any of the parties. "

During the negotiating period, your continuing reassurance of the strong American-Israeli relationship and your continuing concern for Israel's security and well-being will ease the minds of the community and clear the air of disinformation concerning your aims in the peace process. I have strongly urged Prime Minister Shamir to call you and begin to restore a relationship of trust and friendship."

On November 12, I gave him both good and not-so-good news. "The Jewish community welcomed and applauded your opening address to the Madrid Conference. They support Israel's loan guarantee request, and are divided on your call for a halt in settlements." I pointedly reminded him that Shamir would be in the U.S. over the next week with a program of addressing Jewish audiences and urged Bush to invite him to the White House. I then gave him my thoughts on the worsening economy with some ideas about what could be done to strengthen real estate values. I closed, "I write not as an economist, not as a politician, but as a friend."

Unfortunately, in the absence of willingness to move on Shamir's side, the 120-day-cooling off period did not lead to the needed compromises between the two sides. By early 1992, with both Israeli and American elections looming, it appeared that the issue would only be resolved by the fall of either Shamir or Bush. Meanwhile, in early March, 1992, old wounds between the Administration and the organized Jewish community were exacerbated when former New York Mayor Ed Koch caused a sensation by asserting to the Washington Post that he had it on good authority that Jim Baker had recently been overheard to say, "F—— the Jews, they don't vote for us anyway."

The story caused a sensation, although Baker never confirmed having made the remark. Even if he had, indeed, said it, that could have been the kind of rough-hewn banter that goes on among top political professionals in the privacy of small group meetings. I know Baker well and was convinced that his tough-minded approach to the Israelis was hurting Bush in the Jewish community.

At the beginning of March, I again visited Shamir in his Jerusalem office and with Bush's authorization, told the Prime Minister "...that the President still sought a compromise of the loan guarantees issue, but that Bush was not prepared to make a 180 degree turn in his position that settlements should stop." I had a subsequent meeting with Foreign Minister David Levy, but as I wrote Bush a few days later, I "received no encouragement from either party." I then suggested a possible compromise to the President I had heard talked about in Israeli political circles, namely that the U.S. agree to allow "natural growth" at an established percent at several settlements that have a security reason for their existence. Beyond that the President would be in a stronger position to demand a halt to all further settlements or expansion of settlements.

Knowing that Bush was unlikely to agree to my suggestion, I gave him some news I had gleaned in Israel, namely, "My sense is that since Yitzhak Rabin has been elected head of Labor, there is a good chance Labor will win enough seats in the June 23 elections to head a new government or form a unity government with Likud. Rabin told me except for security-based settlements and East Jerusalem, he would halt further settlements."

I then broached the painful Baker matter, commenting ever so delicately, "The remarks about Jews and their voting habits alleged to have been made by Jim Baker have added to deteriorating relations with the Administration. I spoke to Jim and suggested a direct meeting with some 20 Jewish leaders to clear the air, as I begin my campaigning for George Bush. There are so many positives to put forward that have gotten lost."

Just how badly those positives were getting lost in the Jewish community was borne home to me in political soundings I took over the next several weeks. I had known things were not good, but now I could see they were well nigh catastrophic. I realized that it was my duty to give my friend the President the unvarnished truth as I saw it and did so in as difficult a letter as I have ever written him, before or since.

I began, "I write this anguished over the loss of support

I am finding in the Jewish Community. The anger is centered on the issue of loan guarantees, but it reflects a series of events starting with the Bush news conference on Sept 12 of last year to the remarks allegedly made by Jim Baker, to the series of suddenly appearing reports of illegal arms transfers [from Israel to China]...Much of the community anger is directed against Jim Baker, but it is being increasingly transferred to George Bush."

What could the President do at this late stage? I offered a few suggestions; an upbeat Passover message that should "reflect your commitment to Israel and the resettlement of Jewish refugees." I urged that the Republican Platform Committee draft a plank on Israel that should strongly affirm America's commitment to Israel. I repeated my oft-stated position that the Administration should cease to refer to East Jerusalem as "occupied territory."

Campaign 1992

Then there was the problem of Bush's rival for the GOP nomination, Pat Buchanan, who had humiliated the President the previous months by besting him in the New Hampshire Primary. By late March, Bush had won a string of primaries and all but sewn up the GOP nomination and Buchanan was reduced to nuisance value, but Bush was paying a price by ignoring Buchanan's not very thinly veiled anti-Semitism and racism. I wrote, "Be aware of the [Jewish] community's concern over the anti-Israel remarks and the isolationist positions of Pat Buchanan."

While the President's political prognosis continued on a downhill slide for much of the spring and early summer, to the point where he found himself running behind Democratic challenger Bill Clinton and barely ahead of Independent Ross Perot, there was some good news on the Israeli front. During the Israeli elections in late June, the Labor Party headed by Yitzhak Rabin decisively defeated Yitzhak Shamir's Likud. Rabin quickly reaffirmed his campaign promises not to resettle Russian Jewish immigrants in the occupied territories, and at the end of July was invited to visit Bush in his retreat in Kennebunkport, Maine. After a cordial meeting, Bush confirmed that he now approved of giving the loan guarantees to Israel.

Political observers said that even with the resolution of the loan guarantee issue, it was unlikely Bush would be able to do much with the Jewish vote, especially versus Clinton who had struck very positive chords among Jews. Still, I was as upbeat as I could be in an August 12 memo to the President, noting that not only had the community responded well to the Kennebunkport meeting but also that roundtable interviews Bush held with some of the leading members of the American Jewish press had come off well. There seemed at least to be reason for cautious optimism.

Alas, it was not to be. The Republican Convention in Houston was dominated by Bush's vanquished rival, Pat Buchanan, whose fierce speech declaring "cultural war" on those not sharing a militantly Christian conservative perspective was a huge turn-off, not only for Jews, but for millions of moderates and swing voters across the country. The economy was still sour and try what he could, Bush, who only a year before had been the heavy favorite to be re-elected, now appeared in serious peril of losing the election. Bush's hope that his debates with Clinton and Perot would turn things around also fell flat.

On October 18, with the debates behind and things looking ever more desperate, I sent my last memo to the President, advising him to reach out to the women's vote by mentioning the funds he had directed to breast and uterine cancer research and by addressing the problems of single mothers, especially child care. I explained that he should address the interests of women, a voting group that is needed to win; he might visit some women's hospitals, talk about their role in shaping the morals in the country through the teaching of their children. I urged him to address the issue of jobs by going to an automobile plant and talking about expanding markets and his success in opening the Chinese and Japanese markets. I urged him to talk about the environment, and to visit a church or synagogue to denounce religious bigotry in any form, and to go to a homeless shelter, to speak about welfare reform. I added, "Return to the George Bush of 'a thousand points of light,' of a 'kinder, gentler America.' This message worked. It can work again...The Bush programs are so good and offer so much hope for all Americans. Please dramatize them, concentrate on them, and let's win with them." I closed by saying, "Please understand that these thoughts are presented by one who deeply cares for you, who values your friendship, who is working the 'street' for votes and who wants you to win."

The next day, I received back a hastily scrawled but heartfelt note that I shall always treasure. "What would I do without friends! Thanks for the Oct 18 fax. On to victory. Your kinder, sometimes gentler friend, George Bush."

There is something deeply poignant about that salutation as I consider it today, and not only because we now know how that 1992 election came out. George Bush's personal instincts were all about being kinder and gentler, but he found himself immersed in a political culture on the American right which was anything but kind and gentle, but was instead deeply fearful and resentful of modernity and demanded a President who responded to its agenda. The irony was that though he wooed the right, they turned on him, especially after he took the fiscally sane and necessary step of raising taxes. My friend, George Bush, the New England patrician could never really win over the southern and western right wing base.

One of the sadder aspects of the first President Bush's

failure to win re-election was that he did a superb job in foreign affairs, winding down the Cold War and presiding over the collapse of the Soviet Union in a way that kept the peace of the world. His response to Saddam Hussein's challenge in Kuwait was masterful and I believe he was absolutely correct to have stopped at the border and not sent the U.S. Army on to Baghdad. My friend, the first President Bush, knew a potential morass when he saw one, and preferred to hem Saddam Hussein in with sanctions and no flight zones than to put American boys and girls into harm's way in the twisted alleys of Mosul and Falluja.

As to the troubles between the Jewish community and Bush, it is clear in retrospect that mistakes were made on both sides. I knew him as a man of greater kindness and sensitivity to Jewish people and who was deeply loyal to his Jewish friends, as someone who helped saved Ethiopian and Soviet Jews and cared deeply for Israel's well being. He was, after all, the man who got rid of "Zionism is Racism" and who brought about the first peace conference between Israelis and Palestinians. It was very unfortunate that few other Jews were given the chance to see how much he cared for our community and concerns.

Looking Back and Moving Forward

Celebrating the culmination of the 350th Anniversary of Jewish life in America, a dinner was held at the National Building Museum in Washington on September 14, 2005.

As President George W. Bush said that night: "We're a better and stronger and freer nation because so many Jews from countries all over the world have chosen to become American Citizens."

Riding on the train back to New York with my grandson, Dr. Ken Stein, I considered the President's words. Yes, America has been good to us, and we have been good for America.

I have been around for over a quarter of the time that Jews have been in this country. I have participated as fully as possible in both American and Jewish life. I involved myself in my synagogue, in the political life of the Jewish community, in the world of business and, together with my beloved wife, Jean, in building a fulfilling family life. I tried to fulfil the obligation incumbent on every Jew, to undertake acts of *tikkun olam* (repairing the world).

With the benefit of my years and experience, I would

like to share here some brief reflections related to American Jewish life, to Israel, and to the lessons I learned from my own life experiences.

I am concerned that all of American Jewry, but especially the Conservative movement within which I spent my religious life, are seeing our numbers seriously diminished by the problem of intermarriage. The Conservative movement is especially susceptible to this blight, because in our movement, unlike the Reform movement, there is no satisfactory provision or mechanism for helping non-Jewish spouses to feel at home in our synagogues and eventually to become Jews. I have repeatedly called this problem to the attention of the leaders of the Jewish Theological Seminary and the United Synagogue, but they have chosen to focus their efforts instead on strengthening the commitment of existing Jews to Conservative Judaism.

I respect their view, but believe the Reform movement took the right step when it adopted the principle of patrilineal descent 20 years ago. They accept children of Jewish fathers as Jews, just as it recognizes the children of Jewish mothers. That step made a lot of sense, because it kept many more people within the Jewish fold and helped them resolve vexatious identity issues. After all, Judaism is basically a patriarchal religion. The Torah presents patrilineal descent as the accepted pattern for a Jewish marriage, and our tribes traced their religious origins to the Bet Av, the Father's house, whenever there was an intermarriage.

The rabbis changed to matrilineal descent early in the Common Era, because during that terrible epoch for the Jewish people, so many Jewish women were being raped and impregnated by Roman soldiers that it was decided to base the identity of the children on the fully Jewish identities of their mother. There is, thankfully, no such need today, and it seems to me that the Conservative movement ought to resolve that if a couple in which one or the other parent is Jewish commits to raising their children as Jews, the Jewish religious community should fully accept and lovingly embrace those children.

Maintaining as large as possible a number of Jews is a positive in itself, but that is only one reason for the Conservative movement to come up with an effective response to intermarriage. The problem is not just one of demographics and statistics. Intermarriage also causes great personal grief to untold thousands of Conservative Jewish families.

It is clear to me that the Conservative movement needs to look at our conversion procedures to make them more acceptable, or to use modern lingo, more user-friendly, to intermarried couples. It has been many years since I was in the retail business, but I remember well what we used to say; that you can't sell your products, unless you can bring the customers into your store. We in the Conservative movement need to bring intermarried couples into our store.

At the same time, I have to admit and we have to recognize that any substantive change that does not have an unified consensus among Jews could be divisive and has the potential to create different "classes" of Jews.

However, more than 42% of the Jewish members of Conservative congregations enter into interfaith marriages. While they are at college or beginning their careers, many establish a loving relationship with a non-Jewish partner and decide to marry. The parents of the Jewish member of such couples are often shocked, chagrined and unsure of how to respond. Some even stop coming to synagogue because of a feeling of shame that their beloved child, who became bar or bat mitzvah at the synagogue and is known to the entire membership, is about to marry a non-Jew.

The parents of such children should be invited to visit their rabbi to discuss the situation and to talk through the conflicting emotions so many of them endure. The rabbi should also meet with the soon-to-be interfaith couple and discuss with them both the basics of Judaism and, specifically, conversion to Judaism for the non-Jewish partner.

I would prefer to see a more modern approach to conversion, one that might not include, for example, the use of the *mikveh* in women's conversions. However, these changes may take a long time until they are fully accepted.

Rabbis need to candidly discuss the complicated issues involved in intermarriage and conversion not only with couples contemplating that step, but also with their entire congregation. Intermarriage touches a huge number of Conservative Jews, and making it a taboo, an unmentionable subject, does nothing to reduce those numbers. The focus needs to be upon finding a way to bring interfaith couples and their children to Judaism and into our congregations.

At the same time, we in the Conservative movement are being confronted with an issue that may become nearly as contentious as intermarriage; namely advocacy on behalf of same-sex marriages. In recent years we have even seen the advent of a growing number of gay synagogues. In the face of these trends, our movement has firmly maintained a policy of not ordaining openly gay Rabbis. Nor do we permit our Rabbis to officiate at same-sex marriages.

Although I do not believe our Rabbis should enter further into the issue of gay marriage, they should certainly not stigmatize as less moral than ourselves those who are gay or advocate gay marriage. If God has chosen some of our children to have different sexual desires and relationships than other children, then that is God's choice. It is not for us to impose our beliefs on another human being as to what his or her sexual orientation should be.

Turning to Israel, let me start with the most important issue; the Jewish state's eternal quest for peace. With the death of Yassir Arafat and with his successor Mahmoud Abbas in place, there was hope of Palestinians adopting more moderate positions during peace negotiations.

However, with the radical Hamas taking control of the Palestinian Authority, a concrete wall of separation from peace has arisen. Not only have they set themselves against Israel, but also against Abbas' stated goal to continue negotiations. Hamas considers Israel illegal and does not officially recognize it. I cannot see the peace talks resuming until Hamas accepts the three requirements set by the international community: 1) recognize Israel's right to exist, 2) renounce violence and commit to disarmament, and 3) accept agreements already reached between Israel and the Palestinians.

Ariel Sharon made the courageous decision in 2005 to evacuate all the Jewish settlements in Gaza and four settlements in the Northern West Bank. This was a bold step toward peace. At present, however, the situation in Gaza has become more chaotic. With no strong Palestinian security in the area, weapons of all kinds are entering Gaza along its Egyptian border, and rocket attacks are being regularly launched across Israel's southern border.

Sharon formed a new political party, *Kadima,* and sought re-election as Prime Minister. Sadly, all these plans ended for him when he suffered a stroke that put him in a coma.

His deputy, Ehud Olmert, has succeeded him as Prime Minister and openly committed to continuing Sharon's path,. including an offer to negotiate peace with the Palestinian President, Mahmoud Abbas. The climate in which Olmert will function has already changed. It does not encourage one to feel that peace is at hand.

Olmert has clearly stated his policy: if negotiations with the Palestinians continue to fail, he will start the "convergence," the removal of settlements in the West Bank at the same time he completes the security fence and provides for Israel's security needs along the Jordan river. If that fails within a specified timetable, he will undertake a unilateral effort to provide peace and security to Israel. He will determine the borders of Israel, complete the fence or security barriers on the border, and there will be a "separation."

To be sure, there remain fundamental issues to overcome on the Palestinian side. One is the drift of much of the Palestinian population to a more radical and violent observance of Islam and specifically to the belief that if any land within the Islamic sphere (*Dar al-Islam*) is lost to non-Muslims, it is incumbent upon Muslims to launch a jihad to reclaim it. It should never be forgotten that this volatile mixture of religion and nationalism plays a major role in the thinking of Palestinians, and that reality helps to explain why the Palestinians rejected the Camp David Accords and refused to make a final peace with Israel.

Having said that, I am not without hope for peace, mainly because I refuse to live without hope. I cannot reconcile myself to saying there is no hope for Israel, or that Israel will go through another 100 years of conflict. It is true that I have seen so many openings to peace that have gone a glimmering during my lifetime, yet I refuse to become discouraged. I am hopeful that, in time, a more worldly generation of Palestinians will emerge and accept the State of Israel as a neighbor. Some might say that is a long shot, but I won't write it off, even if the odds against it are 99-1. After all, we've already been through a lot of failures, and that one percent chance has only to happen one time in order for Israel to achieve peace.

As for Israeli domestic issues, I believe it is extremely important for Israel's future to finally rid itself of the institution of the Chief Rabbinate. Israel must transform itself into a fully democratic state with a Constitution. That would strengthen the fabric of the country by making all Israelis, including the ultra-Orthodox, full members of society. I believe they should go to work every day like every other citizen, and should participate in the defense of their country.

In addition, having a State of Israel that is committed to only one branch of Judaism—the Orthodox one—as is the case today, leaves no room for non-Orthodox Jewish movements. I felt personally insulted that my long time spiritual leader at Temple Israel, Rabbi Mordecai Waxman of blessed memory, who was highly respected not only in the Conservative movement but throughout the American Jewish community for his religious erudition and personal decency, and who played a historic role in building relations between Judaism and the Vatican, was not allowed to perform marriages in Israel.

In terms of relations between Israel and the American Jewish community, I believe Israeli students should be taught in school something about American Jewry and its institutions. We are a community that contributes so much to Israel, and yet Israelis often relate to us mainly as a perpetual source of funding. For our part, American Jews should more carefully monitor how the money we are sending to Israel is being spent. Many of us do not want our money being used to finance the expansion of settlements or the creation of illegal outposts, especially at a time when there are efforts to negotiate peace.

On the other hand, while the Israeli government has certainly done things over the years with which I did not agree, I have always recognized that on matters in which the security of Israel is at stake, I have no right as a Jew living in the Diaspora to take Israel publicly to task. I've been always been sensitive that the Israelis themselves will be called upon to put their lives on the line to defend the strategic choices they make, while I will sit back and watch it all on CNN. In any event, I have never had the self-importance to believe that Israel will ever make any decision regarding its security based on what I have to say.

Israel is still a very young state that, over its 58 years of existence, has had to integrate an enormously diverse population from around the world under conditions of war or the constant threat of war. During that period, the population of Israel has grown 10 times since it's founding, from 600,000 to over six million. By any standard, Israel is an enormous success story. In just over half a century, Israel has developed a commercial, industrial and research base far beyond anything in the surrounding Arab world; on a par in many respects with what is being done in far richer countries like the United States and Western Europe.

I made my first visit to Israel in 1954, and have returned scores of times since; always relishing the opportunity to watch the progress being made there. I remember on that first visit, Jean and I stayed at the Dan Hotel, then the only quality hotel in Tel Aviv. In 1972-1973, while chairman of the Presidents Conference, I also served as chairman of Israel's 25th Anniversary celebration in the United States. I have done my best to inform Americans about how far that gallant little state with few natural resources besides its brainpower had come in such a short time.

Looking back on my early visits to Israel, I wish I had bought real estate there, when prices were still very reasonable. I missed the chance to do that, but am nevertheless proud I was able to make a contribution to the development of tourism in Israel as one of the founding partners of Isratours. I later sold my share of the company to an Israeli, and Isratours, like the State of Israel itself, has gone from strength to strength.

I am also proud to have played a small role in the great historical process of helping to free the Jews of the Soviet Union. There is no question that the arrival in Israel of over one million Soviet Jews—a predominantly secular and technologically adept group that now represents about 20 percent of the total population—is transforming the Jewish state in fundamentally positive ways.

One reward for my decades-long, high-level involvement in the organized American Jewish community's advocacy efforts on behalf of Israel was the opportunity to form friendships with some of Israel's great leaders, from David Ben-Gurion and Golda Meir back in the 1960's to people like Ariel Sharon and Shimon Peres in more recent times. Ben-Gurion and Meir articulated to me the soaring Zionist ethos of the founding generation; Sharon helped me to understand the elemental Israeli commitment to strength and constancy in order to overcome Arab rejectionism, and Peres communicated the vision of a shared economy between Israel, the Palestinians and Jordan as an indispensable element of a new and peaceful Middle East.

Ultimately, I think, that Israel is an amalgam of its varied great leaders. Today, the majority of Israelis may think more like Sharon, or even a Netanyahu, yet when the time comes for peace—hopefully in the not-too-distant future—the protean efforts of Peres to build a network of human ties and mutual interests between Israel and its neighbors may come to be evaluated very highly by his countrymen.

On a personal level, I am pleased that I was able to succeed in the real estate business. I was fortunate to be in the right place at the right time: to be in real estate on Long Island as that area experienced its period of most sustained growth during the 1950's, 1960's and 1970's. I deeply enjoyed the challenges involved in the day to day process of acquiring and selling real estate, and was blessed to have two hard-working, genial and profoundly decent partners, the late Max Staller and Ben Kasper, who allowed me to take considerable periods of time away to attend to Jewish affairs. Max was a highly assimilated Jew and Ben was not Jewish at all, yet both were totally supportive of my involvement in Jewish activities.

People often ask me why I devoted so much time and energy throughout my life to Jewish religious and political life;

pointing out correctly that I would have made a great deal more money if I had focused more intently on my business career. I don't have an answer to that question in words, only in my heart. It goes back to my childhood in Poughkeepsie where my family attended a modern Orthodox synagogue and I received a very serious Jewish education four afternoons a week. Even though I later became a Conservative Jew, the rigorous modern Orthodox education I received in Poughkeepsie as a child and in Brooklyn played a major role in molding me into the Jew I am today. That education gave me both the necessary basic Judaic knowledge, as well as a great pride in being Jewish and a personal commitment to making a contribution to the betterment of my people.

As a young man running clothing stores in places like Kansas City, I was exposed to anti-Semitism, which disturbed me deeply. After my father died in 1942 and Jean and I moved to Great Neck, I searched for a synagogue in which to say *kaddish* and found Temple Israel, a recently created Conservative congregation with only 35 members. I came to identify quickly with the Conservative philosophy; a traditional form of Judaism that fully embraces the modern world, and the very smallness of the Temple Israel membership at the beginning allowed me to quickly become involved in leadership roles; a member of the board and soon, president of the synagogue. From there I moved on to become President of the New York Metropolitan Region of United Synagogue, the national lay body of Conservative Judaism. That brought me to the Jewish Theological Seminary, the intellectual heart of Conservative Judaism, where I became attached to and worked closely with Chancellor Louis Finkelstein, one of the giants of Conservative Judaism.

I never imagined when I was starting out that I would rise to the top position in the principal umbrella body of American Jewry, yet, as it turned out, one step led naturally to the next. Throughout my involvement in Jewish religious and political life, I felt in sync with the great majority of people with whom I collaborated. I relished the challenge of helping to overcome the very difficult problems we faced. Most of all, I felt privileged to serve my people and make a positive difference for American Jewry and Israel. Having the opportunity to accomplish that touched me very deeply and led me to make considerable personal sacrifices, such as putting my business career on hold for extended periods.

During my time as Chairman of the Presidents Conference, when I was defending the Nixon Administration's balanced approach to freeing Soviet Jews while maintaining détente with the Soviet government, I was loudly accused by some in the Jewish community of putting the Administration's interests over those of Soviet Jews. I endured similar personal attacks while serving as White House liaison to the Jewish community during the battle over the Reagan Administration's sale of AWACS to Saudi Arabia; and a decade later when I mediated between my close friend, President George H.W. Bush and the organized Jewish community during the struggle over loan guarantees to Israel.

I knew then and know today that the charges made against me of undercutting Israeli and Jewish interests were utterly false. Throughout my long career in Jewish organizational life, my bottom line commitment in everything I did was to protect Israel's security and well being. Yet I was also a pragmatist who understood that the long-term safety of Israel was inextricably linked to the maintenance of a strong U.S.-Israel relationship. Amidst the tumult of the struggle over the Jackson-Vanik Amendment in the 70's and during the epic battles over AWACS and loan guarantees later on, moderate voices like my own tended to be drowned out by hard-liners whose credo seemed to be "scream loudly first and think about the consequences later."

I stick to my guns when I know I am right, even at emotionally charged moments such as the one in the early 1970's when a group of young Jews disrupted a meeting of the Presidents Conference under my tenure, denouncing me as a *shtadlan* (court Jew) and other less printable epithets. I was angered by that uncivilised behavior, yet reminded myself that those who took part in that action were young American Jews who had dedicated themselves to the cause of fellow Jews in peril behind the Iron Curtain. They were convinced they had the right answer and that the political line I advocated was wrong. I could appreciate and even admire their zeal even if I felt it was misdirected. I knew that my approach was getting results; that thanks to the Nixon Administration's policy of constructive engagement with the Soviet government, which we supported, the number of Jews getting out of Russia had risen in a few years from almost zero to more than 35,000.

In that situation, as well as in the later contretemps between the Jewish community and Presidents Reagan and Bush, I believe I played a positive role in helping to prevent emotions from spinning out of control and irretrievably damaging the overall texture of U.S.-Israel relations. Despite some difficult moments, that did not happen, and today those relations are stronger than at any time in history.

Certainly, I am proud of the work I did on behalf of Israel, yet would point out that my Israel-related involvement was only a part of my overall work on behalf of my people. I was always a proud and loyal American Jew, whose work on behalf of my people has always been as much about my efforts on behalf of Temple Israel and United Synagogue as about my efforts to strengthen U.S.-Israel relations.

I am proud that back in the early 1950's I pushed hard in collaboration with Rabbi Waxman to make Temple Israel as egalitarian as possible. I joined in doing away with the synagogue's separate Sunday School for girls, during those years, ensuring that boys and girls in our synagogue's would study together and receive the same high quality of Jewish education. Access to equal Jewish education led more and more women to go on to study at the Seminary and to make careers within the world of the synagogue, including the rabbinate. Today, Temple Israel has a female rabbi, Rabbi Sarah Cohen, and half the class in the rabbinical school at the Jewish Theological Seminary are women. I am pleased to have played a small role in that transformation.

Jean and I helped to spread the message of the Conservative movement, when, late in our lives, we contributed several thousand copies of the *Siddur Sim Shalom* and presented them to Temple Israel. A few years after that, we provided a similar number of copies of the *Humash Etz Chaim* and several years later of the *Machzor for the Yomim Nora'im (*High Holidays*)*. Certainly the presentation of those books made it possible for the synagogue to make available the principal prayer books of our movement to every member of Temple Israel. Jean and I proudly dedicated the contributions to the memories of our parents, Samuel and Bella Stein and Michael and Eva Cohen. We dedicated the *Machzor* to the memory of the spiritual leader of Temple Israel for more than 50 years, Rabbi Mordecai Waxman, a rabbinical giant of our era, whose friendship and moral guidance meant so much to Jean and myself.

I had other involvements through the years that give me a warm feeling as I look back on them. Back in the early 1980's we bought a condo in a beautiful planned community called Lakeridge in the rolling hill country near Torrington, Conn. There Jean and I enjoyed many wonderful weekends filled with swimming, boating and hiking. As we began to put down roots in the community, I got involved in local real estate. I bought and upscaled a local shopping center and developed some other land parcels in the area. Jean and

I also made contact with the local Conservative synagogue, which was struggling due to the fact that many members are businessmen who don't come to services because they need to keep their businesses open on Shabbat.

During the late 1980's, I was asked to join a committee for the establishment of a Holocaust Memorial and Educational Center in Nassau County. The United States Holocaust Museum in Washington had opened several years earlier, and a number of communities around the country with large Jewish populations saw the need to also create local Holocaust centers to reach large numbers of people who might never get to the museum in Washington with a message about the horrors of the Holocaust and the danger that something like it could happen again. In addition to myself, members of the founding committee included such people as Boris Chartan, Msgr. Donald Beckman, Rabbi Myron Fenster, Simon Zarah and Rev. John McGann, Bishop of the Diocese of Rockville Centre.

That committee debated long and hard over the course of many meetings the question of how to create a Holocaust memorial on Long Island that would be something more than a pale imitation of the Holocaust Museum in Washington. Eventually we decided that the best way to accomplish that was to make our institution more of an educational center than a museum; a place where school children and others would come to learn the lessons of the Holocaust and the principles of tolerance and understanding between people of different ethnic and religious backgrounds.

We were also unsure about where to locate our facility until Nassau County Executive Thomas Gulotta made us the offer of a wonderful old estate in the middle of the 200-acre Welwyn Preserve in Glen Cove. There could be no better place for our new Nassau County Holocaust Memorial and Educational Center than the place Gulotta found for us; a gracious mansion in a bucolic setting with plenty of space to accommodate the busloads of schoolchildren who come there each day.

After opening the Nassau County Holocaust Memorial and Educational Center, we focused our efforts upon hiring a first rate teaching staff of dedicated professionals who instruct new generations of school children on how the Holocaust happened and how to keep anything like it from ever happening again.

In 1996, I was asked to serve on a three-person committee that was being set up to investigate the situation at the Jewish National Fund, after revelations of financial mismanagement damaged the image of that venerable agency. For 100 years, the JNF has been responsible for planting most of the forests of Israel and acting as steward of the natural resources of the Jewish state. In the wake of the resignations of several top officials at the national office of the JNF in New York, the audit committee was asked by the JNF itself to undertake a thorough investigation. We worked long hours with a sense of great responsibility, informed by an awareness that we were dealing with a serious matter concerning the integrity of a flagship Zionist institution that continues to do a great deal of important work for Israel.

After several months of investigation we issued a report showing abundance of mismanagement, including the fact that only 20 percent of donations to JNF were reaching Israel, despite the agency's claim that 70 percent was going there. Certainly there was sloppy accounting and poor management, but no solid evidence of criminal activity.

In the wake of the scandal, my friend and past-Chairman of the Conference of Presidents, Ronald Lauder, became president of JNF and commenced a concerted, highly successful campaign to re-establish the agency's integrity. Today, Ron Lauder is still at the helm of JNF and the agency is doing better than ever. I am gratified to have played a role in helping JNF to overcome its financial and management problems; thereby allowing that important agency to get back on its feet.

I served as a member of the Dead Sea Scrolls Foundation Board of Advisors. Westin Fields, Executive Director of the Dead Sea Scrolls Foundation brought me into this activity, and I became interested in our early Jewish history and in the mystery of the Scrolls. The scrolls were found at Qumran, an area near Jericho and the Dead Sea. The origins date from 135 BCE with some scholars dating it as early as the Maccabean uprising of 167 BCE.

The Scrolls, or fragments found show two complete copies of Isaiah and fragments of nearly every other book of the Bible. Life in the Qumran caves centred around Divine worship and the residents of the caves of Qumran observed the traditional Biblical festivals. They, unlike the mainstream Jews, lived by a solar calendar of four periods of thirteen weeks. The failure (66-71 CE) of the revolt against Rome marked the end of the Qumran sects existence.

I found this continuing experience very pleasant and enjoyed enriching my knowledge of ancient Jewry in Hellenistic and Roman times.

Once a year, members of the Presidents Conference, including former chairmen like myself, travel together to Israel for meetings with the Prime Minister and other leading officials. On the way to Israel, or after we have been there, we often stop off in Europe or Asia, sometimes visiting countries in the former Communist bloc or in the Arab world, where it was previously impossible for pro-Israel groups like ours to venture. Thus in 1996, we made the first-ever visit by an American Jewish delegation to Qatar, an oil-rich emirate on the Persian Gulf.

As on many other Presidents Conference trips, other participants and I brought along our spouses. While in Qatar, we were treated with meticulous courtesy by the government of the Emir, which went to great lengths to make sure we would be comfortable and our dietary needs would be met. In the luxury hotel where we stayed in the capital city of Doha, the hotel manager, who said his grandfather was an Egyptian Jew, provided us with brand new serving dishes and individually wrapped brand new plates, glasses and utensils for every member of the delegation. We had arrived from Israel with kosher meals pre-packed on paper plates, and welcomed the hospitality of Qatar.

As it turned out, while everything went smoothly with the Qataris, we had plenty of controversy within our own delegation. When we gathered for Friday night services, we learned that our executive vice president, Malcolm Hoenlein, as well as other Orthodox members of the delegation, were insisting that we should make our Friday night *kiddush* with wine, as is normally done, despite our being guests of a rigorously Islamic state, where alcohol is strictly prohibited. For my part, I urged Malcolm that we drink grape juice instead of wine in deference to the sensibilities of our hosts, especially given that the purpose of our visit was to smooth the way for strengthening still-fragile Israeli-Qatari relations. Yet the Orthodox members of our delegation insisted that we stick to Judaism according to their own rites, no matter what the possible consequences. Finally, Hoenlein arranged for those members of the delegation who felt the need to have wine in their kiddush cups to assemble in a small, closed room.

I swallowed that one, but I made a ruckus the following morning when Jean and I came to the room set-aside by the hotel for Shabbat services and found that a *mechitza* consisting of tables had been placed down the middle of the room to separate men and women. I had originally joined the Conservative movement back in the 1940's partly because that movement allowed mixed seating at services, allowing me to sit with my wife, and I told Malcolm that I wanted to sit with my wife and stand with her as she said Kaddish for her recently deceased father. I objected strongly to being separated from Jean during the service. After our discussion, a compromise was arranged by which the *mechitza* would extend only to the middle of the room so that couples who wanted to pray together could do so by sitting further back. It wasn't an optimum solution, but the compromise allowed the service to proceed and the members of the "sitting-together" delegation felt comfortable during the Shabbat service.

In thinking over the course of my life, it almost goes without saying that I have been blessed with wonderful children and grandchildren. Their love and caring for Jean and myself gave us enormous support and sustenance through the decades of our life together, and, of course, helps to sustain me now, when I no longer have my life partner by my side. It certainly gave Jean and I great pleasure to watch our children and grandchildren grow, and we reveled in their educational and professional achievements.

Our three children, Richard, Stuart and Linda, have lived purposeful and loving lives, animated by the values Jean and I sought to transmit to them. Their own children in turn, are doing very well, active in their professions. Jean and I were happy to contribute to the success of our children and grandchildren by helping to pay for their educations beyond high school.

Our oldest son, Richard and his wife Roselle Shubin, have twins, Dr. Beth Shubin Stein and Dr. Kenneth Shubin Stein. Today, Beth holds a fellowship as an orthopedic surgeon at the Hospital for Special Surgery, while, Kenneth left medicine for a career on Wall Street. He is presently the manager of a major hedge fund. I guess I shouldn't be too surprised that Ken ended up in finance, as he was always entrepreneurial, coming up with schemes to sell candy to his fellow students in high school and tee shirts in Columbia college. Richard's daughter Beth has a son named Charles, or C.J., as he is more popularly known.

Stuart and his wife Pepi, have two daughters, Heather and Marissa, both became lawyers. Stuart's daughter Heather has two children, Abigail and a new baby, Julia, born just last year. Marissa, the youngest of our grandchildren, is employed by a major law firm.

Our daughter Linda, a registered nurse, now helps me to run Jacob Stein Realty, Inc. Linda and her husband Jack Whalen have two children, Sara and Debbie. Sara was a superb athlete who became a skilled Olympic soccer player. She was a member of the United States National soccer team, which won the 1999 World Cup championship and won a Silver Medal at the 2000 Olympics in Sydney, Australia. Shortly thereafter, Sara badly damaged her knee and retired from athletics. She is now finishing a degree in clinical psychology at Fordham University. For her part, Debbie opted to be a traditional stay-at-home mother and put her husband to work. She is the mother of three of my great grandchildren, Samantha Jean, Zachary and Alexis. I have a total of six great-grandchildren, at this witing. Four of whom Jean got to know, and two who were born after her passing. My granddaughter Sara Hess tells me that she has the seventh in her womb.

Today, in my 90th year, I have few regrets. Yet I am beset by a deep sense of grief and loss at Jean's death in October, 2004. Jean and I were partners not only in raising our children, but in every other important aspect of our lives; in the real estate business, in the life of Temple Israel of Great Neck, in the United Synagogue, and in the political world. I was very pleased and proud that Jean was appointed by President George H.W. Bush to be a Member of the Board of the United States Holocaust Memorial Council, a position in which she served for seven years. During the 65 years of our marriage, Jean and

I were truly one, and now that one of us is gone, it feels like there is only half a person left.

As noted, my children and their families have been a source of considerable consolation to me as I have struggled to cope emotionally with my loss of Jean. I am grateful, too, that Judaism offers beautiful ritual, proverbs and healing prayers to help Jews deal with the loss of a loved one including, the *kaddish* (mourning prayer), the seven days of mourning called *shiva* and the *shloshim* (30 days of mourning). Yet nothing so far has helped me to find the answer to the question I ask again and again: why? I always believed that I would die before Jean, and therefore am having a very hard time dealing with losing her. I find myself often blaming the Almighty, while at the same time, acknowledging the harsh truth that we are all born to die. At my age, how do I summon the strength to continue forward with the balance of my life?

A lot of well-meaning people have said to me, "You should be grateful and feel blessed that you and Jean had 65 wonderful years together." There is much truth in that. 65 years is a long time to be together, more than most couples are given. Yet especially after such a long marriage, in which being with that one special and irreplaceable person became my way of life, it is that much harder to go on without her. So, no, quite honestly, I don't feel blessed right now, and have not received the answers I am seeking. At least not yet.

During the weeks that Jean lay near death in Mt. Sinai Hospital, I sat by her bedside whispering words of encouragement in her ear, not knowing if she was able to hear them. I recognized in those days that our world is like a small room adjoining the room of the limitless heavenly world we enter upon death. Each day, as Jean's condition deteriorated, I could see the door separating the two rooms opening wider and wider. The day that she stopped breathing, I saw that the door had opened all the way and when I looked at my wonderful wife, I understood that she had gone into the next room, the heavenly room. She was truly an *ayschit chayil*, a woman of valor. All I have left of Jean now are wonderful memories of the lifetime we spent together, memories I will take to the grave.

I have lost the guiding figure of my life. Jean was the person who became as one with me and her passing leaves me now less than whole. I question why I go on doing certain things. Whatever lies ahead holds little interest for me; I feel that my future was my past. Every single day I think of Jean and miss her deeply; wherever I find myself, I feel alone. I like to talk, but the walls of our house, now sadly my house, do not respond. I certainly do not feel it is "my" house. This dwelling was Jean's palace of activity. I enter the house and call loudly upstairs, "Hon?" But there is no response.

Several times during the week I start my day with a visit to the cemetery where Jean lies. There I talk with her, knowing that I am standing as close to her as I possibly can be. I talk about the children and the grandchildren, and have told her that she recently became a great-grandmother again with the birth of our sixth great-grandchild, Julia, who was given the Hebrew name *Yocheved* in honor of Jean.

I am not yet able to open Jean's dresser drawers or to empty her closets. I am told by many people that "time will ease you." And so I go from day to day trying my best to hold myself together. I apply the maximum effort to every undertaking of what remains of my life, whether large or small.

I realize that I must go on. So I continue to take on commitments in the area of modern Jewish life, wherein much has changed.

Sixty-three years ago, Jean and I joined Temple Israel of Great Neck, a Conservative Jewish congregation. Over these passing six decades our membership has grown from 35 families to 1200 families and each member has customized Conservative

Judaism to meet his or her needs and desires. Today, driving to Temple and then taking the car to the Supermarket after the Sabbath service is almost universal.

The meaning of *halacha* (Jewish Law) and its standards is a matter of serious consideration. In the past, Conservative Halacha has approved egalitarian actions: the driving of our cars to Shul, use of electricity on Shabbat (Microphones, so we can hear) and some questions of marriage after divorce. It has not been revised to meet the fullness of positive growth and actions of the Jewish community and establish realistic standards and procedures for bringing intermarried couples into the synagogue and Judaism.

I find that Jewish education for children and adults has much advanced since the 1960's, when my children started in Hebrew school. There is a continuing interest in our history; scores of books are available for children and adults to learn of any aspect of our history; the first and second Temple, the Pharisees and Essenes and the Sadducees, Judaism at the time of Jesus, the Crusades, the development and meaning of Islam, the tragedy of the Holocaust and our current need to maintain the wall of separation of religion and state.

Today there is an encyclopaedia of Judaism on the Internet. We can find kosher recipes, the meaning of the high holidays and gifts for Hanukkah and other events. We can read of the history of Jews and the events that have influenced us. Many universities have Jewish programs on campus.

America is a fine place for us. We have participated actively in society; Joseph Lieberman was a candidate for the office of Vice President. Senators and Congressman are Jewish, and Jewish doctors, lawyers, and engineers are common in almost every city. We have university presidents, deans, and professors in greater numbers than ever. Our hospitals and homes for the aged and other institutions are providing help for Americans and are visible signs of philanthropy. All of these things make me very proud to be a Jewish American. I feel at home.

People sometimes ask me what I see as my legacy. I can think of no better example than my experience with my grandson at the 350th Anniversary dinner with the President. I asked Ken to come with me because I have long sought to strengthen the interest of my children and grandchildren in Jewish history. I was moved to see how much my grandson enjoyed that evening of immersion in our past. Sharing that event with Ken gave me a palpable and reassuring feeling of the connection between my own life and that of my children, grandchildren and great-grandchildren, and with the larger pageant of Jewish history and American history. Each of our individual lives is fully bound up with the destiny of our people.

I certainly didn't reinvent the wheel, either in relation to Jewish life or the real estate business. But I do feel that I did my part and pulled my weight. I was able to contribute to the growth of America and the development of Jewish life in America and to the security and well-being of Israel. I hope I will leave a good name among my friends and know I will remain in the memory and love of my family. Soon I too will be going into that heavenly room, where I pray I will be reunited with Jean.

Index

I

J

K